Praise for *Through the Eye of the Tiger*

"The song Jim and Frankie wrote, 'Eye of the Tiger,' was So Amazing that when I first heard it I had to make sure I was not dreaming— a heart pounding timeless Rock Masterpiece!!!! ... Thank you, you made Rocky even more Heroic."

—Sylvester Stallone

"Joe Thomas introduced me to Jim Peterik almost twenty years ago and we've been friends ever since. The first time I met him we wrote a song together while sharing a spaghetti dinner at my favorite Italian restaurant. Somewhere between the garlic bread and the crème brûlée I knew we had a hit...sure enough, that song, 'That's Why God Made the Radio,' became the title of the Beach Boys' highest-debuting record (#3) in over forty years."

— Brian Wilson

"I got the opportunity to meet Jim Peterik when he invited me to play on his *World Stage* record. We did a funky bluesy version of his number 'Vehicle.' I knew the song but never really knew whose song it was. I was immediately impressed with Jim; he was a true musician and lover of music. We come from different worlds, but we speak the international language ... M-U-S-I-C. Since that recording I have come to know and respect Jim as a peer. When I do my annual run of shows at my club Legends, Jim has joined me on many occasions and jammed with me and my band. No rehearsals, just music. Before the show, he will hang out with me and have a shot and talk about old times, music, and cars. I am honored to share a stage with him and call him friend. He's my Vehicle."

—Buddy Guy

"Jim Peterik is such an extraordinary songwriter, musician, and human being. I believe he was put here on this earth to inspire us all with his words and melodies and he's done just that. Jim, you wrote a great book ... great storytelling ... such an adventure to read. Jimbo rides again!"
—**Mindi Abair, Concord Records singer/saxophonist/songwriter and president of the L.A. chapter of National Academy of Recording Arts and Sciences**

"For all of his encounters with the likes of Led Zeppelin, The Beach Boys, and of course Sylvester Stallone, Jim Peterik remains resiliently down to earth and refreshingly aware of his roots. *Through the Eye of the Tiger: The Rock 'n' Roll Life of Survivor's Founding Member* by Jim with journalist Lisa Torem is a fascinating, revealing, and riotously entertaining book from a musical legend."
—**John Clarkson, editor of Pennyblackmusic.com**

"Jim Peterik takes his surroundings and experiences to build songs wherever he is. Both in the UK and while hanging out in Chicago, I have witnessed him stop in mid-sentence to whip out his personal recorder and start humming a melody or a snippet of lyric into the microphone—the beginning of his next masterpiece. Through reading his memoirs, I have learned the inner workings of the man behind so many timeless classics."
—**Andrew McNeice, melodicrock.com**

"I've known Jim Peterik for almost fifty years, and in that time saw him go from gawky teenage boy who wanted to be a rock-and-roller into one of the giants of that industry. This book tells it all, and this hometown boy couldn't be prouder."
—**Joe Mantegna, star of stage, screen, and television and star of the hit series** *Criminal Minds*

"If you bought a record with a Jim Peterik tune on it, chances are that would be the one you'd find yourself singing along with before the first chorus ended. Even if you can't sing along with *Through the Eye of the Tiger*, Jim's autobiography is powered by the same boundless enthusiasm and way with a hook that have helped his greatest hits endure for decades. This is one entertaining read."

—Jeff Giles, UltimateClassicRock.com

"It's no coincidence that Jim Peterik's most successful band was called 'Survivor.' *Through the Eye of the Tiger* is Peterik's rock 'n' roll saga, the engaging autobiography of a hit-making musician and songwriter who pursued his music with passion, power, and persistence. The soundtrack to his life includes the classic rock hits 'Vehicle,' 'Hold on Loosely,' 'The Search Is Over,' and 'Eye of the Tiger,' and his new book tracks the highs and lows of his life in rock, with equal parts honesty, insight, and irreverence."

—Ken Paulsen, music journalist,
editor of Americana Music News

"In a tenacious business that eats its young and spits them out every fifteen minutes, Jim Peterik has proven to be the ultimate music survivor. *Through the Eye of the Tiger* offers proud testament to his enduring gift as an artist/songwriter, hard-fought integrity, and unyielding passion for his craft."

—Ken Sharp, award-winning music journalist
and *New York Times* bestselling author
of *Nothin' to Lose: The Making of KISS (1972–1975)*

"What is it that makes a listener turn the volume up when a song comes on? Energy? Excitement? Emotional connection? Jim Peterik's songs have all that. But there's an extra 'it' factor—that 'something else' in his songs. Same way with Jim himself. Jim continues to impress me with his generosity of spirit and humanity as he strives to inspire others to find their own 'Eye of the Tiger.'"

—Sherrill Blackman, multi-time winner
of Nashville Song Plugger of the Year

through the
eye
of the
tiger

through the eye of the tiger

The Rock 'n' Roll Life of Survivor's Founding Member

Jim Peterik

WITH LISA TOREM

BENBELLA BOOKS, INC.

DALLAS, TEXAS

Copyright © 2014 by Jim Peterik and Lisa Torem

BENBELLA

BenBella Books, Inc.
10300 N. Central Expressway
Suite #530
Dallas, TX 75231
www.benbellabooks.com
Send feedback to feedback@benbellabooks.com

Printed in the United States of America
10 9 8 7 6 5 4 3 2 1

Library of Congress Cataloging-in-Publication Data
Peterik, Jim, author
    Through the eye of the tiger : the rock 'n' roll life of Survivor's founding member / by Jim Peterik with Lisa Torem.
        pages cm
    Includes bibliographical references and index.
    ISBN 978-1-940363-16-5 (trade paper : alk. paper)—ISBN 978-1-940363-56-1 (electronic) 1. Peterik, Jim. 2. Rock musicians—United States—Biography. 3. Survivor (Musical group) I. Torem, Lisa, author. II. Title.
    ML420.P459A3 2014
    782.42166092—dc23
    [B]

                                                                                    2014003378

Editing by Glenn Yeffeth and Katie Kennedy
Copyediting by Eric Wechter
Proofreading by Brittany Dowdle and James Fraleigh
Cover design by Ty Nowicki
Cover photo by Marc Hauser
Text design and composition by John Reinhardt Book Design
Printed by Lake Book Manufacturing, Inc., Melrose Park, IL

Distributed by Perseus Distribution
www.perseusdistribution.com

To place orders through Perseus Distribution:
Tel: (800) 343-4499
Fax: (800) 351-5073
E-mail: orderentry@perseusbooks.com

Significant discounts for bulk sales are available.
Please contact Glenn Yeffeth at glenn@benbellabooks.com or (214) 750-3628.

There's a Story in My Eyes...

Dedicated to the first cool guys in my life,
Binky Cihak and Johnny Babinek—
on Wesley Avenue we learned about cars, ukuleles, marbles,
scooters, and the wonders of rock 'n' roll.

Contents

Foreword

I FIRST MET Jim Peterik in 1968, or was it '69, hmmmmm…

The roads are windswept and slippery as our tour bus creeps up I-57 headed for a snowbound Chicago. At 4 a.m. I am eyes open in the back lounge, iPad in hand, rummaging through my weary head for the exact memory.

…I believe it may have actually been 1968, after an Ides of March show at The Blue Village teen club in Westmont, Illinois, one of many psychedelic-themed live music spots which were popping up all over Chicagoland at that time. Through the black-lit haze, in a moment certainly tattooed on Jimmy's brain, some pimply-chinned high school kid walked up to him as he was packing up his guitar, and said, "Hey man, I'm in a band too, and I think 'You Wouldn't Listen' is a really good song." Jim Peterik was already a local rock star by then and could have easily blown me off…but he didn't. Since that fateful night I have gone on to do everything from booking Jimmy and The Ides at Brother Rice High School's prom in 1969, to forging a long-term friendship while co-writing and recording a number of Peterik/Cronin songs with my band, REO Speedwagon.

For as long as I have known him, Jimmy has always been a stand-up guy, prolifically talented, smart, quirky, naturally funny, a fair and honest collaborator, and a loyal friend. We share the same Midwest work ethic, a love and respect for songs and their creation, as well as an undying belief that music is our salvation. We both still feel the thrill when that final word of a new song magically travels from pen to notebook, when that perfect master mix explodes from the studio monitors, when at last you hear your record on the radio so you pull off to the side of the road, roll down the windows, crank it up full blast, and dig the moment!

Jim has largely flown under the global rock radar. He remains as underrated a singer and guitar player as he is well respected by his songwriting peers and beloved by his fans. He knows everything there is to know about writing a hit song and has a whole bunch of 'em under his silver-studded leather belt to prove it. He is constantly scribbling notes or dictating song ideas into one handheld device or another, totally committed to his craft. When together we have stumbled upon that precise lyric line or unique chord progression we are searching for, his whole being lights up with a love of the music-making process … a rarity in this digital age.

Jim possesses a personality that is built for artistic success … a delicate balance of insecurity and self-confidence, of strength and vulnerability, of unstoppable drive and love of the journey. He has chosen the life of both professional musician and devoted family man, and has figured out how to succeed at both. I want to know his secret.

All that having been said, it is my belief that most, if not all, creative people have a darker inner world from which their art springs. My guess is that by the time we finish reading this book, you and I will also have gotten a glimpse into that part of Jimbo's life, as that is where a lot of the cool stuff happens. Songwriting is more than an art and a craft. It is where songwriters go to give form to our scariest feelings, to seek answers that elude us in real life, and for help expressing our anger, fear, and self-doubt in a functional way. In other words, it's where we go to rock!

Kevin Cronin and me.

I know him pretty well, but I want to find out more about where Jim goes to rock. I want to understand how it all got started for young Jimmy Peterik of Berwyn, Illinois, how he has kept it going strong over a nearly fifty-year span, and most incredibly, how he got his beautiful wife Karen into that Vehicle!

So here we are, at a time in most guys' careers when they are cashing out and looking into retirement plans; Jimbo is dyeing his hair purple, writing a book, and still schmoozing up a storm! Some might think he's a nut, and maybe he is, but that is why we are such kindred spirits and why I love the guy like I do.

rock on brother … kc

There's a Story in My Eyes...

I WOULDN'T TRADE LIVES with anyone. Every day has been a singular journey that has brought me to this moment in time. Writing this memoir has been like writing the diary I never kept. Fortunately and maybe not so fortunately, my brain is not equipped with a "delete" button, so most of my remembrances are either painfully or joyously intact.

As I leafed through my mental notes, I discovered what makes my life tick: the reasons I found success and the reasons even greater success has so far eluded me. I consider myself the luckiest guy I know—not because I have been blessed with wealth or fame, but because I have been touched by a wealth of people I can truly call friends.

I'm sure all autobiographies are cathartic for the writer, but perhaps even more so for me. Before tackling my memoirs, I was never the type to examine life as it happened, preferring to live in the cozy cocoon of creativity.

Songwriting has always been my escape, but it has also, too often, been my excuse for dealing improperly with many interpersonal and business relationships. Writing this book has forced me to harness my powers of recall and to look for answers to the complex questions I never thought to ask myself before.

You'll find those answers right here—no holds barred. The complex patchwork of my life is drenched with drama and reward, Sturm und Drang. My book tells the tale of a Czech kid from a small Chicago suburb who, instead of denying his humble heritage, chose to glorify it. In fact, here's how I still introduce us: "Hi everybody. We're The Ides of March from Berwyn, Illinois!"

It's a story about a boy whose rise to success reflects that of Rocky Balboa in the very song he co-wrote for *Rocky III*: the now iconic motivational anthem, "Eye of the Tiger."

I feel I was put on this earth to express my heart through the songs I write. Songs thoroughly define me. They have been both companion and sage counselor. They have made me a ton of money, yet have cost me a small fortune as I chased dream after dream to promote them.

Mine is a life that shatters the stereotypical "sex, drugs, and rock 'n' roll" archetype. Maybe that's why I'm still here and still coherent.

It is why my high school sweetheart and I have now been married for forty years. But the contradictions and complexity of my psyche are all here in living color. My various quirks and neuroses have informed my songwriting and created a kind of petri dish of cultures. I believe that if you never fail—if you never fall—then you are playing life too safe, and that's not who I am. Not at all.

I carry the strength and sometimes overconfidence of my gift, and yet I honor and protect that gift with every fiber of my being. I've always felt that if I fully appreciate the life I've been granted, He will let me keep it. So far, so good.

I can be endearing or annoying (depending on who you talk to), self-serving or self-deprecating, stingy or generous, overbearing or laissez-faire, humble or pretentious. But I always try to be genuine and treat people the way I'd like to be treated. By relaying my experiences as honestly as possible, I hope I have given you reasons to judge me fairly.

Here I rip the lid off many issues I have avoided for years. In the process I learned a lot about myself.

You will get to know more about many of the people I have been fortunate enough to work with through the years: The Ides of March, 38 Special, Sammy Hagar, Brian Wilson, The Beach Boys, Kevin Cronin and REO Speedwagon, The Doobie Brothers, Cheap Trick, Night Ranger, Dennis DeYoung, Reba McEntire, Henry Paul of Blackhawk, David Hasselhoff (!), Johnny Rivers, Lynyrd Skynyrd and, of course, Survivor. You will get a feel for the kind of people I love to work with and find out why I stay close to them even after all these years.

As I enter my seventh decade, I am still evolving—still pushing the envelope, sometimes achieving success, other times falling on my ass. I'm one of the few people I know who has acquired a nickname at age sixty: Jimbo. I've shed forty pounds and I've kept it off. I work out three times a week; I've added a swash of purple to my hair, tight, spray-on jeans, and a confident swagger that is in stark contrast with my history of shrinking from the light for so many years...

Why now? Why the reinvention? And, most importantly, will it last? Well, you've got to read this book and then decide for yourself.

People often stop and ask me, "Jim, what's your best song?" I'm sure they expect to hear me name one of my big hits, perhaps "Eye of the Tiger," "Hold on Loosely," "The Search Is Over" or "Vehicle."

Instead I tell them, "I haven't written it yet." And I'm dead serious. It's always day one for me—the first day of the rest of my life, and I intend to live to 100.

I've got too damn much to do, too many committed goals, too many songs to write, and too many emotions to express. I've got too much love to share, too many slushy martinis to sip, bone-in fillets to sink my teeth into, young rockers to mentor, too many vintage guitars to collect and memories to reflect upon. But most of all, I have the motivation to maybe even make a difference in your life.

Hopefully, I will touch you with a shared experience or perhaps mirror your own life in some way; maybe I will even shed some light on a problem you might be having. I have found that as I write, I become my own shrink—so I'm saving a bundle there.

At this very moment, sitting at the computer in my kitchen, I'm writing a song called "Delusional" for the group I founded, Pride of Lions, which features me and the amazing vocalist Toby Hitchcock.

It's a good one that concerns the sometimes careless medication of "hyperactive" kids when they become a nuisance to their parents and society. It's my belief that except in extreme cases kids should be allowed to be kids, exhibiting all the characteristics that make them unique individuals.

The lyric brings that point home:

"He gets up early each morning rushes down to the field
By the power of will he's a man made of steel
He says he's gonna be a football star
yeah they all say the boy's delusional

She sings into her hairbrush in front of the mirror
At the top of her lungs—her passion is clear
She says she wants to be like her idols on the screen
Ah they shake their heads—the girl's delusional

Then they come up with initials
for not doing what he's told
Giving her prescriptions—to fit into the mold"

Chorus:

"Let the boy dream—let him believe
Live and breathe—let him be delusional
Let the girl grow
Question all she's been told
Wild and free
Let them be unusual—Delusional

These are the rule breakers—the rain makers—the game changers
These are the restless souls that shape their destiny
These are the earth shakers—the risk takers—the storm chasers
These are the crazy hearts taking hope to history

Now here's to all with a vision beyond what is known
The ones who fight the whole world on raw courage alone
The ones who never listen when they taunt and they tease
One flash of their eyes—you can see what they see
It's the curse and the cure of the dreamer's disease
Do you know what it means to be—Delusional."

So here it is—with all its warts and beauty, holy water and spit—the world as I see it—"Through the Eye of the Tiger."

—Jimbo

In the Light of 1,000 Smiles

WHEN JIM PETERIK writes a song, he not only captures life's extraordinary moments, he sanctifies them. By penning the lyrics of "Eye of the Tiger" and "The Destiny Stone" (from Pride of Lions' 2007 release) he has made the distant dream attainable. Maybe we weren't raised to be boxers or political strategists, but Jim assures us, through his empowering words, that we have the power to succeed.

His talent does not stand still. "Ghost Orchid" (from his first Lifeforce CD) is shrouded in sensitivity, yet holds up to the strongest feminist anthem. "The Search Is Over" was inspired by a news story (but was informed by his own life's search), one that many might have read, but few would have synthesized.

Because the songwriter and the man are not two distinct entities, Jim's life story is as genuine as the solid, brick bungalows constructed in his native Berwyn. He's got roots, but he also has wings, which he has used to soar above some of pop culture's most transformative, yet harrowing times. Many of his contemporaries died—sadly, senselessly—before the age of thirty. Maybe that's why he doesn't take for granted one single day.

But survival, of course, isn't enough. Jim, who once skated danger-ously close to a spirit-crushing depression, had to find the strength to spring back. Songwriting, his close-knit friends, and his high school sweetheart, Karen (who eventually became his wife), meant the world to Jim back in Berwyn, but these loved ones mean even more today.

Because of their shared history, they understand his words and, moreover, his need for introspection. Soul-searching requires time. To Jim Peterik, silence seems to brilliantly simmer; perhaps it opens the gates to wondrous images and thoughts or to those lyrics that motivate and move us. Jim Peterik uses words and space to make the mundane fierce, strong, and gorgeous.

Jim and I met for the first time at a songwriting workshop in the late '80s, although I really doubt Jim remembers me; one of many emerging artists in a crowded room, I was buried behind a note-book. (*Author's note: I do distinctly remember this inquisitive and bright girl!*) I was struck by Jim's knowledge of the music business, but I also recall how the successful, Grammy-winning songwriter stayed around to field additional questions well past the targeted ending time.

What struck me, too, was how warm and personable Jim was, even after what must have been an exhausting afternoon. "Approachable" is how many of his fans would describe him. Jim sees himself as a people person. Even the shortest dialogue with a fan or a server at a local diner seems to excite him; his dad, Jim Peterik Sr., also a work-ing musician, taught, by example, that no one trumps another—we're in this life together. I believe that Jim feels we have to embrace our commonalities.

I never forgot that personality. Years later, when I started writing for the popular British webzine *Pennyblackmusic*, I was in a position to interview many of my favorite artists. I sought out Jim to find out how he had successfully navigated his post–Ides of March and Sur-vivor days and how he had sustained his career in an industry that many might call cutthroat.

I initially called to request a twenty-minute phoner, but I was incredibly pleased when Jim invited me to spend the afternoon in his recording studio, "Lennon's Den" (named after one of his biggest heroes), to watch a session and to conduct a more extensive interview in his contemporary, sun-drenched home in the western suburb of Burr Ridge, Illinois.

For several hours I observed Jim, along with Larry Millas, his long-standing boyhood friend, fellow Ides of March band member, and engineer of the day's session, at work. They overdubbed solos with several outstanding session musicians, and I then interviewed Jim for another seamless hour. Finally, we grabbed lunch at his favorite haunt, the Moondance Diner.

We touched on many themes that afternoon: songwriting, career building, and the production of his hits. Jim also relayed emotional challenges that he had faced as a result of growing up ahead of his peers. Though we went deep, the time went by in a flash. For that reason, I wasn't too surprised, after I typed up my notes, that we had discussed enough for a comprehensive two-part interview.

Earlier this year, Jim got in touch and asked if I would help him write his memoirs. A project that could have been daunting—documenting a life!—was made endlessly enjoyable because of Jim's charm, humor, and talent.

Before I came along, his life and music had already been immortalized through endless awards, discographies, and personal testimonies, but now I had the enviable opportunity to find out, through first-person narratives, how he had achieved his goals, and whether his journey would be better described as a struggle or a methodical game plan.

For Jim, I believe, this collaboration required incredible stamina and honesty; the courage to face memories that at times were painful, and the resolution to favor deep thought over superficial judgments. A life story is not an easy one to tell, but Jim's high degree of emotional intelligence, and surprising ability to recall key events, make him a stellar narrator.

In my opinion, *Through the Eye of the Tiger* was not intended for a singular audience. It is a fascinating read for anyone looking to propel a dream, as well as for the obsessive rock music fan, music historian, or emerging songwriter.

Jim, aside from his accomplishments, remains, for many of his fans, the quintessential Midwesterner who resisted life on both coasts, the guy-next-door who married his dream-woman and life partner, Karen.

As the rare, remarkable artist who has reshuffled the deck of the American dream, Jim has redefined his talents, consistently, in an industry that is as unpredictable as the temperamental Chicago climate.

To enjoy Jim's story, though, you must redefine the term "rock star" because, while it's true that his flashy wardrobe stops passersby on any city street, the parallels end there.

This songwriter's glories are not built upon endless visits to rehab nor dalliances with star-struck fans. Jim Peterik, the father, husband, brother, uncle, mentor, producer, performer, and singer/songwriter, remains aware that, with his celebrity status, he can offer creative inspiration to others, and he takes that precious gift seriously.

—Lisa Torem

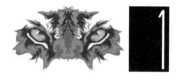

Rising Up to the Challenge

THE PHONE CALL that shook my world came on an otherwise ordinary day, the way life-altering events usually do.

The '77 VW Scirocco I had just picked up from a repair shop in Maywood, Illinois, should have had a Sunkist logo on it—that lemon had left me stranded all over the U.S. But now the old junker was finally fixed, and after a long afternoon fielding traffic, I pulled into the driveway of our ranch home on South Stone Avenue in La Grange.

I walked inside and gave way to my everyday ritual. I pressed "play" on my enormous answering machine.

"Jim, give me a call, it's Alice Anne. What are we getting Mother for her birthday?" *Click.*

As I casually listened I laid my shoulder bag on the counter, and started shuffling through the mail. Lotsa junk mail as always.

Next: "Jim! Salzman. You gotta hear the new one by Rundgren. It's sick. Call me." *Click.*

I picked up a Les Paul Gibson and started idly picking. I was tired and only half-listening when I pressed the button to retrieve one last call.

"Hey, yo, Jim. That's a nice message machine you got there. This is Sylvester Stallone. Give me a call. 604..." *Click.*

Rewind. Click. "Hey, yo, Jim. That's a nice message machine you got there..."

Rewind. Click. "Hey, yo, Jim. That's a nice ..."

Time froze and I gathered my thoughts. Maybe it was a gag. It's true that we had formed a new group, Survivor, and that by early 1982 we had established a good reputation with two albums under our belt. We had also toured with the likes of Jefferson Starship, Kansas, and Triumph. But, Stallone? What would he want with me?

Was it even Stallone? Or could it have been Sal, our Italian road manager, doing a dead-on impersonation? I had to find out. But first, I called up Frankie Sullivan, the lead guitarist in Survivor, and told him to come over right away. I explained that I thought I had just gotten a call from Sylvester Stallone!

Frankie came right over and we strategized. We manned two separate phones; I dialed the Los Angeles number and we got a quick response. "Yo!"

"Is this Sylvester Stallone? This is Jim Peterik and Frankie Sullivan of Survivor."

"Yeah, but call me Sly," he answered.

"Okay, Sly," I stammered.

Speaking in his now trademark Philly accent he told us about a new movie he had just shot. It was the third in the Rocky series, *Rocky III*. The film was now finished except that they still needed to choose the music.

I hurriedly scrambled to find a piece of paper to write on until my hand landed on the *Beatles Songs Easy Piano Series: Volume One* songbook that Karen had been playing. I grabbed the thin book, still focused on every word Sly was saying, flipped it over to a mostly blank backside, and started scribbling notes as he spoke. I was jotting words, phrases, and concepts even as we went along. I wrote around another long-forgotten song I was working on called "Take These Memories" and put his phone number down next to the name Syvestor [sic] Stallone!

"Tony Scotti [CEO of Survivor's label, Scotti Brothers] played me your song, 'Poor Man's Son.'" (It was a cut off of our 1981 release *Premonition*.) "That's the sound I want for my movie's title song. It's raw, it's street. It's got energy and it's got exactly what I need. Do you think you can help me out?"

By this time I felt like I was levitating and looking down at the room from a hundred feet.

"Ummm. Absolutely," I answered.

Sly added, "I want something for the kids, something with a pulse. I'm going to send you the first three minutes of the movie. That's the montage. That's where I need the song."

He went on to explain that he had tried to obtain the rights to use "Another One Bites the Dust" by Queen for that spot, but they had refused to grant him the license. *Thank you, Queen!* I thought to myself.

"That's the song you'll hear on the rough cut I'm going to send you. That's the one to beat, but I can only send you the first three minutes. The rest is top secret," Sly intoned.

Click.

I stared at the music book. The thing looked like it had been caught in a brainstorm. Ideas, both random and dictated, spread from top to bottom and side to side. I recently rediscovered this artifact and it immediately took me back to that day. That pivotal moment.

I looked over at Frankie, he was half grinning, half in shock, and we slapped each other five. This was the chance we had been waiting for.

Frankie was a young, unproven guitar hotshot from the industrial town of Franklin Park, Illinois, and I was already a conquering warrior fighting on the frontlines of rock 'n' roll for fifteen years, looking for my next victory. As band members and individuals we were ready for what might turn out to be our defining moment. We agreed that Rocky Balboa's story was a lot like ours: Against the odds, a band on

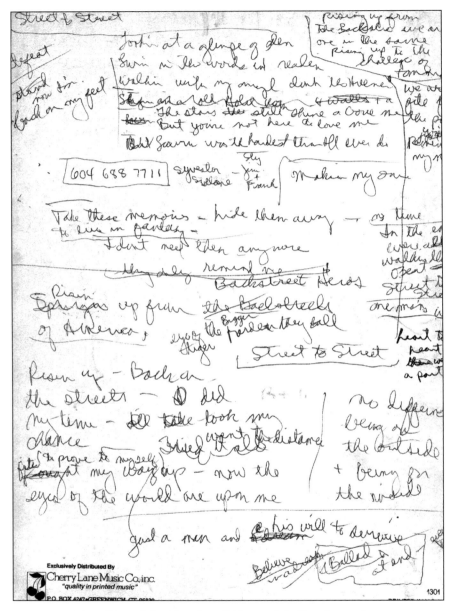

First "Eye of the Tiger" scribbles and Stallone's number.

a small label tries to fell the giants, Foreigner, Journey, Kansas, and other melodic rock heavyweights.

That afternoon I went out and rented a pro Betamax player—a then state-of-the-art video machine that was about the size of a small refrigerator. I hooked it up on the kitchen counter and waited for FedEx. When the tape arrived at my doorstep the next day I called Frankie to come over quick and we wasted no time loading it in.

Here I was, at the ready, my white Les Paul electric guitar casually slung around my neck waiting for lightning to strike. Suddenly, the kitchen was charged with electricity. The Mohawk-headed Mr. T rose up like the commanding threat he would soon become; his dramatic entrance was contrasted by Stallone resting on his laurels doing Master Charge commercials and enjoying the spoils of his success. This quick-cut film montage was accompanied by "Another One Bites the Dust" by one of our favorite bands, Queen.

I rolled my eyes and wondered out loud how we were going to beat that masterstroke of a song. Queen's smash hit seemed to work so perfectly. We watched it again, this time with the sound off. That's when I started playing that now familiar, muted, sixteenth-note figure: *digga digga digga digga digga digga digga* and then started grabbing chords from thin air; C minor, B flat major, C minor. Then C minor, B flat major, C minor, C over G, A flat. Repeat. The slashes seemed to coincide with the punches being thrown. I even put one slash in an unorthodox beat to match a punch. This irregular beat would become the scourge of drummers for all time! Later in my career, when I'd audition a drummer, if he couldn't grasp this weird measure I knew he was probably not gonna cut it.

At just the right moment, without saying a word, Frankie and I headed for the piano room at the front of the house. This very cozy, yet inspiring room held my small, but growing guitar collection, which hung on the wall. A beautiful Ibach grand piano took up a good portion of the tiny room. (I still have that piano—it's lucky.)

Frankie switched to guitar and I dashed over to the piano. I hammered out a chord progression that was actually quite R&B inflected. Frankie held down the fort with the rhythm we had established. Now, we had the groove and some of the chords, but then we hit a wall.

What was this movie about? How does it end? What should be the focus of this song? We called up Sly and begged him to send us a rough cut of the entire movie. He reluctantly agreed to do so but only under the condition that we send it back the very next day, overnight delivery.

The entire *Rocky III* movie arrived by FedEx the next morning. We sat there spellbound as we watched the dazzling action and humorous yet meaningful dialogue. It was filled with soon-to-be-famous Stallone catchphrases: "Go for it!" "Knock you into tomorrow!" Then we heard it: the Big Hook. Rocky Balboa's trainer, played by the gravelly voiced actor Burgess Meredith, tells the main character, "Rocky, you're losing the eye of the tiger." Bingo. There was our title, the focus of our game-changing smash.

The next day, we reconvened. We sat in the music room wondering where this lyric could start. Frankie broke the ice. He mumbled, "How about, 'Back on the street, doing time, taking chances'?"

I liked the sound of those words. I thought about the script and Rocky's quest to stay on top. I countered with, "How about this? 'Rising up, back on the street, did my time, took my chances.'"

We had our start. From there the lyrics just seemed to flow with the storyline. The next few days as I jogged (an every morning ritual) I sweated out words and phrases.

"So many times, it happens too fast, you trade your passion for glory." Yeah, great line. I would recite it into my Radio Shack cassette recorder. "Don't lose your grip on the dreams of the past; you must fight just to keep them alive." Yup, that'll work, too.

When I had the bulk of the lyric and Frankie's approval, we booked time at Chicago Recording Company (CRC) to record the demo. We rounded up Marc Droubay, our drummer, and Stephan Ellis, on bass, who were both living in a house that my wife, Karen, and I owned at the time. Stephan obviously didn't understand the magnitude of the project. In fact, I remember how he groused about going down to the studio just to record "some movie music."

The guys heard the song for the first time as I was pounding it out on the Yamaha grand piano in studio A. We set up the drums in the storage room in back of the studio to get that raw, ambient, John

Bonham–style sound. The Led Zeppelin drummer was Marc's main influence. You could hear it in his attack.

When it was time to record, Frankie sat in the control room next to our engineer, the late Phil Bonanno, to make sure the sounds were going down right. Frankie's great set of ears always helped us get the most out of an engineer and a studio.

We found a click tempo, which is like a metronome that we would hear in our cans (headphones) to keep our tempo steady. We were concerned because the tendency for most musicians is to rush the tempo. In this song, that outcome would have been deadly.

As soon as we lit into the song I felt the surge of magic. Oh, my God! Marc laid down the groove with four on the floor, the kick drum pounding on every beat and the jackhammer snare that Frankie and Phil had dialed in just right. Steph laid down the steady plod with his amazing pick style, and, on piano, I supplied the expansive chording; my goal was to fill out our song and make it move.

Survivor's lead singer, Dave Bickler, did not know the song well enough yet to sing a guide vocal so we just kept the melody in our heads as we played. The second take was magic. It felt like history was going down; we were achieving a solidity of sound I had never heard before and rarely since.

Frankie declared it was a "take" and we filed into the control booth for a very loud and powerful playback. The overdubs went quickly the next day. I laid down the sixteenth-note *digga-digga-digga* muted guitar figure to the bottom using my white Les Paul Custom running through my 1959 Fender Tweed Bassman amp and an Electric Mistress chorus effect—this device mimics the sound of an electric twelve-string—then I meticulously doubled this part, which Frankie panned far left and right in the stereo spread to make it sound huge.

Now it was Frankie's turn. He did the first two passes on a tobacco sunburst Les Paul, which he christened "Firewood," through his Marshall fifty-watt half-stack. Then, he layered on top two tracks of Fender Stratocaster to give shimmer to the raw slabs of power guitar. (A few years later at a music/tennis event, the amazing Alan Parsons asked me how the hell we got that incredible guitar sound. Do you think I told him?)

Two days later it was Dave's time to shine. He sang as if his life depended on it.

> *"It's the eye of the tiger, it's the thrill of the fight,*
> *rising up to the challenge of our rival*
> *and the last known survivor*
> *stalks his prey in the night,*
> *and he's watching us all with the*
> *eye...of the tiger."*

Dave hit that high E on the word "eye" and made this one of the most exhilarating moments of my life and in rock 'n' roll history. Everyone in the control room cheered as he walked in for the first playback. No one else could have sung that song as well as Dave. He was born for that performance.

When we sent the rough mix to Stallone, he responded, "Yeah, you guys really did it! This is exactly what I was looking for. But you got a little lazy on me. You forgot to write me a third verse!" On the original demo, we had Dave repeat the first verse a second time in the third verse slot.

So now it was back to the drawing board. After discussions with Frankie, we decided to cheat a bit and grab pieces of the first verse and alternate with new lines. Stallone loved our job of self-thievery.

"Rising up, straight to the top, had the guts, got the glory. Went the distance, now I'm not gonna stop. Just a man and his will to survive." (In a recently discovered notebook, I found that one of my trial lyrics for the first line of the final chorus was, "Rising up, ready to spring!" Ouch!)

I was not totally surprised when "Eye of the Tiger" went on to hit number one on the *Billboard* charts and stayed there for seven weeks, or that it would sell 5 million records in its first year and 30 million to date. Hell, we had a 10-million-dollar video titled *Rocky III* to promote it!

What amazes me most is that this song remains alive and well—stronger, it seems with every passing year. It continues to be a thread in the fabric of millions of lives and it has motivated so many to go beyond their perceived limitations and achieve more than they ever could imagine.

Over the years, "Eye of the Tiger" has given focus and strength to athletes. It has helped people rise from wheelchairs and walk, and it has been part of the soundtrack to the lives of so many individuals from all walks of life.

It seems as if every generation discovers it and claims the song as its own. Truly, in my case, destiny began with a phone call and changed a thousand destinies along the way. It certainly changed mine forever. Now when people ask what comes first for me, the words or the music, I answer, "Neither. First comes a phone call…in my case—from Sylvester Stallone."

Ever Since the World Began

I HAD A VERY COOL CHILDHOOD. Not only was I the youngest child, I also held the status of being the only boy. Nobody knew I was coming. I was a complete surprise. Everyone thought I'd come out as Barbara—they already had a name picked out for me!

I was treasured. I felt completely valued by my parents and sisters. Some people only talk about self-esteem, but I knew that I was special because my family made me feel that way. My earliest memory was being bathed in a white wicker bassinet, which was located right off the kitchen. That shared experience was so special—my whole family smiling and cooing at me was pretty seductive stuff. I think that's why I became a performer. I always loved the feeling of being the center of attention.

When I was about three years old I walked into the living room where my parents and sisters were cooing over a newborn baby that

Happy New Year, 1953.

a relative of ours had brought over. I surveyed the situation with disgust and before storming out the front door to the porch, I muttered, "Why don't you do something more important rather!" I didn't quite understand the explosion of laughter I heard as I slammed the door. You see, only I could be the center of attention. The next day I complained about a stomachache. I received so much concern and attention that I complained of one almost every day after that, to the point that my family took me downtown to the tallest building in Chicago at the time, the Prudential Building, for a raft of allergy tests. As the fine needles scratched my back for about an hour I was suddenly very sorry I had created the great stomachache hoax.

My older sisters, Alice Anne and Janice, ten and twelve years older, respectively, were the typical 1950s teenagers, wearing all the latest styles: fleece poodle skirts, tight angora or cashmere sweaters, faded jeans rolled up to the knee, and capri slacks with the zipper in the back (still love those). Janice was a bleach blonde, Alice Anne a brunette. They alternated hairstyles between Audrey Hepburn short and Lauren Bacall long.

Music was a huge part of my early years. My sisters, I realize now, had impeccable taste in music. They loved Johnny Cash. The country star with the oak barrel whiskey baritone became my first real influence after the girls had brought home these yellow label 45s, manufactured by the Memphis-based Sun Records. I loved "I Walk the Line," "Train of Love," and "I Still Miss Someone." I didn't know it then, but it was the stripped-down simplicity and raw honesty that spoke to my emerging sensibilities.[1]

These little records would churn at forty-five revolutions per minute around the big spindle of the then-revolutionary RCA Victor record changer, which sat proudly on top of the Peterik family's blond-cabinet black-and-white Zenith television set. You would stack up to eight records on the chubby spindle and marvel as the records dropped one by one.

My parents, of course, had their own records, but their tastes consisted of real cornball stuff that I dreaded. There were, however, one or two records of theirs that I could not get enough of. One was Dean Martin's "Memories Are Made of This" and the other a divine instrumental called "Skokiaan" by Ralph Marterie. I found myself gravitating to that major key melodic stuff, though it would be years until I would see the impact in my own writing.

---

[1] My passion for those old Sun Records sides of Johnny Cash extended forward to 1966 when I convinced The Ides of March to work up and record a Byrds-influenced rendition of Johnny's "Train of Love." It was recorded at the same session that spawned "Roller Coaster" and is only being released now on The Ides' 50th anniversary set.

It was the heartfelt and beautiful melodies that always got me. "Big Rock Candy Mountain" enchanted me. This blue vinyl 45 had all of these different cowboy hits on the sleeve, and because I knew that "Big Rock Candy Mountain" was the third cut, I would position myself in my favorite armchair so I could anticipate the cowboy three-part harmony and the lyric I learned by heart: "Oh the buzzing of the bees and the cigarette trees…" (seriously!) "The soda water fountain…" I would let these great melodies seduce and wash over me again and again. Today when I relive these moments there is a chemical reaction inside me that sets off the exact vibration complete with sounds, smells, and intense feeling. (I described that phenomenon many years later in a song I wrote for Lisa McClowry, "Time Signatures"—those sensory cues being the signature of time.)

I liked the spooky tunes, too. There was something very seductive when Art and Dotty Todd cooed "Chanson D'Amour" especially when they went "ra da da, da da"—goose bumps. When I heard the intro to "Mr. Sandman" by the Chordettes I had a brand-new physical reaction. As the girls were singing, "Mr. Sandman, bring me a dream, make him the cutest that I've ever seen" in that sugar-sweet three-part harmony I felt something angular in my pants—something hard and boney. Something strange yet somehow wonderful. I listened to that song a lot just wondering what to do with that protuberance.

Certain other songs through the years had what Neil Young calls "the spook" and had that same effect on me: "Runaway" by Del Shannon, "Sealed with a Kiss" by Brian Hyland, "(The Man Who Shot) Liberty Valance" by Gene Pitney (written by my future songwriting heroes Burt Bacharach and Hal David), "Scotch and Soda" by the Kingston Trio, "Beyond the Sea" by Bobby Darin, "Come Softly to Me" by the Fleetwoods, and yes, predictably, "Spooky" by the Classics IV.

As much as I loved Johnny Cash, he had to play second fiddle when Janice brought home a black-labeled disc with a phonograph and a dog pictured on the label by an artist with a very odd name: Elvis Presley. He had a rawness that just got to the roots of my soul! This is what I had been waiting for. Then when my sisters and I huddled around the "shmee-vee" (my mother enjoyed degrading the TV with that flippant nickname) to watch Elvis on *The Ed Sullivan Show* one fateful Saturday night, I knew that's who I wanted to be. After that day I hound-dogged my parents until they bought me every Presley single they could find: older releases on Sam Phillips' Sun Records such as "Milk Cow Blues Boogie," "Baby, Let's Play House," "I Don't Care If the Sun Don't Shine," and "Good Rockin' Tonight."

Then Alice Anne brought home this giant record with a little hole in it. I had never seen an LP before. "LP" stood for "long playing" and it had not one but up to six songs per side. This purchase coincided with my mom and dad purchasing a freshly minted RCA portable record player. It was maroon red and had speakers built in. It sat on a functionally beautiful gold metal stand. I stared at it in total awe as the arm went down on our very first LP: Elvis Presley's first album.

As I listened I devoured the cover with pink letters that screamed out Elvis Presley. There he was, live onstage, with his guitar slung around his neck, mouth open so wide you could practically see his tonsils. On the back he was wearing a black-and-white polka-dotted scarf. My sisters and I would gaze and listen almost obsessively 'til we knew every word of each song on that album: "I'm Counting on You," "Blue Suede Shoes," "Tutti Frutti" (I knew this version way before hearing Little Richard's original), the wonderfully playful "One-Sided Love Affair," and the super-tough "Trying to Get to You."

One day my sisters brought home "Love Me Tender." I put that record on, and suddenly it seemed as if Elvis was singing right into my ear. I don't know how to describe what I was feeling, but it was very, very intimate. I found out years later that besides the emotion that Elvis put into the delivery, he was recorded absolutely "dry"— that is, without any of the tape slap echo that producer Sam Phillips typically used on his voice. In this dry state it was as if Elvis was right in the room with you, singing into your ear.

When I was three or four my family started going on summer vacations. We'd drive down to Ft. Myers, Florida, to visit my mother's brother, Uncle Raymond and Auntie Florence, who ran one of those soft-serve ice cream stands called the Dairy Dream—kind of a Tastee-Freez wanna-be. We'd hit the interstate, head across the endless miles of cornfields of southern Illinois, and gradually ramble through the steaming heat of the southern states. As we'd wind through the Smoky Mountains, Alice Anne and Janice would take out their ukuleles from the trunk. One was a mahogany Gretsch, which I still have to this day, and the other was a blond Regal that, unfortunately, has long since disappeared.

In the backseat my sisters and I would sing camp songs, such as "The Happy Wanderer" (better known by its chorus chant: "valderee, valderah"), "Smile Awhile," and "Let the Rest of the World Go By." Perhaps our favorite sing-along was "Bye Bye Love" and "All I Have to Do Is Dream" by our beloved Everly Brothers. As I'd sing I'd bite my inner cheeks to simulate their gaunt, sunken cheek look. Our repertoire consisted of the same six or seven songs that we would sing over and over again. I felt secure and loved in the arms of family. Those days are some of the best times of my life.

I first found myself drawn to the ukulele when I was about four years old, but when I picked it up, my hands couldn't even wrap around the neck of the instrument. Then, at about four and a half, when my hands grew bigger, I could finally grasp it and firmly place my fingers around the neck to form a chord. I was jubilant!

Janice and Alice Anne taught me the basic chords: C, G, F, and E minor, which allowed me to strum and sing a tune called "Maybe," made popular by the Chantels in '56. I played that song over and over again and drove my parents to distraction as my sisters giggled.

Then, I learned the other songs they were so fond of singing: "Jada" and "Has Anybody Seen My Gal?" ("Five foot two, eyes of blue. But, oh! what those five foot could do…"). To this day I can play all of those songs and wow my friends at parties or events. When my sister Janice died, Alice Anne and I played our ukes at the wake and sang a bittersweet, slightly out of tune version of "Let the Rest of the World Go By."

That was the beginning of my musical journey: singing three-part harmonies with Janice and Alice Anne and strumming those ukuleles in the backseat while my parents bickered in the front seat.

"You're going too fast, slow down. Do you have to be the first car on the highway all the time?" griped my mom, Alice. But she knew the answer: of course! Ninety-five mph was the typical speed for one of our trips down south.

We didn't care, though. My sisters used to try to "pants" me in the backseat, hit me, kick me, tickle me, and of course, I loved every minute of it.

"Stop, it girls! Jimmie, would you rather be up here with us or tortured in the backseat with your sisters?"

My answer was simple: "Tortured in the backseat with my sisters!" You see, this wasn't torture at all. Having all that attention focused on me set the stage for my strong desire, obsession if you will, to be a performer.

3

Capturing Memories from Afar

I ALWAYS CRAVED the spotlight. As time went on, I became more and more comfortable in the limelight, and then actually needed it to feel like myself.

My sisters, in a way, were the ones who raised me. With my dad busy at work adjusting relays at our local telephone company, Automatic Electric, and my mother doing community work (she volunteered at the Piggy Bank Thrift Shop, a resale store that sold donated clothes and items) in South Berwyn, it fell to my sisters to mind "Fatboy," as they often called me. My belly was so big at age five that I used to lift it up and throw it down like I saw the bullies do in the cartoons I loved. It was the move they'd make when they came "harrumphing" into the room. Because of the many years between us, I was like an only child, but they made me feel like a golden child. I had so much more in common with them than with

"Fatboy" with my dear and gorgeous sisters, Alice Anne and Janice—
Oceanside Miami Beach—Cavalier Motel, 1955.

my parents. They made me feel loved and they doted on me. They
laughed at my jokes and treated me like a rock star even before I
learned to play the guitar.

My parents made me take piano when I was seven. God, did I hate
practicing! Mr. Ulrich was my unfortunate tutor. He was ancient and
smelled like mothballs. I was never prepared with my lesson and one
day he finally looked me straight in the eye.

"You really don't want to do this, do you?"

"Uhh, not really, Mr. Ulrich," I stammered.

When my Uncle Raymond would visit, my mom would say, "Show your uncle what you've learned on piano." I would reluctantly play my scales, but when he started yawning I realized that this wasn't cool. Then Alice Anne would launch into "Clair de Lune" and Uncle Raymond would be all smiles. Piano lessons were a chore. I wanted to play songs!

Just like my dad before me, I'm an ear person. I never liked reading those ants on the page called "notes." Never cared about theory or avoiding parallel fifths (apparently a no-no in classical composing). I quit piano lessons after one long year at the ripe old age of eight. By that point, I knew enough to work out the chords and simple melodies on my own. Soon I began to fashion those chords into primitive songs. I would perform those four or five simple chords mimicking another of my early rock 'n' roll heroes, Jerry Lee Lewis, which included standing up and kicking away the piano bench as I'd seen him do on TV.

I developed a style that is known as a "writer's piano." For me the piano is mainly a tool for writing songs. The keyboard for me has always been more about mood than technique or fast runs. A few years later I'd use the guitar in a similar fashion to bring out the rock side of my songwriting.

There's something so peaceful about sitting down at the piano because it speaks to my soul and inspires me to write about romance and beauty. When I want to rock, though, I crank up the guitar through a Marshall amp and feel a different kind of majesty.

Janice and Alice Anne were polar opposites. Janice was the popular girl in high school. Even though I was twelve years younger, I kind of sensed that she was hot stuff. Very attractive, very happening, and smartly dressed in her form-fitted skirt and cashmere sweater, Janice collected a closet full of the latest styles and a dazzling array of boyfriends. She actually modeled dresses for fashion shows for the upscale Wieboldt's department store in Oak Park, Illinois, where she also sold ladies' hats.

Not that Alice Anne wasn't popular, but she was more conservative and perhaps not the trendsetter that Janice was. For some reason

Alice Anne did not really resemble the rest of the family. Once when we grouped together for a family photo in Miami Beach the photographer shooed her aside shouting, "You, at the end. Just the family, just the family!"

Janice had a mad crush on a high school dropout named Al Kovarik, a slick-looking, James Dean type of guy from the tough Chicago suburb of Cicero. He was my favorite of all her boyfriends because he looked cool and drove a '56 chartreuse and black Mercury Monterey convertible complete with spotlights, blue-dot taillights, and power windows. He would take me and Janice out cruising, some nights stopping at Big Boy, a burger drive-in on the main drag on Ogden Avenue in Berwyn. He'd let me order a double Big Boy and a chocolate milkshake… once he even took us to the drive-in movie way out on Cicero Avenue to see *Apache*. I drove them both crazy putting the power windows and power antenna up and down all night long as they were trying to make out.

Sadly, Janice made decisions with her heart, not her intellect, and her boyfriends tended to be left of center, nontraditional types.

She married the last in that line, a burly trucking magnate whose name could be seen silk-screened on the gravel trucks going to and from the local limestone quarry in Lyons. One of his big Mack trucks bore the name "Miss Janice" on the hood. But things were far from rosy between them and Mother and Dad had to intervene when Janice wanted a divorce. (In my parents' day people mated for life! Divorce was a sin.)

Perhaps because of the marital discord, Janice became a closet drinker, hiding bottles of wine all around the house and spending time in rehab centers. I remember as a child feeling powerless at calming the battles that raged between them. Even though her husband loved her and funded her every whim (archeological digs, her vast collection of African art), money could not make up for a certain emptiness and growing aggression between them.

A lifetime chain smoker, Janice finally found peace on December 20, 1994, when she succumbed to emphysema-induced heart failure at age fifty-seven, leaving behind a heart load of precious memories.

She came to me in a vivid dream the day after she passed. "Jimmie, don't worry about me. It's wonderful here." In my reverie she was restored to the teen queen Janice in her cashmere sweater and pearls long before life got the best of her. From that dream on I felt totally at peace.

Poor Alice Anne (nicknamed "AA") was often the brunt of my mother's sharp-tongued sarcasm, saying she looked like an Indian squaw while Janice would always come out unscathed. If Mom's tactics created competition between the two of them, I sure never saw it. All I saw was a lot of love between them.

The contrast between Janice and Alice Anne was never more apparent than on the family 8-millimeter movie clip where Alice Anne couldn't stay upright for even a millisecond on her water skis. She kept falling hilariously right back into the water, being dragged along helplessly by the speeding boat. Next, the grainy film showed Janice, tan in her bikini, flashing her all-American smile as she glided effortlessly across that same pale, blue lake, skimming the crystal-clear waters with bulletproof confidence, casually waving her free hand.

But Alice Anne is a true gem if perhaps a rough diamond, and to this day my closest friend and soulmate. When Janice passed away in 1994, AA and I closed ranks—a lot of our time together consists of reminiscing and remembering the shimmering spirit that was Janice and those dear old days when it was the three of us just enjoying all life had to offer.

Besides the huge influence of my sisters, my Catholic upbringing had a profound effect. My parents were not extremely religious around the house, but they made sure we went to St. Odilo's Parish for Sunday school. (He must have been kind of an off-brand saint—I have never heard of a St. Odilo then or since...)

When my family went to church, I would tag along. It didn't mean much to me; the priest was just some guy in a black suit droning on about who knows what. At first, the Mass was in Latin. Clear as mud. In Sunday school, I experienced the austere nuns. Their very glance could wither you. It's as if they were taking their whole miserable life out on you.

Sunday school was all about the memorization of the Lord's Prayer, Hail Mary, and the Act of Contrition. After my first communion and confirmation I became defined by guilt. I took to heart that "if you thought about committing a sin, by God, you sinned!"

If I had "impure thoughts" about Laura Strama, that fantasy girl in grade school who always sat in the front of the class, I knew that I was going to Hell. Until, of course, I came clean with the man behind the curtain.

Masturbation was a huge no-no. I knew that if I happened to "fall off the wagon" it felt good, and then I felt bad! At that point, of course, I had to fall on the sword and go to confession. If you did masturbate, here's what you had to say:

"Bless me Father for I have sinned. It has been two weeks since my last confession and these are my sins: I talked back to my mother, I disobeyed my father, I stole a silver dollar from Jerry Kmen's parents' bedroom (that really happened!), and had impure actions with my body."

The priest must have heard this same scenario a thousand times, and then, in a spooky, disembodied voice, he would dish out my penance: "Say ten Our Fathers, ten Hail Mary's, and make a good act of contrition." (As opposed to a bad one?)

Leaving the confessional, I felt that I had been purged, and then, yippee, I was free to go out and sin again! It was like putting gas in the tank of eternal salvation; you had to do it every couple of weeks or face eternal damnation. I have to admit I felt cleansed at least until real life dirtied me up again.

The negative influence of guilt in my life manifested itself in far-reaching ways. In those days they didn't have initials for what I suffered from as a child. Nowadays my behavior would probably be called obsessive-compulsive disorder. Back in the day, I was just "a boy trying to find himself" as my sixth-grade teacher Mrs. Hull told my folks at the dreaded parent-teacher conference. I was also "a chronic worrier."

"Jimmie, don't you be's a worrier!" my mother would often intone, lapsing into a peculiar soulful dialect. I obsessed about everything: the test coming up on Monday, the project due on Tuesday, and even way back in kindergarten, I stressed out about how I was going to button my smock in art class (finally my mother installed snaps on it, thus saving me the humiliation of not knowing how to button a button).

After watching *Dr. Kildare* (starring a very young Richard Chamberlain) or *Ben Casey* (featuring Vince Edwards), two very popular medically based dramas, I contracted whatever disease was diagnosed that particular episode. One week I was convinced I looked pale and, of course, I concluded that I must certainly have leukemia.

Another week it was cancer. It was the disease du jour. I staggered between fear of tornados, earthquakes, thunderstorms, and, after I watched the terrifying TV drama *On the Beach*, which depicted the world after nuclear annihilation, I had nightmares of mushroom clouds on every horizon.

In my later years, I worked on divesting myself of this guilt—unlearning all the BS. We're all sinners and we're accepted anyway. Jillian, a Christian artist who I produced, was a great influence, and a great source of consolation.

She would preach the word of the Lord to nondenominational churches all over the country. One day in the car on the way to the studio she asked if I had accepted Jesus into my heart.

I told her that I went to church almost every Sunday. Jillian again asked me if I had accepted Jesus, and I responded that I wasn't good enough; that I'm a sinner and I don't feel worthy enough. She essentially told me that that was nonsense! She said, "We're all worthy of having Jesus in our hearts. Jesus knows we are imperfect. We are forgiven the moment that we sin."

I'm not crazy about the phrase "born again," but in that moment I felt lighter than air. I felt a new energy come over me. I felt like a child again.

We're not perfect, but we're loved anyway. This epiphany eventually formed the basis for my new way of thinking. But religion was not the only influence in my early life; I was also entranced by American popular culture.

When I was about eight years old I was drawn to Charlie Brown, the self-effacing main character in Charles Schulz's comic strip,

"Peanuts." Whenever I tagged along with my mom on boring shopping expeditions, I would get lost in the book department of the upscale Marshall Field's department store in Oak Park.

There I was, laughing out loud at the antics of those comic strip characters. Charlie Brown was the underdog, an ordinary kid who tried harder but often fell short. I identified with him, and later the message that I clearly stated in "Eye of the Tiger" reflected his belief system.

Like many kids, I loved Captain Kangaroo, who was an iconic father figure. He was a stocky, kindly man with blond bangs that looked like they had been chopped short with pinking shears around an upside-down cereal bowl. The Captain's soft, reassuring voice was something a kid could count on every morning. The jingling of his keys as he walked was music to my young ears. My other faves were *Kukla, Fran and Ollie, Ding Dong School, Garfield Goose,* and a bit later the hilarious Rocky the Flying Squirrel from *The Rocky and Bullwinkle Show.*

Despite my love for those innocent television characters, music still held the trump card. On Halloween, as a kindergartener, I dressed as a pirate, complete with charcoal mustache and plastic sword.

The following Halloween, my dear mother, seeing my infatuation with rock 'n' roll as a whole and Elvis in particular, took it upon herself to apply the name "Elvis" on the front of my ukulele in white surgical tape. When she showed it to me I didn't react the way she expected. I told her that there was no way I would go as Elvis. I felt terrible (and still do) for destroying her expectations after all the time she took putting on that tape. But no matter how she begged me, I was not gonna be a rock pretender. I'd rather go as a pirate again than fake being a rock star.

Every year Hiawatha School would have a Halloween parade. As we would snake through the different classrooms, I felt special because, even though I was just one of the crowd, I had experienced what it felt like to be in the public eye. I liked that feeling—a lot.

Although I looked forward so much to the Halloween parade with my schoolmates, I had other friendships. In my Berwyn, Illinois, neighborhood, I hung around with a pair of great kids, Binky Cihak and Johnny Babinak.

Every kid should have a Binky and a Johnny. Sure, they were a little older, but they were my buddies, and not only did they know a heck of a lot about the opposite sex, they would always bring home new records.

Once Binky sent away to the Beechnut Spearmint Gum Contest, and through the mail came a recording of "Great Balls of Fire" by Jerry Lee Lewis. Unfortunately, when it arrived, we found that the record was cracked. The rockabilly singer repeated "great balls of fire" over and over because the record repeatedly skipped. But the message and echo on Jerry Lee's voice rang loud and clear.

When the chorus would hit, Binky and Johnny would lead a sing along, "Goodness gracious, my balls are on fire!"

My parents didn't like these boys one bit. "They're a bad influence, Jimmie. Stay away from them!" They were actually really great kids—just a bit more mature, and sexually aware.

We collected marbles and played them endlessly at the empty lot at the end of the block that we dubbed "the prairie." I still remember the feeling of those babies in my hands as I thumbed them toward the valley we dug in the mud: cat's eyes, cat's eye boulders (the bigger ones), purees (no colored glass inside), puree boulders, and the heavy steelies and steely boulders. The colors dazzled me: turquoise, coral pink, yellow, orange, and purple.

One day, Binky and Johnny organized a night bike ride. All the boys in the neighborhood made plans to go out in a pack that evening. I could barely contain my excitement until my mother informed me that I couldn't go because I didn't have a light on my bike like the others. I was disconsolate. When my dad got home and was told the situation he quietly affixed our family flashlight to my handlebars with electrical tape, and off I went into the starry Berwyn night. At that moment he reaffirmed his status as my hero.

But our main compulsion was cars. We built scale model, plastic cars, which we raced down the sidewalk. I still remember the somehow seductive smell of the Testors glue we used and the slick flame decals we'd lick and apply carefully to the fenders. Some we would purchase at our local hobby shop, already built, that contained a friction mechanism that kept the car in motion when you gave it a good shove. It wasn't about how fast you could go, but how far we could get them to coast down the sidewalks of Wesley Avenue in front of our houses. If your car made it to the Dandas' yellow bungalow you were doing pretty darn good.

Me, Binky, and Johnny, with miles of unstructured time each day, would perch on the curb on busy 26th Street and report on every car that passed by: "'53 Packard Caribbean—three-tone paint—coral pink, gray, and white, two-door hardtop, V8, white walls; '54 Buick Skylark, convertible, wire wheels, whitewalls, V8, no portholes" (the normal Buicks had three or four of these mock portholes on the front fender depending on the prestige of the model). We would talk over one another trying to blurt out the info first.

We didn't much care about the workings of the engine; it was all about flashy design, and color schemes. I'm still a car nut and recently could afford to relive those days by buying myself a mint-condition 1955 Chevy Bel Air convertible and a 1958 Corvette convertible—both in coral red and cream, both with matching interiors and V8 engines and power windows! Someday I'd like to own a 1956 T-Bird (with Continental kit) and a chartreuse and black Mercury convertible— just like Al Kovarik's.

Binky and Johnny and Alice Anne and Janice were my life until I turned seven, and then we moved up in status to a brand-new location only about a mile away. Suddenly, there was a whole new group of kids, and though the new crowd made me feel light-years away from Binky and Johnny, I made new friends and quickly adjusted to my new surroundings. But I always maintained a soft spot for my Wesley Avenue digs—the real cradle of civilization for me.

As I said, 2647 Oak Park Ave. was a move up the social ladder for my folks. There was more money in the Peterik family coffers and my parents wanted to move closer to my Auntie Clara, my mother's twin sister. Auntie Clara was Gracie Allen to my mother's Barbara Stanwyck. They both came from affluence (Mother's father, Jim, was the butcher of choice in Hawthorne), but my mother was all sophistication, and Clara all over the deck. Auntie worked behind the long luncheonette counter at Murphy's five-and-dime in the Berwyn Cermak Plaza. At any given time of day you could hear her shouts resounding though the entire store: "Murphyburger." "Murphyburger Deluxe." I would bring friends there just to have them hear my mother's twin's ear-splitting voice in full song.

Growing up had its challenges. By the time I was eleven, I had become a target for bullies. Maybe it was the black-rimmed glasses with the tape mending the bridge that made me look kind of nerdy or maybe the bullies just decided to pick on me because I was the musician, "the guy in the band." I had started playing in the grade school band with those gaudy uniforms and I felt I was scorned upon by the "hard guys." It seemed they were lurking everywhere in Berwyn and Cicero. One Christmas when I finally got that Schwinn Jaguar bike I had been lobbying for, it wasn't more than two weeks before it was stolen from our garage. After the police retrieved the bike, it was stolen once again by three thugs who followed me from Cock Robin Ice Cream to G.C. Murphy's where it was stolen for the final time.

My true nemeses though were two brothers, Gary and Tom Booth, good-looking Irish-Catholics who slathered pomade on their combed-back hair. These boys had lots of swagger and got kicked out of school constantly for truant behavior and failing grades. They tried to make up for their lack of discipline and antisocial tendencies by becoming the kingpins of their own amateur gangster world.

Their henchman, Mike McKenzie, was way nerdier than I was, but since he aligned himself with the "Booth Boys," his status grew. He became "their guy," their lackey. Mike McKenzie had wisely bought himself protection.

One day, I was shooting baskets in my driveway when Mike McKenzie yelled, "Hey, want to take a walk to the park with me?"

"Yeah," I said, excitedly.

Here was this cool henchman who wanted to hang with me. I glanced at the huge beds of colored, dried autumn leaves that were piled up high. Not only was it a gorgeous fall day, but also I was finally being accepted and appreciated for the cool guy I really was. One of the Booth Boys had shown up at my house to meet me!

But when we reached the park, my luck changed. Mike McKenzie shoved me into another pile of leaves, leaving Tom Booth free to shove his frigid switchblade toward my neck.

"I never want to see you again! Never walk past my house again. If you do, I'll slit your throat," he said, in a threatening tone that I'll never forget.

I shook and trembled as Booth lunged over me, thrusting his silver blade closer to my throat. I managed to croak, "Okay" as my young life flashed before my eyes. These hoodlums finally let me go and, though they didn't actually injure me physically, the mental scar will be with me forever.

After that experience, I made great pains to avoid going past that house. I created a whole new route home just to avoid them. From what I heard, the Booths ended up becoming petty criminals. Tom died recently. God only knows where Mike McKenzie is today.

My days being the brunt of bullies came in handy recently when I got a call from an old record company buddy of mine, Bobby Tarantino, who was looking for an antibullying song for the group he managed, Ariel & Zoey & Eli, Too. This group of twin fourteen-year-old girls and their eleven-year-old brother had already made a name for themselves with their own variety show on The Cool TV network. The song I wrote and produced for them, "Hey Bully," would eventually go viral on YouTube with their creative video. Maybe I have the Booth brothers to thank for giving me the ammunition I needed to write that song.

I never used the music as a selling point, though, not until about fourth grade when I picked up the sax and played "Wiggle Wobble," which was a popular tune that year by Les Cooper. When I played it for the class, the girls started giggling. They started looking at me differently. The guys sat silently in awe, looking a tad jealous. My teacher looked surprised. That day my course was set.

4

Fortunes of Our Fathers

MY DAD, like his father before him, was a natural born musician. He mastered violin in his teens and was known all over the Hawthorne district of Cicero, Illinois, as the best around. He looked like actor Robert Young (the adorably incompetent patriarch in one of my favorite shows, *Father Knows Best*) and became popular with the local girls with his sidewalk serenades.

In the late '40s he switched to saxophone and formed a group dubbed the Hi-Hatters. Their repertoire consisted of popular standards of the day as well as the required Czech and Polish polkas. I have fond memories of hearing the sweet strains of "Tea for Two" (the group's opener) as Dad warmed up in the basement workshop of our Wesley Avenue house, which was part of his routine before he left for a "job," as such gigs were called in those days. His tone and vibrato put chills right through me even from down in the basement.

He had that effect on his audience, too, the ladies flocking around the stage to see and hear this handsome sax man. He blew into his sax from the side of his mouth—a very incorrect embouchure to be sure but his sound was spectacular just the same. He was in the best mood as he tinkered in the workshop, oiling the pads and adjusting the action on his Martin tenor and Conn alto saxes.

Sometimes my mother would threaten the sanctity of his warm-up ritual with sharp criticism or chastisement. "Alice, this is my job; I have to be in a great mood," he'd say. "I can't play sweet tonight if you're nagging me about something and putting me in a bad frame of mind!"

In the basement, he stored the bandstands with the words "Hi-Hatters" carved out in vibrant blue and gold. I posed proudly with the whole band in front of one stand the first day I got my very own saxophone. There was my dad, on tenor and alto sax, Joe Delfino on trumpet, Irv on drums, and a really talented accordion player named Al Tobias. Later on, Al was kind enough to let me use his amazing Magnatone amplifier with a cool vibrato feature.

For a while, my uncle George Peterik played drums with my dad's band, before he moved to California, and then the band had to change drummers. Though I was too young to remember, they say that that band with the two Peterik boys was a ferocious entity. Irv took his place, but he was no George Peterik, and the musical bond my father and my uncle had developed was gone forever.

By day, Jim Peterik, Sr., was a relay adjustor at Automatic Electric Telephone. I have a picture of him at the desk painstakingly fine-tuning these delicate pieces of gear in his black-rimmed bifocals. Without these relays tuned just right, the telephone of the day would not have functioned properly.

Automatic Electric had a factory parallel to the Eisenhower Expressway, near downtown Chicago. My father soldiered to the bus that took him to the train early each morning, despite the elements. I'd wake up to the familiar farm report blasting from our clock radio, which had become his makeshift alarm.

"The grain is up fifteen points and soybeans are down five," bellowed a voice from the airwaves in a monotonous tone. The voice was loud enough to wake the dead—and my dad and the entire household.

I'm still an early-morning guy, and that is probably because of my dad's impenetrable work ethic and that droning call-to-arms. But these rituals bonded us. Each day when he came home, I would greet him as he ambled down Wesley Avenue from the bus drop-off.

As we'd walk he'd tell me stories about his work buddy "Skinny" who was always doing hilariously stupid things. Sometimes he'd talk about an upcoming job with the Hi-Hatters at the VFW or the Moose Lodge in Blue Island.

When I finally got good enough on sax (around sixth grade), I would tag along with my dad to his various gigs—bar mitzvahs, men's fraternities like the Elks, Lions, or Moose clubs, weddings, anniversary celebrations, and the lot.

For a while they were the featured band at Melody Mill on First Avenue in suburban Riverside. With my alto sax I would hide behind one of the wooden Hi-Hatters bandstands and play harmonies to my dad's sweet tenor sax.

I had no union card and was underage so I kept pretty scarce. By the way, my dad played "by ear." He never learned to read music, but it never held him back. He was equally adept at concertina (like his father) and fiddle, and his ear was deadly accurate, his tone was sweet, his vibrato wide, and his soloing was as good as his hero's, Wayne King, the popular sax player from Wisconsin to whom he was often compared. In some circles he was known as "Young Wayne King."

Another one of my favorite memories was doing a job at the VFW or the Moose Lodge with my dad and his buddies and then going out for White Castle hamburgers. It was the only place still open at midnight when the gig was through. I felt so grown-up, being in sixth grade and hanging with the guys at these gleaming white burger palaces.

I must have meant a lot to my dad. The day after my birth, my dad boasted to Skinny and Zichek, another friend of his from work, on the bench at Automatic Electric that he now had "a son!" It was somehow the validation my dad needed to make his manhood complete. That phrase, "a son," echoed through Berwyn for days to come!

My birth did little, however, to still the constant and accelerated bickering between Alice and Jim, my mom and dad.

"Alice, quit belittling me! You're baiting me again!"

"Jimmie, all you do is lay around the house doing nothing. Can't you be useful? And why do you spend so much time in the bathroom? You've got some magazines in there with some pretty dandy pictures. I can imagine what you are doing!" My mother's intimation of my dad's masturbating in there was not lost on me as I grew older.

"Go jump in the lake!" he would respond, among other unprintable phrases. I got used to the slamming of doors and the feeling that all was not right in the world after all. It shook me to my core. Music became my asylum, my safe house.

As I grew up, I learned how to create a protective shield from the often negative spirit of their marriage. I think it was actually this kind of behavior that made me more determined that I would never be like that. When my sixth-grade teacher, Mrs. Hull, asked me what I wanted to be when I grew up, I answered, without hesitation, "a good husband."

For the same reason, I never smoked cigarettes. I had spent one too many Sundays at home tolerating what I called my "Sunday Headache," which I discovered much later came from inhaling secondhand smoke from my father. He chain-smoked unfiltered Camels all day, lighting the next one with the glowing butt of the last one 'til he died of heart failure at the age of seventy.

My mother and dad always seemed distant from each other. It felt as if some dark secret existed between them—as if there was an elephant in the closet that no one saw or at least acknowledged.

When Daphne, my mother's pen pal, visited from Australia we all went to the Brookfield Zoo. Although I was only about eight, I noticed something unusual happening—my mom and dad were holding hands. I had never seen that happen before. They were clearly putting on a show for Daphne.

That simple display of affection was so unlike them. I know there must have been a lot of love there, but there was never any demonstration of it. My parents were not huggers. They didn't hug me, and they didn't hug each other. In fact, it seemed like nobody hugged back then. Still, I never had any doubt that they loved me—unconditionally.

Every time tempers got really hot and my mother needed ammunition, through her sobs, she would lay out her trump card: "It was seventeen years ago (or eighteen, or however many years it had been at the time), Jimmie, but I remember it like it was yesterday."

Many years later, my mother finally cornered me and told me what "it" was. "You think your father is so great—well, let me tell you about the affair he had when we had only been married a few years!"

That encounter didn't change my respect for my father, but it did explain the fights and icy silence between them once and for all. It affected me greatly for years and made me vow not to repeat this pattern of holding onto hurt and using it as a weapon. Inversely, it taught me the vital importance of forgiveness.

My own sexual education was sketchy at best. In sixth grade my buddy Jerry Kmen told me all he knew about the opposite sex. He said something about a girl having "three holes." And the main one was called a "pussy nose." This was before I had my first orgasm so the thought of taking off my clothes in front of a girl sounded just plain embarrassing. He described masturbation but I couldn't quite put all the pieces together.

One day I was at the park with my friends and for some reason I started climbing the poles that supported the swings. When I got near the top I felt a very odd and unfamiliar sensation between my legs. I wasn't sure if it was pleasurable or not at first—just different. The next day, trying to recreate that feeling at the poles, I clearly decided this feeling was good—*very* good. I developed strong muscles after that from climbing those poles almost daily! But I still didn't put that feeling together with what Jerry Kmen had described 'til one day while gazing at a very sexy cartoon in *Mad Magazine* I figured it all out. Oh, that's what that pole thing was! Little did I know at that time that I'd be chasing that feeling from that moment on.

My parents were no help in the sex-education department. One day my dad handed me a dark green book called *Moving into Manhood.*

He kind of averted his eyes as he slipped it to me. After glancing through it I still knew nothing about the actual process of sex. The book said things like, "when the sperm meets the egg…" How the hell does that happen, guys? I still was not quite ready for one of those three holers.

It wasn't 'til I was with The Ides on one of our first road trips (this one to Savanna, Illinois, to play the Road-Runner Den) that I connected all the dots. One of the guys had acquired some grainy black-and-white porn tapes from the '50s and we watched them in our seedy sleeping quarters above the club owner's office on the projector we had brought with us. The men in the films were all Brylcreem, white legs, and black socks. The gals were overweight, pasty white, and over the hill, but at least I saw the act in motion. My line, now famous in the pantheon of Ides of March lore, was, "Hey guys, it's like jagging off—in a girl!" Prior to this I thought you just put it in and waited motionlessly.

For as long as I could remember, my mother had one big dream for me. "Jimmie, you be's a doctor," is what my mother always said. For some reason, she spoke this phrase in a kind of "Porgy and Bess" dialect.

My mom actually had a metal box exclusively earmarked for my post–medical school career. "After each patient, you put the money in," she explained, opening the box and carefully arranging the bills for visual aid. It was never about saving mankind; it was about the money I would make that would go into this strong box.

"You be's a doctor!"

I heard my mother's tirade year after year until, at the age of ten, I could stand it no longer. I finally stood up to her and said, "Mother, let me be what I want to be, okay?" The anxious expression on her face eventually broke into a smile. She finally realized that I was my own man, and she never brought it up again.

That's how I am with my son, Colin, too. I believe that if you raise a child with good values and you set a good example, that example goes beyond words, beyond lectures. I trust him so much that I don't lecture, just as my parents didn't lecture. Nobody ever said, "Jimmie, don't drink and drive. Don't smoke pot." Nobody ever told me that.

They knew I wasn't going to go there—it was just that unspoken trust.

My reaction to the stoners and drinkers was, "Why do that?" It was never a temptation. In fact, I think I felt a tiny bit superior because I had the willpower to resist that course.

I've seen too many of my rock 'n' roll brothers fall to drugs. They're some of the most evil substances known to man because they totally take you over, change your personality, and ruin your body. I once had a writing session with the lead singer of a very well-known group from the '70s. He said, "Jim, you know, my problem is that I've never had one great song idea when I wasn't doing coke." It's a voice inside many of us that says, "I am not enough—I need a crutch." To silence that voice is my everyday challenge.

I tried to tell him that those creative juices are "you"; it's not the work of the drug. You can access those inner chemicals in a natural way by engaging in physical activity, eating right, sharing your talents with others, embracing loved ones, and doing nice things for people. He said, "Yeah, but I still need the coke." This man ultimately lost his wide vocal range and ability to perform onstage.

I've seen way too many examples of this. When I give master classes at a Camp Jam seminar,[2] I always tell my cautionary tale of the time The Ides of March were invited to the aftershow party hosted by Led Zeppelin after our triumphant gig opening for them in Winnipeg, Ontario.

Here's what happened. We knocked on the door of the band's hotel suite. (They stayed at the fancy hotel in the area—not the lowly Holiday Inn where we were staying.)

Robert Plant came to the door in his bikini briefs and welcomed us in. As we walked in, we spotted half-naked groupies cavorting on the bed in a pillow fight. Pot was being smoked, cocaine snorted, John Bonham was in a stupor, and booze was everywhere. Jimmy Page was in the bathtub with a young lady going through some uncomfortable-looking contortions.

---

[2] Camp Jam is the wonderful organization that Jeff Carlisi of 38 Special and Dan Lipson currently run. It's designed to mentor budding musicians, ages nine to sixteen, coast to coast in weeklong classes. "No canoes—lots of rock" is their slogan!

I looked at Larry (The Ides' rhythm guitarist), Larry looked at Mike (Ides' drummer), and we turned on our heels and said, "Thanks guys, see ya later!" This was not our scene at all. We repaired to a donut shop across the street from the hotel. We were back in our comfort zone.

When I tell that story at a master class, believe it or not, the kids always cheer. I tell them it's probably why I'm still here talking to you right now. You can't keep the party going at all costs.

My own Czech heritage also impacted my childhood. About twice a year, usually to commemorate the day someone had died, we would visit my ancestors at Bohemian National Cemetery on Pulaski Avenue and Foster.

Before the age of expressways, this would be a day-long expedition, ending with a feast at one of the authentic Czech restaurants on Cermak Road in Berwyn or Cicero. At the cemetery, we would be spellbound by the elaborate gravestones, which carried hard to pronounce names like Vosacek, Vlcek, Krahulek, and Klitpetko. These names were always dense with consonants.

Nowadays, many American parents take great pains to teach their children their native tongue, but back then, the goal was to assimilate. When my parents didn't want me to understand what they were saying, they would speak in Czech.

They whispered little Czech phrases under their breath when they wanted to be secretive. Though I didn't understand a word they were saying, I could pretty much decipher the meanings by their inflection, tone, and decibel level.

My strongest connection and fondest memory of my Czech heritage was the Bohemian cuisine. My mother mainly prepared Czech food. Dinnertime would become another time during which I would get teased and get called "Fatboy." (My mother had to shop with me in the "husky" section of the department stores where you could find any color of corduroy pants you wanted as long as it was brown or navy blue.)

About once a month, the family would go out for an "eating party" (a phrase I apparently coined at age four). Some of our favorite destinations for Bohemian food were Klas in Cicero (the sidewalk in front shimmered with shards of colored glass), Old Prague, and the Dumpling House in Berwyn.

My family bought "bakery" (always used in place of "baked goods") at Vesecky's on Cermak Road (kind of the Rodeo Drive of Berwyn and Cicero). There we'd stock up on *hoska*—wonderful, eggy bread studded with slivered almonds and laced with dark and light raisins.

We'd also buy plenty of *kolaches*: doughy rounds made with cream cheese and targeted with apricot, cheese, and prune fillings, or my favorite: poppy seed. Cermak Road was a street lined with the most savings and loans and banks per block of any one city—Bohemians were a frugal lot, that's for sure.

Little old Czech ladies wearing colorful *babushkas* (scarves) would wheel their shopping carts from butcher to baker. For meats, there was Vlceks (also on Cermak) for your pork loin and chicken and my favorite sausages called *jelitzy* and *Jaternice* or *Jitrnice*.

One was blood-red, barley sausage in a casing; the other was a light-colored veal sausage. You would squeeze it out of the casing (half the fun of it, really) and mix these garlicky, fatty meats with mashed potatoes and gravy. Talk about a triple bypass plate!

Since that time, of course, the area and the demographic have changed radically. The neighborhood is now largely Hispanic. The homes are still meticulously kept, but many of the restaurants now specialize in amazing *flautas* and enchiladas. The population has changed, but the smells are still intoxicating.

A little while back, I took my friend and Facebook guru, Paul Braun, on a walking tour of my old stomping grounds of Berwyn. Paul is not only a great friend, but also a music historian whose grasp of rock history is second to none.

We started with a visit to my first home at 2529 Wesley Avenue; the empty lot that is now a police station; the Tastee-Freez (still there!); and my second abode, the big ritzy house with the ornate stained-glass windows at 2647 Oak Park Avenue. We walked up its stairs and peered through the window. All of the walls had been torn out and "modernized." What a shame.

We walked past Karen Moulik's family home on Clinton where I used to spy through the front window as I passed, hoping to catch a secret glimpse of my future wife. One night I got more than I bargained for: it was Karen's enormous father—"the old water buffalo" as I used to call him—in his undershirt and boxer shorts. What a letdown!

I walked Paul past Hiawatha Grade School where I attended kindergarten and first grade and past the school where much of my maturation took place—Piper Elementary. Three things really stood out during my six-year tenure at Piper Elementary: an amazingly caring teacher named Mrs. (Helen) Hull, who was perhaps the first to recognize my potential as a human being; Laura Strama, the object of my affections who kept me up nights and provoked my fantasies; and my nemesis, Piper School Principal, Hugh Biddinger.

Exactly three times in third grade (but who's counting!), Laura picked me out of all the other boys to help her take off her shiny, white winter boots! (She would ordain one of us every day in the snowy winter months.) This was an honor too great to be believed. I still remember the smell of that rubber and the feeling of being that close to Laura's calf—that close to any female, for that matter.

Recently, I had lunch with Laura after not seeing her for about forty years. Now I know why I was especially attracted to the American actress Sandra Bullock—Laura could be her sister.

We caught up on old times and she even remembered those white boots! The last recollection was darker; it had to do with the tenuous relationship that had developed with Mr. Hugh Biddinger.

What a foreboding figure! He stood at six feet, four inches tall with long ape-like arms that hung down well below his knees as he swung through the blackboard jungle of Piper Elementary. Mr. Biddinger had a permanent scowl on his face and a diabetes alert bracelet on his wrist.

He really showed his true colors when one morning he joined in our favorite playground game, kickball. He joined the other team's side to make up for a missing player. As Biddinger rounded the bases to home plate, he was tagged out.

Of course, after I spotted that play, I yelled, "You're out!"

He screamed, "I'm safe, Jim Pet!!"

I repeated, "No, you're out!"

The LIFE   **Page 16**   **Sunday, June 7, 1964**

PIPER'S BEST—The Piper School Boy and Girl of the Year, Jim Peterik, son of Mr. and Mrs. James Peterik, 2647 Oak Park ave., and Sue Sellers, daughter of Mr. and Mrs. George Sellers, 6841 Rivesride dr., are shown with Principal Hugh Biddinger. Peterik is holding the plaque given by Mrs. Emil Venclik, on which his name will be enscribed. The plaque was given in honor of Emil Venclik who lost his life in World War II. Sue is holding the cup given in memory of William Rockett, former board member of the Piper School and long time president of the board of education. Both are honor students and active in school affairs. They were voted outstanding graduates by their peers and their teachers.   (LIFE Photo)

Boy of the Year.

He then came over to me and walloped me hard in the back of the head with his clenched fist. I was knocked dizzy, but managed to run to the nurse's station to report what had happened. You don't expect your bullies to come in the form of school principals.

From that moment on, our relationship changed. Biddinger knew I had the goods on him. When I came up for the honor of the coveted

"Boy of the Year" award in eighth grade, he made sure I was taken off the bench and put into action at the last basketball game of the season.

After that game (where I literally fell flat on my face) I now had all the qualifications necessary to be voted "Boy of the Year." The day I won the honor was one of the proudest moments of my life. The plaque still hangs above the water fountain in the gym. I only wish Laura Strama had won the "Girl of the Year" honor, instead of the very bookish and straight Sue Sellars—then we could have ruled our little Czech Camelot together.

Finally, I took Paul past the gas station where AZ & R bowling lanes once stood. Every Friday afternoon, Hugh Biddinger would march the whole eighth-grade class over to the lanes to bowl three games.

One particular Friday afternoon will be eternally engraved in my memory, not for the too-salty hot dogs, Green River soda, or the pungent odor that emanated from the shoe rental counter.

On this day, whether you got a strike or a gutter ball hardly mattered because everything grinded to a halt. A voice on the loudspeaker announced that President John F. Kennedy had been shot.

Everyone from that era remembers exactly what they were doing on that Friday. Grim-faced and disheartened, after having our day of playful innocence violently interrupted, we slipped back into our street shoes, grabbed our winter coats, and slunk, dazed and confused, back to the shelter of our homes.

A Bad Guitar and a Simple Song

IT WAS NOT JUST the intense politics of the day that created a sense of heaviness during this time; there were other tensions in the Peterik household, and, at times, it felt like my only saving grace was my music. When my parents would fight—and that was often—I headed for the asylum of my tiny bedroom and lost myself in the four or five chords I knew on the ukulele. Years later, "In My Room" by the Beach Boys resounded with meaning for me.

Soon the four-string instrument gave way to the guitar. I knew Elvis Presley's guitar had six strings; I cleverly counted them as they appeared on the cover of his iconic first album.

I started begging my parents for a guitar when I was about seven. For Christmas, I finally got my wish. My first guitar was made entirely out of plastic. It was horrible, and it had this device on the neck. You pressed down on one of the buttons of the contraption that was clamped onto the neck and it made chords.

I looked under the chord device to find out which strings had to be held down and on which fret. Then, I would attempt to substitute fingers in order to start making my own chords. I could see that this guitar was just like a ukulele, but with two extra strings. All I really had to do was figure out what to do with the extra two!

I would strum the C chord on the ukulele and play "Love Me Tender" and then play it on the guitar. So that's basically how I learned to play the guitar. I based the guitar chords on the chords I had learned on the ukulele.

By next Christmas, my parents knew I had to move up. My first semi-cool guitar was a Harmony acoustic model with a tacky painted-on sunburst finish—but it was my Stradivarius. I would get up every morning at 6 a.m. and go over and over the basic eight-bar blues progression. I practiced that series of chords so relentlessly that it got to the point that my sister Alice Anne would scream from her slumber, "Shut up with that same progression!"

You forget, after you've been playing for so long, how hard it was at the beginning to hold down those strings when you're first learning your instrument. It took me months to get enough strength to clamp down the strings to the frets and form a barre chord, which is the basis of practically all advanced chords on the instrument.

I was very influenced by a group in this pre-Beatles era, The Ventures, who played wicked instrumentals; kind of surf music meets spy music. They were like a human aurora borealis: they wore matching sharkskin suits and played Fender electric guitars finished in custom colors. When I finally purloined a Fender catalogue from Balkan Music in Berwyn I learned the correct name for these dazzling Duco finishes: Lake Placid Blue, Candy Apple Red, Foam Green, Fiesta Red, Salmon Pink, and, of course, Shoreline Gold.

I would pore over my Fender catalogue for hours on end to view the guitars played by my musical heroes. I can still feel the glossy pages of the book, as the corners brushed across my fingertips; pages filled with images of beautiful, smiling teenagers enjoying their instruments together, on the beach and on the bandstand.

I imagined how it would feel to cradle one of those contoured Stratocasters or Jazzmasters in my arms. I woke up thinking about these immaculate instruments, scheming ways to coerce my folks into buying me one.

I was mesmerized by the steely twang of Don Wilson and Bob Bogle's Fender Stratocasters and Jazzmasters, their use of the vibrato arm to simulate Hawaiian steel guitar sounds, and how they would use the palms of their hands to create a muting effect that deadened the strings and made the sound pop. I also loved the sound of Mel Taylor's snare drum, which he played in rim-shot style, thus combining the sound of the drumhead with the sound of the metal rim of the drum. It gave the backbeat a unique metallic gunshot sound that I could not get enough of. I had first heard that sound years before on "Jailhouse Rock." The drum was played to sound like a gunshot ricocheting off the hard prison walls. Nokie Edwards played his sunburst Precision bass with a pick to give the bottom end a powerful snap.

I used to haunt The Balkans music store. It was located on Cermak Road and Clinton Avenue (one block from Karen Moulik's family dwelling—the future Karen Peterik). Balkans was not only known for carrying a broad selection of ethnic sheet music, but it also carried a great array of electric guitars. There was a door that led to an actual recording studio. The big red light flashed "Recording" when a session was in progress. I didn't dare ask the proprietor, Mr. Slavico Hlad, to enter those sacred confines. That was for music pros, not us little kids. One of the store's highlights was a glass case that held the cream of the current guitar crop. I remember a red Gibson ES 355 that stayed there 'til the store closed its doors years later. I wish I'd been the one to finally buy it. Once when I ran in I was stopped in my tracks by an entire wall of Gretsch hollow body electrics. At first, I was riveted by a blood orange model until my eyes caught sight of one finished in a pale green with a darker green back and sides. That one became the focal point of my fantasies. Years later, in Minneapolis on tour with Survivor and REO Speedwagon, I bought a Gretsch just like that one. It was called the Anniversary model, from Pete of Pete's Guitars, one of the several vintage guitar merchants who would meet groups backstage, tempting us with their wares.

Of course, I always had to go home to face my own el-cheapo guitar. Finally, as Christmas was closing in, my dad caved in to my incessant nagging and said, "I think it's time we got you a decent electric guitar."

The accordion player in my dad's band, Al Tobias, did business with a store on the legendary music row down on south Wabash Street in downtown Chicago. That store imported not only fine ornate Italian-made accordions, but also began to import very bizarre-looking electric guitars, also from Italy.

I was beside myself with excitement the day my dad decided it was time to go downtown to the now-familiar district and check out some guitars. I raced up the narrow flight of stairs, ahead of my dad, which led to the music showroom, and found myself face-to-face with rows of shiny electric guitars. This was Mecca to me!

Dad whispered Al Tobias's name to the proprietor of the shop, after which he proceeded to hand me an abstractly shaped, sparkly white Wandre. It said "Noble" on the headstock, but that was just the name of the importer. It was actually a Wandre designed by the eccentric Italian luthier, Antonio Pioli.

When I plugged this oddity into an amp, even with my limited experience, I realized it was a pretty lame instrument, even though I was only eleven. The strings were impossibly hard to hold down and the sound was kind of soft and wimpy. But then the owner handed me a Gibson, a higher priced brand. When I plugged this one in, the vibrant and piercing sound came shooting through the speaker. I was electrified!

We left the shop not knowing which guitar my dad would choose to put under the tree for me that Christmas, though I was hoping with all my heart that I would get the Gibson.

On Christmas morning, I was the first one to wake up, and, still in my pajamas, I spotted a red guitar case under the tree. Breathlessly, I opened it up to find, not the Sunburst Gibson of my dreams, but that modern, Danish coffee table of a guitar—the Wandre! My dad chose it not only for the sweet deal that was offered to move these beasts, but also for its warp-proof aluminum neck. Practicality like that spoke volumes to my father's generation.

Christmas morning with the Wandre.

When my parents finally got up, I feigned excitement and posed happily for them. I cradled the guitar in my arms. I have that Wandre to this day. I love it—not only because I cut my guitar chops on it in those blissful, halcyon days, or because it has now become a valuable collector's item, but because my dad bought it for me with his hard-earned money.

In addition, I realized that I had inherited my dad's respect for a bargain. He shared my dream at that moment, and buying me that guitar made me love him even more.

From that moment on, that ugly first guitar and I became insepa-rable. I still didn't have an amp, but Al Tobias came to the rescue and let me borrow his high-end Magnatone when the band wasn't gig-ging. The amp had a dazzling vibrato effect built right in. You'd hit a chord and the sound went, *wah wah woosh*, as it swirled around the room. It made even a simple E chord sound profound!

At that time, I had just written my first song, which I had started to play in front of the grade-school kids. It was a derivative of a Chuck Berry tune. I called it "Hully Gully Bay." The popular dances of the time were the Hully Gully and the Mashed Potato, so I decided to write a song about an imaginary place where you would go and dance and party (somewhere sunny and exotic) or maybe even a barely discovered archipelago. That extraordinary getaway was "Hully Gully Bay."

"Come with me, my babe
Where the sea is choppy
and the tide is high
Come with me, my babe
Where the seagulls rock and the riverboats fly
Yeah, Yeah—hey hey
Come with me to Hully Gully Bay
Where the sea is choppy
And the waves are rocky
And the hully gully seagulls are winging our way
Come with me, my babe
to a place called the Hully Gully Bay"

Copyright Jim Peterik/Bicycle Music ASCAP

When I performed this original for my seventh-grade class, I sud-denly became the hit of Piper Elementary. I had experienced once again the rush of performing. I liked the way it made me feel and I couldn't wait to do it all again.

There was another guitar player at Piper whose name was Scott Sindelar. I heard that he played pretty well, and one day he invited

me over to his apartment to show me his brand-new Gibson Les
Paul Special, which was finished in what the Gibson catalogue called
"TV Yellow." The name was penned because of the hue's resemblance to the blond finish on many television sets in the '50s and
'60s. (Recently I purchased one in mint condition. I wonder if it was
Scott's?) We would jack into his brand-new Ampeg Reverb-a-Rocket
amplifier, and before long we could play eight songs from the catalogue of our heroes, The Ventures.

I am quite certain that I chose the Fender Jazzmaster as my next
dream guitar based on the fact that this was the model Don Wilson
of The Ventures played. I found one for sale in the classified ads of
the *Chicago Tribune* and begged my father to take me to Chicago's
exclusive northern suburb of Northbrook to try it out.

When we pulled up to the address, I noticed three brand-new Corvette Stingrays in the driveway. They belonged to the band members
that had advertised the guitar. I was already impressed. For reasons
unknown they were selling a near mint-condition Fender Jazzmaster finished in a vibrant three-tone sunburst: black to red to yellow.
When I first gazed at it, the guitar was languishing in its blond Tolex
(a DuPont registered leatherette) rectangular case with bright orange
plush lining. When they saw this little eleven year old walk in, they
started snickering amongst themselves. But when I sat down, plugged
in, and started playing a note-perfect "Walk, Don't Run," their expres-
sions changed to disbelief, and they suddenly got real quiet.

"Well, you might as well try the tone that made this guitar famous,"
one of the band members said as he positioned the toggle switch to
the center position, thus engaging both pickups at the same time.
He was correct. There was the bell-like ring of the famous Fender
sound!

"We'll take it," I exclaimed, as my dad peeled out the 150 big ones
from his well-worn brown wallet. They're probably still shaking their
heads to this day.

The first time I heard the new Ventures song "The 2,000 Pound
Bee," in '63, I was mesmerized by the sound of that searing lead guitar. It was like no sound I had ever heard—kind of a cross between

a buzz saw and an electric guitar. It actually did replicate the sound that the title suggested—a bumblebee on steroids!

There was a revolutionary device that created that magical sound every time a guitar was patched into it; this $100 device, which was marketed by Gibson as the "Maestro Fuzz Tone," literally changed the face of the electric guitar by adding a snarling sound that could sustain a note until the crowd left the building.

After I heard Keith Richards use this sound on the Rolling Stones '65 smash "Satisfaction," I ran out to The Balkans music store and made one mine. Suddenly, I was a complete horn section. I could also mimic the creamy tones of Eric Clapton (then a member of Cream).

I loved guitars. I felt like Aunt Bea on *The Andy Griffith Show*. Each time Aunt Bea would buy a new hat, she would become a new woman—until it was time for another one. Each new guitar was my new hat. Every time I acquired one, whether it was new or used, mint condition or rough around the edges, I felt that surge of energy coursing through my body.

Sometimes a new guitar would set me off on a twenty-four-hour writing binge. It added spring to my step, a light in my eyes, and a dream fulfilled. "Mother, this is the last guitar I'll ever buy, I promise, oh, please, please!" In time my collection would grow to 172 specimens, each with a unique story, and each inspirational in its own way.

Do I play them all? Yes, I do. When preparing for a session, I will scan the racks in my home for the perfect one to create the sound I hear in my head for that particular song. For screaming, raunchy sounds, perhaps I'll grab my Charvel (the small San Dimas, California, company that Eddie Van Halen put on the map. Just listen to "Eruption" from Van Halen's first album for a piece of sweet ear candy.).

For a funky thing, I might choose my '56 Fender Telecaster (perhaps the Swiss Army knife of guitars for me—it can do just about anything if coaxed properly). For a dreamy, Jimi Hendrix–inspired ballad, I may choose an early '70s vintage Stratocaster, similar to the one he used.

It's not only the sound of these vintage instruments that makes them special, it's also the vibe they possess and the way they speak to you, and inspire you to play. When I play my '54 Strat, I become Buddy Holly. When I strap on my original Gibson Flying V, I channel blues great Albert King. People tell me I have GAS—"guitar acquisition syndrome"! Who am I to argue?

There's a famous Who video in which lead guitarist Pete Townshend violently smashes a vintage Telecaster into his towering amplifier—a Marshall stack. Through the years, Townshend has demolished hundreds of these irreplaceable works of art in the name of rock 'n' roll. Though it's hard for me to witness or reconcile this act of destruction, I understand the desire to thrill one's audience.

One time when I was playing with The Ides in Joplin, Missouri, I threw my own guitar high in the air (as I often did at the end of "Vehicle"). Typically, I would catch it on the last drumbeat, but this time I missed.

My beloved 1968 Les Paul Goldtop went crashing to the floor, shattering its neck. I cried as I picked up the pathetic pieces and laid them lovingly back in the case. I've since had it reconstructed, but I learned a hard lesson that night about respecting your axe.

Flashback to my first public performance: I signed up to appear at the Talented Teen Search at the Cermak Plaza in my hometown of Berwyn. The parking lot was crowded with teens, adults, and "golden-agers" that had come to view the spectacle. When the emcee, Leonard Koenke (why do we remember that kind of stuff!) introduced me, I plugged my Wandre into my borrowed Magnatone amp and sang for all I was worth.

"Goin' to Kansas City, Kansas City, here I come. They got some crazy little women there, and I'm a-gonna get me one."

When I heard my eleven-year-old tenor amplified through the public address system, I basked in the vibrations that echoed across the parking lot. After I was done, and the people applauded, a cloud of happy dust circled around me, filling my every pore. While it's true that I did not even place in that competition, my course had still been set. I knew I had to experience that feeling again and again. That performance even put all of my neurotic worries into remission.

From that moment on I needed to perform every week or so just to keep my demons at bay. The spotlight and the applause was the elixir that stopped the momentum of needless anxiety.

My night terrors also subsided. In the middle of many nights I'd had episodes that did not feel like nightmares. They were beyond that. It felt like I was helplessly ascending through space, never to land. It was terrifying and still is when I summon that feeling. Around these years I also experienced distortions of time and space, usually in the evening, when a sound as common as the ticking of a clock would suddenly be amplified, then intensified, then speed up...and up...and up. I never took acid but from what I've heard, these experiences were not too different. When music and performing finally came into my life all of this thankfully vanished.

Enter The Renegades, my debut into the rock 'n' roll sweepstakes. I was in eighth grade by that time, and determined to go up against the Beatles and the Dave Clark Five—or at least to play the Berwyn Recreation Center, make a few bucks, and (maybe) even impress the girls.

I gathered up Scott Sindelar (the enviable owner of the yellow Les Paul Special), and Eddie Skopek on drums. Eddie was the younger brother of Corrine Skopek, who was in my grade at Piper Elementary. Corrine was the one that pursued me determinedly since second grade. Of course I had no interest in her whatsoever. Our band, which I christened The Renegades (I originally wanted to call the band The Masterbeats but my dad vetoed it vehemently for reasons I didn't understand 'til years later), was pretty terrible. Eddie could barely keep a beat. We also boasted a bass player (whose name slips my mind) who did not know the importance of tuning his instrument.

I guess we were good enough, though, because we convinced my alma mater, Morton West High School, to hire us, pro bono, of course, to perform at the big Fourth of July show at the school's football stadium. This was big! We were terrified, yet exhilarated, when we hit that stage.

As I prepared for the count-off for our first number, "I've Had It," by the Crestones, I felt as if I was standing on the top floor of

Chicago's Prudential Building without a parachute, screwing up the courage to jump. But jump, I did. And we rocked! "One, two, three, four! Blast off!"

A schoolmate of mine named Larry Millas, unbeknownst to me, was sitting in those bleachers with soon-to-be bandmate Bob Bergland. Larry was a tall kid that I had known since third grade. You couldn't miss him because he wore pink-tinted glasses. Fully present that day, he was mentally taking notes. I always wondered why he wore those pink-tinted glasses throughout grade school. I figured it was some correctional thing. About a year ago, I finally asked, "Larry, what was up with those pink glasses?"

He said, "I just thought they looked cool."

Larry was way ahead of the curve with those specs. But, specs or no specs, he was always kind of a cool guy, and in eighth grade, during that performance with The Renegades, he was the one scanning the stage, like a nighthawk, for signs of life. He must have been thinking, *That band is terrible, but that guitar guy plays and sings really well.* Bob added, "Yeah, and he knows all the chords!"

About a week after that event, I heard a knock on the door. It was Larry Millas clutching a guitar case. I recognized him from grade school, but I didn't let him in at the time. He talked to me as he stood outside on the front porch.

"I've got a band and, umm, I think you'd be great in this band," he murmured.

"I've already got a band. Thanks, though. What's the band's name?" I asked.

"The Shy-Lads," he replied. Huge negative.

A week later, I heard that persistent *knock, knock, knock,* and found Larry Millas, again, at the door. This guy just wouldn't take no for an answer!

"I've got this band. We're called the Shy-Lads."

"I know, I know! That's a terrible name," I replied bluntly.

"Yeah, our drummer's dad came up with it. But, really," he said, "come over to Bob Erhart's house. He plays drums and Bob Bergland plays bass."

I already knew Bob Bergland. We had been in the same Cub Scouts and Boy Scouts troop. Our fathers were friends and we were both from close-knit, supportive families. In fact, Larry told me that Bob's mom had recently cashed in her S & H Green Stamps (these were stamps you would receive for purchasing merchandise at various stores that you would paste into booklets and redeem for other merchandise) to buy her son a shiny, new, copper-finished six-string Danelectro bass. The "Dano" was an American brand distinctive for its use of Formica and composite board instead of wood for its body. The magnetic pickups were cased in what appeared to be lipstick cases. I found out later they actually were lipstick cases!

So, finally, I gave in to Larry's persistence and agreed to come and play. A few days later I walked the four long blocks to current drummer Bob Erhart's home, lugging my Wandre guitar and Al Tobias's fifty-pound plus Magnatone amplifier. I would have to stop about every fourth bungalow to rest and shift hands.

In Erhart's tiny attic space, the boys were working on the song "Tell Me Why," a brand-new one from the Beatles (that places the date exactly in time: the summer of '64). Fortunately, I knew this tune very well and joined right in.

I started strumming the chords on the guitar, mimicking John Lennon's rhythm part (even then, Lennon was my favorite), while Larry sang the lead vocal. I noticed right away that when I sang harmony, the other guys did not switch to my part. That impressed me to no end!

The hallmark of a lousy band is when one of the singers is swayed to move up or down to another band member's part. These guys stayed on their own parts! Actually, this was the main thing that convinced me to leave The Renegades behind and join The Shy-Lads. (I didn't want to rock the boat that first day, but something had to be done about both the name and drummer Bob Erhart's clunky-looking 1940s natural-wood drum kit—actually I now realize it was pretty cool!) Plus, Larry had a very good voice. Still, there was work to be done. I knew I had to give these guys a crash course in vocal phrasing.

Now, every Beatles fan knows that the verse in "Tell Me Why" goes, "Well, I gave you everything I had, but you left me standing all alone…"

"No offense, Lar, but your phrasing is all wrong," I said, hoping that I wasn't launching an attack. "The phrase 'I gave you everything I had' is sung bunched up quickly like this [I demonstrated], not sung slowly. Same thing with the words 'but you left me standing on my own,'" I added. "The rest of the line follows from there."

Larry looked at me. I guessed that he was not used to being challenged in this way, and then, after what seemed like an interminable, deadly silence, he replied, "Let me try it that way."

Whew, now I knew I had to be in this band! How could I have known that this day would give way to a fifty-year journey that sees no chance of stopping? From this attic rehearsal, my career would be catapulted into motion.

The next day, I told the members of The Renegades that it was over—I was disbanding the group and joining The Shy-Lads. Though I braced myself for a meltdown, there were no tears. The anticlimactic sendoff made me realize just how uncommitted these guys were to making it big. Obviously, our time together had just been a lark to them!

The next time I got together with Larry and the guys, I sheepishly ventured, "We really should find a new name. The Shy-Lads is really bad. How about The Shondels?"

I had been keeping this name in my back pocket for a while now. I had first seen it in the back pages of a *Melody Maker* newspaper (I treasured these publications because they represented the whole allure of the British rock culture), which Alice Anne had brought back to me after visiting England and Scotland with her Scottish fiancé and future husband, Jim McCabe.

My culture-crazed sister had also carried back these other amazing recordings: The Shadows' *Greatest Hits*, smashes by Freddie and the Dreamers (this was before their dance, "the Freddie," became popular; it resembled a Kingfisher penguin flapping its appendages mindlessly against its thighs), and the debut LP by a new English group called The Rolling Stones! "England's newest hit makers!"

But it was the adverts, in the back of that newspaper, that intrigued me most. It was like being in the London Underground gazing at emerging bands with strange and fascinating names: The Steampacket, The Underbeats, Shane Fenton and the Fentones, and The Graham Bond Organisation (note British spelling!). They were performing in clubs such as the Cavern, the Marquee, and the Rainbow. It was in these back pages I noticed a performance by an obscure group called The Shondels.

They were a small-time British band playing tiny clubs in London. I figured (correctly) that they'd never make it, and history proved me right. But, I also liked the name because it was the last name of one of my favorite artists, Troy Shondel. His hit "This Time" was currently in high rotation on my turntable.

Larry, in his unvarnished honesty, asked, "What's a Shondel?"

I told him that I had absolutely no idea, but added, "It sounds cool, doesn't it?"

"Yeah," Larry said. "It sounds cool!" Everyone else agreed. That day we officially became The Shondels.

That agreement marked the beginning of forever. We rehearsed tirelessly and went from teen club to teen club, from church event to recreation center, offering our services. The routine was exhausting, but it paid off. We soon begged our parents to buy us matching Sears Roebuck Silvertone amps. These were "piggyback" models where the amplifier section was separate from the speaker cabinet and perched on top. It made for easier cartage and more flexibility.

We made our grand debut.

When we hit the Berwyn Recreation Center (known as "The Rec"), we gave our hard sell to the director, Fritz Ploegman.

"Well boys, I'd like to have you play our Saturday night dance, but of course, you'd have to 'donate your services.'" That's not the last time we would hear that phrase from countless teen center managers and club owners.

These performances went really well. I remember the kids dancing, frugging, ponying, and twisting to our repertoire, which included hits by the Beatles and The Ventures. We also covered "Bad Motor-cycle" and "I've Had It" by the Crestones.

Then there was our selection of Beach Boys songs, which offered us a good excuse to show off our emerging harmonies. We did "Fun, Fun, Fun," "409," and "Surfin' Safari." Then we'd cut loose with "Carhop," by the Exports, "Land of 1,000 Dances," by Cannibal and the Headhunters, and even a cover of the Chiffons' hit "He's So Fine" (changed to "She's So Fine"—we loved singing that "doo lang, doo lang, doo lang" hook in three-part harmony!).

We even started sneaking some of our originals into the set: The Ventures-inspired "Corruption" and "Torque Out" ("I'll get the car, you buy the gas, I'll bring the girls…Torque Out!").

After starting out with a wicked snare drum rim shot, I intoned the first song's ominous hook, "Corruption." Then Bob Bergland took over with the "Peter Gunn"–inspired bass line. I continued our Ven-tures homage by adding the twangy lead on my sunburst Jazzmaster.

Time flew by. I became a freshman, and the other guys became sophomores. After being Boy of the Year in eighth grade I was now demoted to nerd boy of the year—at the bottom of the food chain at Morton West High School. When I couldn't find my algebra class on the very first day of school, I slid into the class on my ass, ten minutes late. I had my slick new leather-soled shoes and the floors had just been waxed. "Nice entrance, Mr. Peterik," intoned the old Mrs. Buddeke. "Now find your way down to the dean's office for a detention!"

That same day as I stood saying my name in the gym class lineup, Coach Regan silently came over to me and handed me a pink slip of paper. "Should be in girls PE. Take it down to the dean's office for a detention!" he bellowed. My hair was only slightly longer than the guys around me, but too long for the coach. I was batting two for two on my first day of high school.

Fortunately The Shondels started playing the sock hops after the basketball games at Morton West. In fact, we proudly became the official sock hop band. It was called a "sock hop" because the kids were asked to remove their shoes so they wouldn't scuff up the gym-nasium floor.

The performing was great, but, gradually, tensions were brewing during rehearsal. Bob Erhart's father was becoming a major pain in the ass. There were never enough drums in the mix for Mr. Erhart and his beloved son.

"You're drowning him out with bass and guitars!" he bitterly complained.

After every set, right on cue, he would chide, "Too much bass! Too much bass! I can't hear the vocals, can't hear the drums!"

Our resident Achilles heel would go on and on, night after night. He went from being an irritating paper cut to becoming an oozing incision. But beyond that, we started to notice something else—Bob Erhart was not really getting the new beat of the modern day songs. To him, the bass drum was four on the floor, *boom, boom, boom, boom.*

Mr. Erhart's coddled son just didn't get the whole *boom-boom boom* thing, at all. After putting all the negatives together, Bob Bergland, Larry Millas, and I converged at Larry's house one afternoon to scan the phone book for the number of a drummer in Mr. Boker's grade school band, of which we were all a part (I played sax, Larry played percussion, and Bob played clarinet). This Mike Borch guy, whom we had all noticed, was really on the ball and knew how to smack that snare drum in band practice.

We scanned the pages, "Borchard," "Borchart," "Borch!" We struck gold. He answered right away. After we convinced him to audition, we gave him the directions to what Larry called his "big ritzy house." It was a magnificent place built in the early '50s on a double-wide lot. It was located on the upscale Riverside Drive in Berwyn. We even put up a sign in front boasting, "Big Ritzy House" so Mike couldn't miss it!

When the day came, Mike's audition song was "Game of Love" by Wayne Fontana and the Mindbenders. We had recently tried out this song with Bob Erhart, and it had been a total disaster. But on this day, I counted it off and Mike proceeded to play it exactly like the record. *Boom, crack, boom-boom.* Heaven! Smiles were exchanged around the room and we welcomed Mike Borch into The Shondels.

The Shondels and I used to frequent Chicago's music row, taking the 'L' train downtown from Cicero, and then getting off at Wabash. We would bug all the music store proprietors by asking questions, and then we would beg permission to plug their guitars into amplifiers. These outings also allowed us to observe the burgeoning Chicago music scene as other real musicians plugged in and jammed in the music rooms of Lyon & Healy Music, The Guitar Gallery, or Kagan & Gaines.

We rehearsed every chance we got. We bought sharp, matching red sweaters for our upcoming shows. We rehearsed in Larry's basement. At breaks, we'd shoot pool on Larry's dad's professional table. Dr. Millas was the beloved town physician. He was known for bartering loaves of bread and bushels of tomatoes and unsold shirts for delivering a baby or setting an arm if the family didn't have the means. Everyone in Berwyn and Cicero knew and loved the kindly Dr. Millas.

Early on, we played a variety show at Piper Elementary, our alma mater. We were the only musical act among dancers, comics, and jugglers. We wowed the audience in those red cardigans.

Flush with victory, we walked back to Larry's house a few blocks away. Unfortunately, we got so distracted goofing off and playing pool that we forgot to go back and take the final curtain call with all of the other acts. We learned a lot about becoming professionals that day, and about avoiding fancy distractions—like shooting pool.

Fortunately, we exercised a little more discipline the next time around. On our first professional gig we opened for a fashion show at Morton East High School. Again, we all wore our signature red sweaters and collectively sweated under the spotlights as the houselights dimmed. Soon, the spot zeroed in on me. I sang:

"When I was just a little boy / I asked my mother, 'what shall I be?'
'Will I be handsome, will I be rich?' Here's what she said to me."

My folksy rendition of "Que Sera, Sera" was then rudely interrupted by the sharp crack of the snare drum.

"You ain't nothing but a hound dog!
Crockin' all the time!"

I sang it "crockin'" because that's what it sounded like when Elvis sang the song. Years later I found out he was saying "cryin.'"

The audience roared their approval! That was a defining moment for me. I heard my voice echo through the wonderful acoustics of the Chodl Auditorium. The Shondels were bringing down the house! We were on our way.

Emboldened by the crowd response and our raging teenage hormones, we entered the Talented Teen Search, being held the very next day at the Cermak Plaza. This was the contest I cut my teeth on the year before with my solo rendition of Wilbert Harris's gem, "Kansas City."

We performed the Pyramids' hit "Penetration" (with a few years under my belt, I wondered if that title went a lot deeper than just a reference to the piercing sound of the lead guitar). Unfortunately, we failed to penetrate. We came in at fifth place.

That first year represented our coming of age as a band. Our door-to-door peddling of our musical wares was paying off. We were playing almost every weekend at venues like Berwyn's Red Feather Building, Morton West High School, and Tiger Hall in Lyons. The latter was a wild place where a senior named Val Godlewski would get raunchy and dirty dance with basketball star Skip Hack as we did our ten-minute rave-up rendition of Ray Charles's "What'd I Say."

The greasers from high school came dressed in their "workies" (short, gray work pants rolled up on the bottom), and at about 11 p.m., they decided that they were sweaty and horny enough to tie red bandanas around their heads. They proceeded to bump and grind to our version of "Land of 1,000 Dances." (Our first swirl-finished, green business card read: "The Shondels—Band of 1,000 Dances.")

The big moment came when a club that hadn't even opened yet contacted us. It was to be called The Keynote Club in suburban Lyons, Illinois. Since Lyons was known for its strip clubs and houses of ill repute, the community felt that the addition of a teen club would serve as a breath of fresh air. This venue would lend an air of respectability to a then-sordid outpost.

Plus, the club owner offered us five hundred big ones for a two-day run. This was *huge* money to us. At our first show, just a few weeks earlier, we had only received $25; not apiece, but for the entire band!!

For this show we decided we had to retire the red sweaters. The Shondels rode the 'L' downtown to go to the fabled Smokey Joe's for some groovy threads. "The man who knows goes to Smokey Joe's" was their radio-blasted slogan. We listened to the train announcer through the megaphone-like sound system: "Jackson," "Monroe," and finally "Wabash," where we tumbled out into the stifling humidity of Chicago summer to look for Smokey Joe's.

Suddenly there it was in all its glory on South State Street. The store window burst with color: coats, shirts, and slacks of every shade—from shocking lime green to deep purple. We were by far the youngest and palest people in the store. After we bought our Beatles look-alike sport coats (tan corduroy with velvet lapels) we walked over to Tad's $1.19 Steakhouse a few blocks north also on State Street. For just over a buck you got the juiciest, toughest, grizzliest steak known to man. There was literally a bonfire of flames as the grill master herded these babies from the bin to the grill and onto your baked-potato-laden plate. There was no medium-rare or even well-done—they were all incinerated equally. I can still taste the bitter charcoal laden with salt against the sizzling fat. Now that's eatin'!

Back in Lyons, Illinois, packed on opening night, our newly outfitted bodies and The Keynote Club generated quite a buzz. "The Shondels rock, man!" We had gone beyond the days of playing wimpy songs like "Mrs. Brown, You've Got a Lovely Daughter," which Bob Bergland sang as Larry performed the palm-muted guitar part with a wadded up Kleenex underneath the strings! Now we were jammin' The Rolling Stones ("The Last Time" and "Satisfaction"), and harmonizing the complex vocal arrangements of The Mamas and the Papas with "Monday, Monday," and the West Coast's Beau Brummels and The Byrds.

Sometimes, when we would come off a string of dates, sick as dogs with the flu, we'd line up as good old Doc Millas gave us each an injection of gamma globulin, apparently the very essence of life. I swear I saw microorganisms swimming around in that syringe!

Presto, chango, instant health. We were tapping our toes, ready for the next gig! We called it "The Doc Millas Magic Bullet!" I found out each of these shots contained about $150 of this life-restoring elixir.

With our hot new band playing the sock hops after the basketball games, gradually the cheerleaders began chatting us up. We were invited to sit on "the stage" of the Morton West cafeteria at lunch where all the school's glitterati (the jocks and pom-pom girls and cheerleaders) ate their sloppy joes and drank their chocolate milk.

The Shondels were my E-Ticket to hipness and acceptability. A nerd no more, I even traded in my broken, black, horn-rimmed glasses for a sharp pair of yellow-tinted aviator frames. I was in with the in-crowd and I swore I'd never be outside looking in again.

Great Caesar's Ghost

THE SHONDELS were making some real headway playing some high-profile venues like The Keynote Club and a fancy place in Berwyn called Frank Bond's Supper Club. We had garnered a great deal of performance experience together and felt a surge of energy whenever we got on stage.

But we still played some hellish dives like The J and D lounge on Cermak Road, back in Berwyn, where drunken old men would slur phrases between numbers. "Play a lullaby, dammit!" or "Could you dedicate your next song to the woman who couldn't dance tonight?" One old pervert actually grabbed my ass.

We entered every battle of the bands and talent competition we could find. One contest at the Red Feather Building in Cicero was especially noteworthy. We heard a rumor that there was to be a talent scout in attendance that night. We were breathless in anticipation as we ran through our spot-on cover of the Beau Brummels hit, "Just a Little." As I started the faux horn riff intro on my fuzzed-out Jazzmaster on the Stones' current smash "Satisfaction," I spotted a person way in the back of the auditorium standing coolly in tight capris and dark glasses. The talent scout, no doubt. I motioned to Larry, Larry motioned to Mike. Mike signaled Bob, and we took it up several notches 'til our performance rivaled The Rolling Stones themselves. After the show we were handed the giant trophy. People came up to the stage one by one to congratulate us including the "talent scout." That mysterious woman turned out to be my dear sister Janice who stopped by to support her little brother.

We started making a name for ourselves with our originals. We threw a few into every set: "It Makes Me Blue," "Don't Cry to Me," and "Please Don't Tell Me Lies." We played Sam the Sham and the Pharaohs' "Wooly Bully" in our parents' ornate bathrobes, starting the song with our backs to the audience then abruptly turning around to reveal the ridiculous robes.

I knew that our future did not lie in our Sam the Sham act. It depended on solid, catchy originals. I have always been kind of like musical tofu—I was good at absorbing the flavors all around me. Somehow, though, my own style always shone through. One of The Ides' favorite groups was The Kinks. It wasn't just their cool Carnaby Street wardrobe that captured us; it was great punchy songs with sharp lyrical hooks and sharper-still guitar hooks. "You Really Got Me," "Revenge," and "All Day and All of the Night" still stand out as archetypal guitar riffs.

I wrote two songs just after "You Really Got Me" came out that were heavily influenced by The Kinks. The first was called "Like It or Lump It" and the second was "No Two Ways about It," which was earmarked in my mind for the "A" side of our first single we were planning on recording soon. The guys flipped out when I played these tunes at rehearsal and added their unique guitar phrases, drum accents, vocal ideas, and arrangement touches, and in a week's time the songs were a part of our regular set. In fact, when we played the sock hop at Morton West that Friday night and premiered these new songs, the crowd went crazy. That positive reaction made us feel that these new songs were already hits. (The crowd may have thought they were new ones by The Kinks!)

Finances were always a challenge. We decided to pool the proceeds from the next gigs until we had enough money to buy recording time at Midwest Broadcasting Service, better known as MBS on Wabash in downtown Chicago. We also needed extra funds to press up 300 copies of the 45 to sell after shows.

After jamming our gear into my dad's 1957 Chrysler, and Mike Borch's Ford station wagon, we excitedly set out for the recording studio early one crisp Saturday morning.

We were mesmerized as we walked into the quiet, professional confines of MBS. Expensive German microphones were gathered in the corner at the ready, and, man, were we ready! We cut those two tracks efficiently, and even talked my dad into providing the jangly tambourine part on "Like It or Lump It." My dad was beaming as he rested his arm on the grand piano and played the tambourine part. This was his first time ever in a recording studio and he was lit from within.

As we packed our equipment back up, after what we considered a successful session, the engineer left the control room and sheepishly approached us with an ashen expression on his face. It looked like bad news. "Boys, I hate to tell you this, but we have to do your two songs all over again. We stretched the tape."

At first, we didn't know whether to laugh or cry. We kept playing those words over and over in our minds: "stretched the tape"! We set our gear back up so that we could try to recapture the magic all over again. Back in the day, apparently, it wasn't uncommon to stretch the tape because it was much more elastic than the more durable modern tape that would be used years later.

When the discs finally arrived, we were giddy with excitement. We had even created our own record label, Epitome Records—of course everyone called it Epi-tome!—but we were so consumed with this new recording that the following fact didn't really seem to upset us: Each and every one of our names was misspelled under the printed song titles! "Millias," "Peter ik," and "Broche" instead of "Millas," "Peterik," and "Borch." (There must be some guy hired to mess up the lettering on every band's first release.) Fortunately, though, these recordings, which were available after every sock hop, sold like hot-cakes. In fact, it looked like we would have to reorder soon!

But the best was soon to come. One sunny Saturday morning, I got a call from Larry, whose voice trembled with excitement. He could barely get out the words.

"My mom got us an appointment at Mercury Records! They want to hear our forty-five!"

Anne Millas was an exotic-looking woman of northern Italian descent with a beehive hairdo and dark, flashing eyes. Today you'd call her a diva. She looked and held herself like a movie star complete with a confident air that could sell ice to the Eskimos. Because of Doc Millas's thriving practice, Anne was always dressed to the nines—even at noon.

What? How did Anne score this appointment? How could this be? To us, record companies were for other people; for real musicians, not self-taught school kids. The labels to us were untouchable entities. They were way too big and important to care about a rock band from the western suburbs of Chicago, weren't they?

I incredulously asked Larry, "How in the world did your mom get us the audition?"

He replied calmly, "She looked up Mercury Records in the phone book, gave her best sell job, and landed an appointment!"

I cannot remember a better day than that one. We all piled into my dad's New Yorker and headed down to the Mather Building on Wacker Drive where Mercury Records was located. I remember my dad's corny humor coming through on that ride down. To settle everyone's nerves he said, "What's a Mather…Building?"

Many times, when asked, "What was the turning point of your career? What started your trajectory to success?" I consistently answer that it was the day when Anne Millas got us that meeting. Everything else that happened to me since could be traced back to that one remarkable event. Honestly, my entire career was set in motion by that one perfectly timed phone call.

We sweated it out in the reception area until the secretary waved us into a cramped little office. Sitting behind the desk was a nice-looking gentleman who was wearing a fashionable blue suit. He introduced himself as Dutch Wenzlaff and greeted us warmly, then pointed at an old-fashioned record player next to his desk. Our nerves were already starting to fray.

"Let's hear what you got!" We couldn't have asked for a more rapt audience. When the needle hit the first grooves of "Like It or Lump It," his foot started tapping. He kind of half-smiled—we got the impression that he didn't want to give anything away—but you could tell he was digging the sounds.

Then, Dutch flipped the record over, and the harmonies of "No Two Ways about It" flooded the room. This time, his facial muscles showed no sign of restraint. In fact, he broke into a mile-wide smile...

"This is the one I've been waiting to hear. This is a hit. I'd like to come down to rehearsal next Saturday and hear you boys play live. Do you have any more good originals?"

"Absolutely, Dutch!" we shouted, practically in unison. What we didn't say was that songs like "It Makes Me Blue" and "Please Don't Tell Me Lies" were far below the quality of the material he had just heard. We knew we had our work cut out for ourselves. We had to come up with a few good ones in the days leading up to his visit.

I went to work, furiously strumming my guitar to find some fresh progressions. Out of this seemingly aimless noodling emerged a brand-new song. This one was kind of a cross between the style of The Kinks crossbred with some of the rhythm and blues chord changes of one my favorite acts, Curtis Mayfield and the Impressions. The songs Curtis wrote just went to my soul.

We had recently played a renowned Chicago nightclub called Thumbs Up, which served as the home base of the popular group Baby Huey and the Babysitters. As luck would have it, one night we got called at the last minute to sub for their ailing front man.

We were told to have enough material to fill four sets—from 9 p.m. to 4 a.m.! We had to borrow a high-quality microphone from the studio at The Balkans music store because my mic was a Ham radio throwback from the '40s.

At every break, the club blasted Baby Huey's latest single called "Beg Me." I definitely picked up on some of the changes in that song

My 15th birthday.

(which in and of itself was Curtis Mayfield–influenced) and made
copious mental notes along the way; I was hoping to blend them into
my new song.

The Shondels had a really cool ritual: When one of us had a birthday, we would pull an all-night rehearsal/celebration/sleepover at
either Larry's house or mine. These soirees were a blast.

The day Dutch Wenzlaff was scheduled to come to Berwyn happened to be November 11th, which was my birthday! Perfect. We'd
rehearse and write all night, and when he came over at 11 a.m., we
would have a couple more smashes to play for him.

We worked feverishly on my new one, "You Wouldn't Listen." It
had the seeds of a good song but it just wasn't hanging together.

We all threw in lyrics. After we wrote a good line down on paper, we pasted our rough lyric sheets on the support pole in my parents' dank basement. But the process was coming along glacially.

At around 4 a.m., we decided to pack it in. We were burned out. With a sigh of resignation, we decided that Dutch would just have to hear this version in its unfinished, nebulous state. Or there was always a chance that a few hours of shut-eye would refresh us...

Miraculously, we woke up at around 8 a.m. totally revitalized. Suddenly we knew just how to finish the song. Larry came up with The Byrds–influenced F to C section and the end of each chorus where I would sing, "Now you have gotta pay, you've gotta pay." When 11 a.m. came, we answered the knock and smiled as Dutch glided into the room.

"Play me what you got!"

I counted off and played The Kinks–like opening guitar part on my recently acquired Fender Jazzmaster. Then Mike's drums kicked in along with Larry's chunky rhythm guitar and Bob's booming bass.

Then, it was on to our well-rehearsed vocal dialogue. Larry sang: "I told you, he was a fool." My young voice replied, "You wouldn't listen to me." Back to Larry, "He'll break your heart." My turn, "You wouldn't listen to me. He'll tear it apart. You wouldn't listen to me. So you better get smart. You wouldn't listen to me..."

As our clever call-and-response continued, Dutch's smile grew bigger and bigger, and, pretty soon his leg started keeping time. When all two minutes and forty-three seconds were done, there was a long, suspenseful moment of total silence as we watched for his initial reaction. Finally, Dutch said, "Well, boys, you got yourself a number one record there. All you've got to do is add a modulation."

We all nodded in agreement. Then, as one intrepid voice, we asked, "What's a modulation?"

Dutch went on to explain that this was the musical trick of raising the key of the song, generally up a half or a whole step at a certain point to build excitement. "Try modulating up a half step, going into the last chorus," he said.

We hit the end of the bridge, "Now, you are in mourning. I said that you're in a mighty bad way..." Then I instinctively added a

"Yeah, yeah, yeah" as the band slid up that magic half step. Goose-bump city! We were flush with the final touch that would soon pro-pel this song to number seven on WLS's Silver Dollar Survey, and then all the way to number forty-two on the prestigious *Billboard* chart. Before long that song, concocted on the night of my fifteenth birthday, would be played on stations coast to coast. It would be featured as the spotlight dance introduced by our childhood rock 'n' roll hero, Dick Clark; it would form the basis of the jingle for a popular acne product, Tackle: "Hey, fella. Before you go out, check your oil. 'Cause that's where acne pimples and blackheads start!" That little song to this day is one of the highlights of an Ides of March concert—a perfect time capsule of 1966 and all the innocence of that time and the dreams of four very young men from Berwyn. We even perform it with the same corny dance steps we learned back then.

Dutch could not get his own record company, Mercury, interested in The Shondels, but he passed the band on to his friend Sam Cerami at London Records, whose subsidiary, Parrot, was home to British acts such as The Zombies, Tom Jones, and The Small Faces. They were more than happy to sign our American-by-way-of-England band.

But in the meantime, we had to keep up with the rest of our responsibilities. I sat in my senior geometry class with the secret knowledge that we were about to explode with our own record. The Shondels would soon be on the radio.

Unfortunately, my little reverie was shattered when I heard the pre-sell from one of my favorite disc jockeys, Art Roberts: "Here's a brand-new one sure to catch fire, 'Hanky Panky' by Tommy James and the Shondells!" Oh, shit!

The name we borrowed from Troy Shondel and that obscure Eng-lish band was stolen once again—this time by some guy named Tommy James! Here we were with our first single ready to come out and this setback happens.

We got together and started tossing around names. This routine quickly got hilarious, of course.

"How about Larry and the Roachbeats?"

"No, I got it! Strawberry Tennis Shoe."

On and on, the absurd brainstorming went. But this was no laughing matter. London Records was freaking out. We had to come up with a new name, and quickly.

We were in the lobby of the Chodl Auditorium waiting to see a high school play when Bob Bergland got us in a huddle, "Guys, I got it. I'm reading *Julius Caesar* now in senior literature class and suddenly I see our future name. In this one part, Brutus warns Caesar, 'Beware the Ides of March.' How about 'The Ides of March'?"

"Sounds like a name!" crowed Larry.

We loved the new moniker immediately, and on that day we were rechristened forever.

One night, we had just finished packing up our gear after a particularly sweaty sock hop at Morton West. We had stirred the crowd into frenzy by performing the new Strangeloves song, "In the Nighttime."

We had already felt euphoria after that set, but it turned out that the biggest thrill was just around the corner. On the way to Larry's "big ritzy house," emanating from the oval speaker in the dashboard of his black 1957 Cadillac limo (The Ides always traveled in style!) came Art Roberts's commanding but familiar voice.

This time, though, the popular DJ spoke the words we'd been waiting to hear our whole lives: "Okay, get ready, Chicago. Here's the new one from a new band on the scene. It's my Art Roberts pick to click: The Ides of March—'You Wouldn't Listen.'"

As I heard my crisp Jazzmaster riff coming across the AM airwaves, I experienced a feeling like no other. I was born for this moment. As the band kicked in, the other Ides, cavorting in the backseat, rolled down the windows and started shouting to anyone in earshot, "That's us, that's us!"

The record sounded incredible, as it streamed through the warm night air. We headed down Cermak Road past Vesecky's Bakery, Lincoln Federal Savings and Loan, the Berwyn Theater, the Olympic Theater, all the way down to Troy Store before the song finally ended, with Art Roberts practically shouting, "New from The Ides of March!"

There is something about the sound of a song coming through the limited bandwidth and heavy compression of AM radio that screams,

"Hit Record!" And there's something about that night that lives forever in me. I still use that moment to inspire me and remind me of why I do what I do. It's the feeling of transporting your heart and soul through space and time. (Forward to 2012 when I harnessed these emotions to inform the lyric of the title song I co-wrote for the Beach Boys, "That's Why God Made the Radio.")

And a hit it was. The next day at Morton West the word had spread. People started to treat us like we were something special. The cheerleaders and pom-pom girls, previously out of my league, asked me questions about the band. I couldn't help notice that they were kind of flirtatious. I could get used to this! Suddenly I felt even more worthy of my place on the stage in the cafeteria where all the jocks and popular guys and girls got to sit.

A moment I will never forget (only recently rock historian Clark Besch supplied me with a DVD of this) was watching one of my favorite shows, *American Bandstand*, when on air the squeaky clean host put in a call to the Chicago disc jockey at WCFL, Ron Riley, to mention a song that was currently "making noise" in Chi-Town. He talked about one that was tearing it up by a local group The Ides of March called "You Wouldn't Listen." "Well then let's hear it, shall we? Now for our spotlight dance, the new smash 'You Wouldn't Listen' by The Ides of March!" The spotlight dance = holy crap! We were made men.

Unfortunately, all of our newfound prestige was wasted on the captain of the hall guards, the short, stocky, Brylcreem-haired, Mr. Magro (derogatorily nicknamed "Little Al"); he was dreaded and feared by all.

Because of Morton's strict dress code, The Ides had to appear before The Don (he really did look like a Mafia boss) every Monday morning to prove that our hair did not go over our collars or ears. Well, seriously, you couldn't be a rock band if you had short hair, so before school each Monday, we would stop at Larry's house, slick our hair back with Dippity-do and water, and tuck our locks inside our shirts. Then we kind of pulled our shoulders up a bit. We must have looked like quite an odd squad as we all slinked into his office. But it worked every time.

"Well, okay, you guys look 'okay,' to me. But keep it cut!" he warned. The only problem was that after we went in the bathroom to towel all that glop off our hair, we'd have to find alternate paths to every class to avoid him. I couldn't even eat in the cafeteria after that. I brought my lunch from home and ate it in the back row of my previous classroom. That's how determined I was to keep my Beatles cut!

But rock hair was getting even longer and soon our Beatles bobs looked tame. Groups such as the Jefferson Airplane, The Byrds, and The Rolling Stones now set the bar for rock hair. One day, our manager at the time, Mike Considine, who had somehow horned his way into that first recording session as a friend or stalker of Sam Cerami, told us that our record was climbing the charts. Though we thought of him as old, Mike was probably only around twenty-four at the time. He also informed us that a hot club in Algonquin, Illinois, wanted us to headline the following night. We had heard the legend of this club, called The New Place, from all of the coolest people we knew. We were completely psyched until Mike laid this one on us, "But you can't arrive with that corny, short Beatles hair. Tomorrow afternoon, before the show, I'm taking you to The Wig Wam to get long-hair wigs."

We did not like this idea, not one bit, but the next day we found ourselves in swivel chairs at this teepee-styled structure just off of I-94. Bob came out of there looking like Mother Mary with hair all the way down his back; Mike looked like Jesus Christ. Larry at least resembled someone from this century—he looked like a latter-day John Lennon.

I bore a passing resemblance to Debby Sherry from my homeroom class. When we showed up at The New Place, we looked like poster boys from some fictitious new horror flick, *It Came from the Suburbs!!*

The kids who had jammed up to the stage couldn't believe what they were seeing. Suddenly, we launched into our first number, "The Kids Are Alright" by one of our favorite groups, The Who.

"I don't mind, other guys dancing with my girl," we sang, with our scintillating three-part harmonies. We closed the show with our big hit, "You Wouldn't Listen." That night, The Ides could do no wrong; the crowd ate us up. Unfortunately, after the set we discovered

Chicago Musicians Union, Local 10, tough guys waiting in the wings to see our union cards. Although we were officially members of the Musicians Union no one told us we had to carry the cards with us at all times. It took months of red tape and fines to get that one behind us. Welcome to the music biz—Chicago style!

From that fateful night, The Ides had no trouble getting gigs. We would play WLS- and WCFL-sponsored teen shows with celebrity disc jockeys such as Dick Biondi, Dex Card, Ron Britton, Ron Riley, Larry Lujack, Barney Pip, or Art Roberts hosting. We even did an Art Roberts television variety show, *Swinging Majority*, with an unknown group from Gary, Indiana, boasting a six-year-old whirling dervish of a dancer, Michael Jackson, singing lead in front of his brothers—The Jackson 5!

We headlined every week at a different Chicago-area teen club, each one with a name more fantastic than the next: The Green Gorilla, The Pink Phink, The Purple Cucumber, Dex Card's Wild Goose (four locations!), The Valley View Young Adults Club (well, not all of them had happening names), The Deep End, and then, of course, our area's version of Liverpool's Cavern Club: a tiny haunt in the basement of a power plant, The Cellar, in Arlington Heights.

This club was ground zero for The Ides. We had played there once as Batt Mann and the Boy Wonders. That brilliant marketing scheme, concocted by our Svengali manager, Mike Considine, was construed as a way to capitalize on the burgeoning Batman craze. Because we showed up sans costume, Larry (Batt Mann) had to announce, "Sorry, our capes are at the cleaners!" (The rarest of rare Ides singles is a promo copy "You Wouldn't Listen" by Batt Mann and the Boy Wonders.)

This time around, as The Ides of March, we took that place by storm and joined the ranks of other Cellar alumni: The Shadows of Knight, The Males (featuring a teenaged Hawk Wolinski), Saturday's Children, HP Lovecraft, and even huge iconic bands such as Cream and Buffalo Springfield.

I feel so fortunate to have been a part of the emerging Chicago music scene back in the '60s when The Ides were cutting their teeth. Competition always seems to make bands sharper and these bands were some stiff competitors.

The Ides were the new kids on the block being a few years younger than the rest but we soaked it all up like dean's list scholars. We were merely fans at first, rushing to the Blue Village in Westmont to make sure we stood right in front of the stage to see our hometown heroes, The Cryan' Shames. Lead singer Tom (Toad) Doody was the classic Irish tenor with a vibrato that I nurtured until I could do a dead-on impersonation of him singing "It Could Be We're In Love." Jim (J.C. Hook) Pilster, who loaded his birth-deformed arm with a wicked metal hook, shook his tambourine and danced like a man possessed. The Ides learned four-part harmony from the intricate vocal arrangements of guitarist Jim (now James) Fairs. I considered him on a par with Brian Wilson and Jimmy Webb.

Suddenly as our "You Wouldn't Listen" climbed the charts we found ourselves sharing the stage with some of Chicago's best: The Buckinghams, whose "Kind of a Drag" would become a nationwide smash, perhaps the first breakthrough of a local band. This was soon followed by a string of huge hits including the Jim Guercio–produced "Don't You Care," "Mercy, Mercy, Mercy," and "Susan." They proved to all of us suburban wannabees that it could be done.

We all competed for prime slots at the various teen clubs such as Desplaine's Green Gorilla and Arlington Heights' Cellar. We kept on trying to top each other with our latest cover version or brand new original. Whenever a band scored a hit there were congratulatory back slaps but also a committed goal to beat them with our next recording.

Also on our thrill list was opening for The New Colony Six (where one Karen Moulik saw me play for the first time!). They were a terrific band boasting two lead singers and using the groovy gimmick of patching Jerry Van Kollenberg's lead guitar through a spinning Leslie organ cabinet. Their breakthrough hit "I Will Always Think About You" sung by Ronnie Rice became many a high school's prom theme.

But The Ides saved our biggest accolades for The Exceptions, a band of seemingly impossibly tall guys who took the stage like they owned it. Their blond lead singer/bassist was none other than Pete Cetera (later a founding member of CTA, subsequently renamed "Chicago") who commanded the stage with his magnetic personality and cutting tenor. Jimmy Vincent (another six-foot-plus giant) played guitar in an amazing jazz rock style that I had never heard before. Billy Herman thundered on drums.

At the Teen World Fair after our set we were treated to the premiere of their version of the just-released "Good Vibrations." In those days, a dead-on cover was as envied as a hit record. The Ides raised our bar due to the amazing bands we had to go against. We and the Shames would trade chord formations and vocal arrangements. We learned the arrangement the Shames used for their version of the Nashville Teens classic "Tobacco Road." They borrowed liberally from our stage patter and song catalogue. The suburbs were rife with rock 'n' roll and became The Ides' Liverpool.

School was out. It was the summer of 1966 and we had a record breaking coast to coast. The heat was literally on, but we had no doubt that we could rise above the expectations.

We found ourselves on a train heading for a string of dates in Florida, where our record was charting Top 10. This was officially our first tour and I still can't believe our parents let us go unaccompanied on this adventure. I was just fifteen! That's just how much our folks trusted us, and we never betrayed that trust.

Wearing heavy, dark-green corduroy suits that we purchased at the hippest boutique in Chicago—Old Town's, The Man at Ease—dress shirts, and ties, we sweated through the tropics of Florida at various teen clubs. By day we would visit radio stations that were playing our song. We shook a lot of hands and made a lot of friends in radio with our confident but polite style. Our total commitment to our music shined through everywhere we went. Our authentic camaraderie was apparent even to the casual observer. We were a family.

Though much of it seems like a blur, one club date stood out above all of the rest, in my mind. In Daytona Beach, right on the ocean next to a beached ocean liner, we stood slack-jawed as we viewed the opening band.

They were a properly scruffy lot, called The Allman Joys, which featured a tall, blond guy playing a black Les Paul Custom guitar. They played some wicked blues and some note-perfect Stones covers. The blond lead singer perched behind an old Hammond B3 organ had a gruff tenor voice that sent chills right through me. That lanky guy played a sweet slide guitar through a fifty-watt Marshall half-stack. But when they hit the three-part harmony on The Impressions' "I've Been Trying" we compared the goose bumps on our arms.

We followed their set with our set of lightweight covers such as "California Dreamin'" by The Mamas and the Papas, "Bus Stop" by The Hollies, and even the lame "Popsicle" by Jan and Dean. Luckily we had the radio hit "You Wouldn't Listen" to close the show. That one saved our butts that night. But after witnessing The Allman Joys, The Ides knew where the bar had to be set. A few years later that group, with a few personnel changes, became the mighty Allman Brothers Band.

But we had other troubles. Those wigs! Once, at the Young World's Fair in Minneapolis where we followed local favorites The Unbelievable Uglies, we took a deep bow after "You Wouldn't Listen," and my trendy wig slid off my head and fell into the crowd that was pressed up close to the stage. One young girl rescued it and sheepishly handed it back. Needless to say, that grand unveiling was kind of a buzz kill as we rushed off the stage.

When we played the Pink Phink on Sheridan Road back in Chi-Town, we noticed some cool, long-haired guys watching us intently in the audience. Afterwards, they introduced themselves as The Flock.

We were already huge fans of this great north side of Chicago band. We had seen them play at our own Morton High School a few weeks earlier, performing their brass-powered local hit, "Take Me Back" and their dynamite rendition of The Supremes' Motown classic, "Come See about Me."

Leader Ricky Kanoff did the talking: "We really dig the way you guys harmonize. Could you come by our rehearsal tomorrow and teach us how you do that?"

We jumped at the chance. The next day, we found ourselves ringing Ricky's doorbell. He lived in an upscale house on the tony north side of Chicago. When he opened the door, though, we were greeted with a blank stare.

He clearly did not recognize us. "Who are you guys?" I thought maybe he was tripping on acid or something until I realized we had shown up without our long, flowing wigs. I could see the disappointment in The Flock's faces. They thought we were some mutant race from the western 'burbs. But now, we resembled the Four Freshmen.

Nonetheless, we tutored them as they worked out the intricate harmonies of the Beach Boys' gem "Good Vibrations." But the illusion had been shattered. Not too long after that, those wigs found their way to the Dumpster, much to Mike Considine's chagrin.

When the single had run its course, we were rushed back into the studio to cut a follow-up. Since we had cut "You Wouldn't Listen" at the technically advanced Sound Studios on Michigan Avenue (no one stretched the tape there to my knowledge!), we were eager to do our next session there. The chief engineer, Stu Black, was the man behind many Chicago band hits around that time, such as "Sugar and Spice" by the Cryan' Shames and "I Confess" by the New Colony Six.

I had recently written a song called "Roller Coaster" and it was killing 'em at live shows. But it took some work to record it. With Mike Considine nervously pacing around the studio, we did take one of the song.

"No, No, No," Mike bellowed. "I want it exploding. I want it to sound like 'Summer in the City' by the Lovin' Spoonful." He was so driven to prove his point that he instructed Stu, "Run the meters in the red, bury the sound in a reverb wash and compress the living bejesus out of it!"

Take two was a sloppy, frenetic mess. We were out of meter and out of tune. Boiling over with frustration inside, but trying to smooth things over, I said, "Okay, Mike, we tuned up and we're ready for take three."

"Guys, that was the one!!" he exclaimed. We drove home feeling a little sick over what had just taken place. But that queasy feeling would only intensify...

As we pulled up to Larry's house with the radio blaring, we heard, "Now, hot off the press, the new smash from The Ides of March, 'Roller Coaster'!" Whaaaa?

We found out later that Mike had mixed the track in five minutes and had hand-carried the acetate over to WLS just down the block—this kind of thing could not happen in today's pre-programmed world.

We were giddy with joy until we heard the sobering results of the song we had cut not much more than an hour ago. It didn't sound anything like "Summer in the City." That production had power and clarity.

"Roller Coaster" was a cluttered mess—guitars and voices drowning in a sea of reverb. We were not surprised when the record stalled at number fourteen on the WLS Silver Dollar Survey and just barely broke the Hot 100 on the *Billboard* chart. When I listen now I like it a lot better than I did then. It kind of previewed the type of music that became known as punk. Since then "Roller Coaster" has become a cult classic.

We had learned an important life lesson. We would never again trust anyone with our future who knew less than we did. Our pact was now written in stone and hermetically sealed. From then on, we would take the reins.

Under the Spell of the Hot Lights

THROUGHOUT THOSE FEW MONTHS, I got a crash course in entertaining a crowd. I went from standing on stage as stiff as a board just kind of taking up space, to moving around, dancing, emoting, and traveling as far as my coil guitar cable would take me.

Tutored by some of the nation's best performers—Michael Jackson, Duane and Gregg Allman, and Jimy Sohns of The Shadows of Knight—I began to recognize that stage performing involved more than just standing like a wooden Indian and reciting the lyrics. I had to connect.

After this realization, I started talking to the crowd between numbers. I would get down on my knees for a lead. The more I engaged in this kind of behavior, the more the crowds started to expect that kind of thing from me, and I was more than happy to oblige. I became known for leaving each show drenched and drained and loving every minute of it. I was the mouthpiece of the band—the Energizer bunny—lead singer and lead guitarist all rolled into one. And behind me was an unstoppable engine of rock 'n' roll. Every man to the man gave it 150 percent every night.

I even started including a little solo comedy bit where the band would leave the stage and I would do what I called "The Teeny Bopper Medley." The bubblegum music craze was in full force around this time and songs by Bobby Sherman, The Archies, The 1910 Fruitgum Company, and Crazy Elephant were climbing the charts. Many of these so-called groups were, in reality, studio concoctions put together by two savvy East Coast producers: Jeff Katz and Jerry Kasenetz.

The Ides were not big fans of this genre, to say the least. But my main point was that, underneath the seeming innocence of these records there lurked heavy double entendre. More recently, I pulled the bit out of the trunk at an Ides show at Moraine Valley College and it went over as big in 2012 as it had in 1970.

In my medley, I'd do a verse from "Chewy Chewy" by The 1910 Fruitgum Company. I'd sing, "Chewy's such a sweet thing, good enough to eat thing, and that's just what I'm gonna do." Then, I would stop playing suddenly, look puzzled, and say, "That's hardcore pornography!" I wound up the bit with my own teenybopper song, which I am publishing here for the first time, right before your very eyes. It's called "Bit O' Honey."

"Slippin' kinda saucy down Sacramento Avenue
She slips into the hearts of every boy she sees
Oh, yeah, that's my Bit O' Honey
Now a little bit of honey's got a little bit of me

Chorus:
Yeah yeah, that's my bit of honey
If you have one mouth, she lasts all day
Yeah, yeah, for a little bit of money
A little Bit O' Honey goes a long, long way"

Copyright 1970 Jim Peterik/Bicycle Music ASCAP

One day, The Ides were summoned to the headquarters of our booking agency, Beacon Artists, which we called the Brain Factory. We were scared speechless that they were delivering bad news. "Roller Coaster" had stiffed. The gigs were drying up. We were deathly afraid that we were about to be dumped by our agency.

The head of Beacon Artists, Herb Gronauer, sat behind a huge desk. He was chomping a cigar, wearing a road-kill toupee, Hai Karate aftershave, and an ill-fitting sharkskin suit. This guy was right out of central casting. Despite his appearance, Herb had an ear for platinum hits and a heart of gold.

He beckoned us all to have a seat. We sat trying to look calm as he began, "Well, boys, we have a lot of acts on our roster and we only have room for so many [long pause]. But I've got to tell you, we have been getting nothing but rave reviews from all the promoters around the country who have booked you."

Our collective blood pressure dropped about fifty points. "I'm going to introduce you to a couple of guys that have started a management company called Lee Productions. Their names are Bob Destocki and Frankie Rand. Bob's a promo man with Warner Brothers Records and Frankie's with Columbia. When they approached me looking for acts to manage, I only gave them one name: The Ides of March."

Suddenly, we felt that all those nights sweating in those damn corduroy suits were not in vain. The word was getting around—and the word was good. Herb went on to tell us that we had just landed the opening slot at the Neil Diamond show at Leyden East High School, and Bob and Frank were going to be there to check us out. Could good news get any better?

We drove home in Mike Borch's station wagon and went right down to Larry's basement to work up a new set of material for this momentous show. It was a mere two weeks away.

"Work up a new show?" you ask. What was wrong with the show we had been polishing for the last year? That set that was slaying the crowds coast to coast?

Well, just listen to the sage words of the author of this book: "Guys, we need a new show if we're opening for Neil Diamond. We've got to learn some brand-new stuff!"

Since I was the musical leader of the band, the guys dutifully went along. They were probably thinking, "This guy is nuts! There's nothing wrong with our current show. We'll never be ready in time!"

But, I raved on, "There's a huge song on the charts right now, 'Those Were the Days' by Mary Hopkin. I can get our buddy, Bob Solone, to play violin and Al Zak [The Ides' head roadie] to play baritone horn. Bergie, could you lend Solone your old wig?"

I was on a roll. "There's another great song by Gary Puckett and the Union Gap. It's called 'The Reverend Mr. Posey,' and I just wrote a new killer called 'Watch My Smoke and Fan My Fire.' We'll encore with that one."

We rehearsed practically every night until the day of the show. That night, I learned some life lessons that I have never forgotten. I share the nine rules with you here.

Rule One:	Never try out new material for the first time at an important gig.
Rule Two:	Never assume playing in front of a live crowd can be simulated by merely rehearsing in the basement.
Rule Three:	Never let your roadie play baritone horn.
Rule Four:	Never play an encore unless the crowd demands it.
Rule Five:	Make sure Bob Solone can actually play violin.
Rule Six:	Never use a new guitar onstage until it has been set up properly.
Rule Seven:	Tune your instruments carefully!
Rule Eight:	Be sure not to suck—especially if you've invited prospective managers, record company execs, or talent scouts.
Rule Nine:	My Golden Rule of Rock 'n' Roll . . . I'll get to this in a minute.

When we ambled off stage after performing our unrequested encore, we ran smack-dab into Neil Diamond, who was standing alone backstage. He had been watching our show.

"Well, what did you think of the set, Mr. Diamond?"

When I asked this question, it was almost as an aside. I was brimming with confidence—somehow I had no idea how bad we were that night.

Neil took a long, commanding breath before he responded, "Next time, boys, only play your best material."

His comment was conveyed so simply and so eloquently that the message stays with me to this day. "Only play your best material." That, my friends, is Rule Number Nine.

Why hadn't I considered that factor before? Though I felt slightly humiliated, I knew I had to move on, and as hard as those words were to swallow, I had to agree. I had let ego get in the way. Though it would not be the last time I would let my impetuous nature get the better of me, I had certainly been dealt an incredibly humbling, life-changing lesson. In a great full-circle moment, in 2007, I signed my new publishing deal with the company Neil Diamond founded, Bicycle Music. Obviously I took his advice to heart all those years ago.

As bad as the night was, Bob and Frankie still saw some redeeming qualities in us. Bob was his typical, low-key, diplomatic self in the dressing room. "Well, you guys definitely need some revamping, but we see something in you we can work with." Whew!

"We want to get you in the studio right away to record a demo tape for Warner Brothers Records. On my recommendation, they've agreed to foot the bill."

Oh boy—oh joy! We had, remarkably, already gotten over Neil's comment. Now, we were mentally preparing a song list for the session.

We circled the wagons the next day at Larry's house.

"Okay, guys, what do we got?" I asked.

"Well," said Bob. "We've got that one we tried out at The Blue Village in Westmont, 'Something Coming On.'"

"Okay. That's a good call. What else?"

Mike ventured, "Jim, what about that song you wrote about Chicken Little?"

"Oh, you mean, 'The Sky Is Falling'?"

The Ides of March add brass.

"Yeah, that one."

"Cool! That tune really shows off Chuck Soumar and John Larson." The recent addition of Chuck and John meant that we now had a smokin' brass section.

"We need one more tune," said Larry. "What about that one that went over so well at the Valley View Young Adults Club last Saturday?"

"The dance floor filled up immediately!" John reminded us.

"No," I said. "That was a good live tune, but it would never make the cut for radio."

"What was the name of that song again, Jim?" John chimed in once more.

"Oh, that one? That's called 'Vehicle.'"

After forty years of continuous airplay in all fifty states and almost every continent, it seems so obvious now, that after going number one in 1970 and then again in 2007, when it was recorded by *American Idol* star Bo Bice, and after being heard coast to coast in General Motors commercials, in movie soundtracks, and after being played, at least once a month, by Paul Shaffer and the NBC Orchestra on *The Late Show, featuring David Letterman*, that we should have showcased the song at that time.

But at the time, "Vehicle" was just another song on our set list; one that I had written in about an hour and a half, inspired by an unintentionally hilarious, antidrug pamphlet that was being circulated around school that showed a sketch of the "friendly stranger" driving slowly along the curb to lure in kids with drugs, etc.

But the real motivation for writing that career-making, game-changing song is the stuff of suburban legend—and my personal history.

Such Complete Intoxication

I WAS A SENIOR at Morton West High School. Karen Moulik was a sophomore at Nazareth Academy, an all-girls school in La Grange. I think I had seen her sitting with her family in the pews of St. Odilo's Parish.

One of my favorite bands, The Turtles, was to appear at Riverside Brookfield High School in nearby Riverside and I was determined to see them in concert. I was also hoping to find a date. There was a girl named Donna Hetman who was in one of my classes. She was a real doll, with big blue eyes and long, silky brunette hair. I had walked up to Donna ready to ask her to the show, but when the time came, I got all tongue-tied and never got the words out.

It was kind of cool out that evening, April 9, 1968, so I had put on my navy blue peacoat hoodie and headed out alone. That night it was open seating: first come, first served. I wanted to get good seats, so even though it was an eight o'clock show, I got there at about ten minutes after six.

I was one of the first people in line. And, as I was standing there, I noticed a gaggle of girls, each one was cuter than the next. And, even though there were four of them, I distinctly noticed this living doll in orange culottes, saddle shoes, and a crisply starched lacy white blouse.

This girl's reddish blonde hair was secured with a barrette. She looked like a young Brigitte Bardot, with those big, blue eyes. There she stood, her head tilted down but her eyes looking up. It was almost as if there was a light that shone on her alone. All of her girl-friends were cute, but this one was beyond cute: She glowed with an inner beauty. There was something special about this girl.

I peered down her blouse discreetly to see what I could see. Nice, I thought. I sized up her long, creamy legs. Real fine. I figured though that she was way out of my league and probably one of those stuck-up Riverside Brookfield girls raised by rich parents and spoiled rotten. Just then she turned to me and said,

"Are you Peterik?"

"Yeah. How did you know?" I responded, trying to sound casual.

"Jim Peterik?"

"Yeah."

"I just saw your band, The Ides of March, about a month ago, when you opened for the New Colony Six at Morton West," she con-tinued amiably, with a softness in her voice that sounded like music. "You guys rocked. My name's Karen."

As we talked I felt like I'd known this person all of my life. Or maybe from another life. There was something very familiar about her somehow. I was this shy guy who could be brave onstage, but when it came to meeting a girl, that was a different story…yet there I was talking a blue streak with this girl.

We talked about our favorite rock groups like the Dave Clark Five and the Cryan' Shames and movies that we'd just seen, books we read, classes we hated. Soon all of those other girls completely disappeared.

Meanwhile, a crowd was forming in back of us and people started pushing. They kept shoving until suddenly a girl in the very front got thrust violently through the glass door. As she dislodged her head and turned around, we all noticed that blood was streaming down her anguished face. She stood there in shock as we all looked on in horror.

I know it sounds strange, but as soon as Karen and I looked at each other after witnessing this, we started laughing uncontrollably. It was one of those paradoxical reactions where you're faced with a sudden tragedy and for some reason your nervous system just goes ballistic.

Karen and I could not stop. We kept trying to hide our hysteria but the more we tried the harder we laughed. The entire crowd was glaring at us as the paramedics came to carry the girl to the hospital. I've always wondered what happened to that girl, and hoped she was alright. Later, Karen and I agreed that this was the moment we realized we were wired the same way—that we were destined to spend our lives together.

After the shock subsided, we rushed to claim a row of good seats near the front of the gymnasium. We waited through the opening act, local favorites, The Second Story, chatting up a storm over the Beatles songs the band covered.

Karen sat down right next to me. This was a very good sign. There I was, virtually sandwiched in the middle of these amazing-looking girls. When The Turtles took the stage Karen grabbed my arm. Oh yeah—love that. They opened with one of their big hits, the super catchy "She'd Rather Be with Me," as the whole crowd sang along. The Turtles were at the top of their game that night, combining great vocals and musicianship with high-camp stage antics: Howard Kaylan and Mark Volman doing a cancan routine bumping butts and hamming it up hilariously. Their third song was one of my favorites, "You Baby." The soundtrack to forever was playing and somehow I knew it.

I was feeling more and more intoxicated by this person next to me. She was wearing Chantilly perfume, which wafted over me like a narcotic.

The Turtles were wisely saving their trump card 'til near the end of their set. The lights dimmed and we heard the minor key guitar riff that formed the intro to their recent number one hit "Happy Together." This was my favorite song at that time. Karen told me it was her favorite too. "Imagine me and you, I do, I think about you day and night, it's only right—to think about the girl you love and hold her tight—so happy together." Just then Karen casually draped her slender leg over mine and said, "Might as well get comfortable!"

"Karen! What are you doing?" her friend, Jan Iverson (nicknamed "Ivey") whispered loudly. Karen replied softly, "It's okay."

Actually, for me it was more than okay. It was life-changing—one of those moments that became a standard bearer against which all moments would be compared. I was falling in love.

After the well-deserved encore, Karen asked if I wanted to walk her and her girlfriends home. They were having a sleepover at Karen Kursija's house just a few blocks away.

Because I got to the show early I'd nabbed a primo parking space right in front of the school's entrance. I was bursting with pride as I showed them the freshly waxed and detailed snow-white 1964 Plymouth Valiant that I had recently purchased from my late cousin Leslie's estate for $350. It had only a couple thousand miles on it. The girls were duly impressed by the oversized wide oval tires, custom Cragar mag wheels, and the black pinstripe I had applied. I offered them a ride but they declined to "hop inside my car."

Outside the other Karen's door before we said good-bye I learned her full name—Karen Moulik—and having no pen or paper I memorized her phone number for eternity: GU 4-8057. "GU" stood for "Gundersen," named after a street in Berwyn—no area code needed back in the day. I promised to call her in a few days on Friday. I walked on air back to my car. I checked my look in the mirror and noticed an unruly shock of hair that must have been sticking straight up all night long. I was hoping this wouldn't be a deal breaker.

When I got home, I told my parents that I had found the girl of my dreams.[3] They looked mildly amused.

---

[3] Though I didn't know it at the time, Karen shared the same "OMG, this feels like destiny" moment as me and painted my name and a rainbow in DayGlo colors on the desk in her bedroom the very day after we met at the Turtles concert.

I said, "No, really, there is something special about this girl. We have everything in common. We laugh at the same things. We love the same movies and the same groups."

My mother gave me her trademark "We shall see" look.

I sat on my bed for hours that night strumming my acoustic guitar looking for words and a melody to express what had just happened to me. "If you like the birds of spring—and if you love the song they sing—then you'd appreciate my girl." That was the first of a lifetime of songs that she inspired.

Friday came. I had Karen's number memorized, but I couldn't get up the nerve to call her. The weekend went by. And Monday came, and then Tuesday came and I realized if I didn't call her soon, I might lose her. I needed to find an angle to help me get over my shyness.

Then it came to me. When she answered I immediately told her how nervous I was. I told her I didn't call her on Friday because I was scared I might blow it or say something stupid. Admitting my frailty had the dual result of diffusing my nerves and charming Karen with my candor. She knew right then that I wasn't your average macho type of guy who would put on a front of bravado just to impress.

After that we had a great conversation as we flowed effortlessly from topic to topic. Lotsa laughs. She suggested I come over to her house the next day.

The next day couldn't come soon enough for me. I made the two mile trip from the Peteriks' yellow bungalow at 2647 Oak Park Avenue past blocks of colorful brick bungalows that lined the Berwyn streets to the Mouliks' house at 2230 S. Clinton Avenue. As I searched for the right number I started singing one of my favorite classic songs, "On the Street Where You Live": "I have often walked on this street before..." And I had—many times. But now it was enchanted. It was Karen's street.

I found the address, parked, and sprinted up the stairs with my guitar without the case. I must have been a sight standing at her door ringing the doorbell. I couldn't wait to see her again. I had forgotten exactly what she looked like. I knew she was a fox, but the details were fuzzy.

When she came to the door she was even better looking than I remembered. Now she was dressed in jeans with a sweater that clearly defined her contours. She invited me in.

We sat on the front room couch together and I played her a couple of instrumental songs I had just written. I could tell she was really enjoying the music when her parents walked into the room. They both had their outdoor jackets on. Karen introduced me to her attractive mom, Esther, and her imposing father, Rudy. Rudy scared me. He weighed in at roughly 350 pounds at that time with a hundred-pound scowl on his face. His voice was not welcoming. "Karen, your mother and I are leaving now, and this boy has to leave immediately. I don't care if Jesus Christ comes to the door. You do not answer!"

I grabbed my guitar and hightailed it out, looking back at Karen longingly. It was a fifteen-minute first date and a taste of things to come.

I reluctantly left, but I called Karen the next day and said, "Boy, yesterday really got cut short. Do you want to see the dress rehearsal of 'Little Mary Sunshine' that my school is putting on? It's just a few blocks from your house at the Morton West auditorium." She thought that sounded like great fun.

That evening I showed up with my Valiant and, again, Karen was a little bit leery about actually getting into the car. So we walked to Morton West, which was fine, because it was only a few blocks away.

We settled in and watched this really corny rendition of the musical. At the time, we didn't understand the concept of "camp." This production was a send-up of old Nelson Eddy and Jeanette MacDonald movies with heavily made-up Canadian Mounties dancing and singing gaily against poorly painted landscapes. Only problem was that we thought it was supposed to be serious. We had such a great time hating it together that it made for a fantastic night.

After we left, we started walking home very, very slowly, until I remembered her mother's words to us. Before we left, she had said, "Karen, I want you home at nine o'clock and not a minute later. You know, I'm a stickler about that."

I thought, *Oh, boy, I not only have to worry about Rudy, but also about Esther. Oh, my God. What am I in for here?*

I warned Karen that it was exactly nine o'clock. She told me not to worry about it. The route took us into an alley, which was a shortcut to her house. Ironically, we ended up right in back of Larry Millas's house.

I stopped to tell her that this is where The Ides rehearse. She shrugged, "That's interesting." We stood there, and, all of a sudden, we found ourselves hugging each other and then Karen gave me a kiss.

Now, I'd had some kisses with my first girlfriend, Marie, and my second girlfriend, Janine. But kisses had always stopped at the lips, and all of a sudden Karen had an open mouth and a tongue that was finding its way to my tongue.

Her technique was very progressive and I took right to it. In fact, I was a quick study. It was my first French kiss. And Karen not only gave it to me, she taught me how to kiss. I was in heaven. I thought I had found nirvana. Time stood still, the world melted away and we were the only two souls on the planet. The trouble was that time really did not stand still and now we would be fifteen minutes late for "the stickler." Karen assured me she'd be fine. I think there was a certain amount of wiggle room built into their relationship.

"We better get you home," I insisted. She grabbed me for another kiss. "Really we better go," I said, raging against my nature. Finally, at about 9:30, we got to her door. Her mother was fine. She didn't mind the thirty-minute lateness, just like Karen had said. I breathed a sigh of relief and I drove home. I had never felt this way in my life and, of course, that evening changed my life. I was head over heels in love with Karen. She not only had everything in common with me, she was an amazing kisser.

"Pussy whipped" was the taunt from the guys in The Ides and I'm afraid I was guilty. We saw each other every chance we had. Once Rudy drove by and caught us locked in a passionate embrace, kissing in the middle of the intersection by Triangle Park. His distrust for me was growing. Another time we parked at Maple Lake, a notorious make-out grove at the local forest preserve, and went at it in the front seat of my Valiant. Unfortunately I had failed to put on my parking lights and suddenly the cold beam of a police flashlight was in our eyes.

"What's going on in here?" the cop bellowed. "How old are you, young lady?" Karen stammered that she had just turned fifteen. "Fella, I could arrest you for statu-airy rape." I told him we were just making out. He replied, "I saw your boxer shorts!"

Well, at age seventeen I never even owned a pair of boxer shorts and we really were just making out. By this time Karen was apoplectic, secretly vowing to enter the nunnery as soon as this night was over. Thinking quickly, I reached in my wallet and handed the officer a crisp twenty-dollar bill.

At that point he said, "Don't ever let me see you two here again!"

Our hearts were pounding as we hightailed it out of the grove. This night would be a secret we both kept, actually, until right now. Because of our respect and fear of authority it affected us deeply for a very long time.

But love was still the conquering hero. Karen and I had Turtles mementos all over our respective houses—paperweights, plush toys, statuettes, candles, and rugs that we bought for each other to commemorate that April 9th when we first met in line to see our favorite band.

We were inseparable until one day we went to the North Avenue Beach to swim, pose, and take in the sun. I had just cut my own hair (a very bad idea, guys—don't ever try it), and I looked pretty hideous. After about an hour in the sun with my shirt off, bright red splotches started appearing on my skin. They were all over my body—arms, legs, chest, face—everywhere. Then, because I drank too much apple cider, I started cramping up with diarrhea, necessitating constant trips to the john.

For a while we pretended that everything was fine but inside I was mortified. The splotches turned out to be a reaction to the sun. I was later diagnosed with a rare form of psoriasis called parapsoriasis. Suddenly Karen began acting differently, kind of distant. When I dropped her off that day, her parting words were chilling:

"Thanks, Jim. I had a good time…I guess."

The "I guess" part was devastating. I've always been very good at reading between the lines. She called me the next day and confirmed my worst fears.

"Hi, Jim. It's Karen. You know, I'm only sixteen and I really think I should date some other guys just to see what is out there. I'm sure you want to date other girls as well. Right? Anyway, I love you, but maybe not in that way. I'd like to stay friends, though."

By this time, my world started melting and swirling into a kind of surreal cartoon. The pop art pattern on the Formica on my kitchen table started pulsing in and out as I tried to get my bearings.

"Uh, okay, like, are you sure?"

"Yes, very sure. But thanks for all the swell times, buh-bye."

I tried to get a grip, but my world was crumbling before my eyes. I looked at my guitar on the stand and it suddenly meant nothing. Was it the haircut? Was it the red spots, the diarrhea, or was it just me?

The next day, The Ides had a show at Brother Rice High School on the south side of Chicago. We were on the bill with The Buckinghams, a group who had just enjoyed major success with "Kind of a Drag." When the crowd demanded an encore, I told the guys, "Blues in A!"

The guys dutifully followed as I poured out my heart, soul, and angst in an interminable, dirge-y eight-bar blues. As we played, the totally bored audience started streaming out of the gymnasium into the street. I came to the realization that I could not perform my therapy at the expense of my band. I never pulled that cathartic stunt again.

One day I thought I saw Karen sitting close to some guy on the bench seat of a powder blue Mustang convertible that was sailing down Oak Park Avenue in front of my house. I had this sinking feeling of destiny being averted—this was just sooo wrong—I could not let this happen. This sighting only strengthened my resolve to win her back. (Postscript: this turned out not to be Karen in the Mustang.)

Despite my heartache, one great thing came out of this female torture: This incident spawned one of the biggest hits of my career. It was about six months after the red splotch debacle when I answered the phone that was mounted on the wall in my parents' kitchen.

"Hi, Jim. It's Karen. Remember me? I'm attending Patricia Stevens Modeling School in Oak Park. Could you and your awesome Valiant come by and pick me up and drive me there this Saturday? This is not like a date or anything, you know?"

Date or not, I felt that I had just won the lottery. After a long second and a half, I stammered, "Sure, why not?" I remember wondering if I could be next to her in the car; if I could restrain myself from grabbing her. If I would be able to not try to hold her and kiss her. I figured, however, that driving her around was better than nothing. I would get to look at her, smell her hair, her Chantilly perfume, and maybe even brush her satiny smoothness in some unobtrusive way—accidentally on purpose.

Maybe I could blow her away with a song. "It Don't Matter to Me" by Bread had become my anthem. And another pattern was emerging...

A few weeks later Karen rang me again. "Hi, Jim. That was really nice of you to take me to Pat Stevens two weeks ago. Do you think you could drive me there again?"

"Sure, why not!"

As I was driving home after dropping her off later that day I suddenly began to feel as if I was becoming her personal limousine service. Mile by mile, I got more and more agitated. Finally, I shouted to no one in particular, "I guess all I am is your vehicle, baby!"

"Vehicle." Hmmmm. I liked the way that word rolled off my tongue. I loved one-word titles because they carried so much impact. "Badge" by Cream popped into my mind.

When I got home I strapped on my red Epiphone Riviera and cranked up my Fender Dual Showman. I started playing the chunky rhythm I had recently heard on the first Blood, Sweat and Tears album, from "I Can't Quit Her." But I sped the tempo way up. Then I heard in my head, the horn riff, which I initially played on a Fuzz Tone guitar (much like Keith Richards of The Rolling Stones did when he dreamed the guitar riff in "Satisfaction"—he had heard it as a horn line).

As my Sony Boom Box recorder spun, I started scatting lyrics: "I got a set of wheels, pretty baby, won't you hop inside my car." Hmmm. Not a bad opening line, but it had no rhythm to it. Then my mind wandered to an antidrug pamphlet I had just seen. I was lab partners in senior biology with a stoner dude named Bill Griner.

Karen's modeling headshot.

He always came to class totally buzzed. Gleefully he showed me the pamphlet he had just picked up at school. It included a small illustration of the "friendly stranger" parked by the curb enticing youngsters with drugs.

Suddenly, I came up with the someday-to-be-historic first line of the song: "Hey well, I'm the friendly stranger in the black sedan, won't you hop inside my car." Yeah, that's the ticket! "I got pictures, got candy, I'm a loveable man, and I can take you to the nearest star." I got goose bumps as the rhythm of the words took hold.

I called an emergency rehearsal session. I wanted to perform this new song on Saturday at the Valley View Young Adults Club in Frankfort, Illinois.

The song came together quickly with Larry switching to B3 organ and Bob manning the tenor sax alongside Chuck Soumar and John Larson on trumpet. Mike came up with a drum groove that to this day very few drummers can cop. He played the bass drum on the after-beats instead of the on-beats. He also innovatively played the hi-hat in the middle of a tom-tom drum fill. As for me, I was emulating David Clayton-Thomas of Blood, Sweat and Tears, who must have been channeling Ray Charles.

Little Tommy, the somewhat annoying neighborhood kid who would always come by to listen to us rehearse, stood there with the classic dropped-jaw pose when we fired up the horn riff that started it all off.

The now iconic brass arrangement came about organically based around my original call-to-arms horn riff, with all the members of the band throwing in ideas. Like all Ides horn charts past, present, and future, not a note was ever committed to musical staff paper: not a shred of sheet music can be found. Even the most complex Ides arrangements were "head charts" stored in the complex synapses of the brass section's minds.

Call it magic. Call it lightning in a bottle. Call it future platinum. It was all that and more. It had a sense of destiny to it. The Valley View Young Adults Club was packed to overflowing the next day with nubile high school girls and tough-talking jocks.

We opened with "More and More," which we had just learned off of Blood, Sweat and Tears' second album. We got a good audience response.

After that came our version of the two-chord classic made famous by Dave Mason of Traffic, "Feelin' Alright." Then we sizzled into our extended take on Buffalo Springfield's "Bluebird." It was then time for the moment of truth.

"Here's a brand-new one that we hope you dig, 'Vehicle'!" *Ba Da Ba Ba Dah!* blared the brass. Immediately the dance floor filled with writhing, pulsating bodies. Ecstasy was a frame of mind, not a drug in those days, and it was in the air. But, of course, in our minds it was just a dance song, a live jam with no potential for radio airplay.

On December 1, 1969, we loaded our gear into the freight elevator at CBS Studios on Fairbanks Ave., in downtown Chicago. CBS Studios was not exactly rock 'n' roll central. In fact, their stock in trade was the production of announcer voice-overs for bank commercials and the lot. Maybe that's why it seemed to take forever for Bob and Frank (now our managers and producers) to dial in the sounds as CBS staff engineer Dick Dearborn set up the mics. There was a behemoth of a tape deck in the control room. This was one of the first state-of-the-art, sixteen-track recorders in the country.

We cut "Something Coming On," "The Sky Is Falling," and a spiritual number I wrote called "Lead Me Home, Gently." As an afterthought, I said, "Let's lay down that dance track we play live. It couldn't hurt. That 'Vehicle' song."

I counted off and the brass entered crisply with their clarion call to arms. *Ba Da Ba Ba Dah*! The hair stood up on my arms as we launched into the song. We could see the excitement build as we peered through the glass of the control room window. Bob Destocki was smiling ear to ear. Frank Rand was dancing his wild "chicken with his head cut off" dance. This was a good sign.

"Okay, guys," said Frank. "Not bad, let's do take two." No problemo! During take one, I had broken a string on my red Epiphone Riviera. Since Larry was on B3 organ, he handed me his beautiful sunburst Epiphone, the one he still plays to this day.

Take two was magic. We could almost feel history going down at fifteen ips (inches per second, the speed at which the two-inch tape would revolve). The band was tight, the brass in tune, the drums cracking, the bass thumping. My lead part was totally spontaneous—nothing had been worked out, I had played it differently each time. I thought it was okay but maybe not very special.

At the end of the solo—this is where I'd usually keep playing—I found that I was fresh out of licks, so I just stopped playing. In that gap, Mike Borch laid in his now signature drum fill, *ba da ba ba dah*, instinctively mirroring the rhythm of the horn riff.

We filed into the control room to hear the playback. It was sensational. Maybe this could be a radio song after all! The sound, coming through the giant Altec Lansing speakers, practically pinned our ears back. So far, so good, except that my solo had been totally buried in the mix. I just assumed the producer had it low in the mix because it was subpar.

I vowed to come back in a few days and redo my solo. When we got back in the studio, I was now armed with my brand-new Maestro Fuzz Tone. I had worked out what I thought was a killer solo. I had orchestrated every note. But on playback, nobody seemed very impressed.

Frank said, "Just for kicks, let's turn up that first solo that you jammed live."

I said, "Sure, couldn't hurt."

There it was, in all its glory, the solo that countless bands have had to learn since that day. Every note was perfect. I didn't even know the licks I played. I must have been channeling a future day, or my hero, Jeff Beck. I found out later that this was one of Jeff's favorite solos!

My fingers had wings for those seconds. Ironically, in order to play that song live, I had to learn that solo, note for note, as if it had been someone else's part!

That same day, I had laid down my final vocal. All the guys, including Bob and Frankie, were in the control room cheering me on. I was in the tiny isolation booth with window access to the control room.

"Take one," intoned Dick Dearborn, with authority.

Now you have to remember how young we all were at this time. I had just celebrated my nineteenth birthday. Chuck was only seventeen. "Impressionable" would be an understatement.

As a band, we had just gone to see Blood, Sweat and Tears at Chicago's psychedelic Kinetic Playground. For five dollars, you could stand on the crowded dance floor, enjoy the plasma display of psychedelic effects projected on the screen at the back of the stage, drink Cokes, and watch as many as three international acts on a given night. One memorable night featured Pacific Gas and Electric, Jethro Tull, and Led Zeppelin—no biggie!

The night Blood, Sweat and Tears took the stage was life-altering. David Clayton-Thomas was in perfect voice that night, sending goose bumps through me on Billie Holiday's classic "God Bless the Child." But David taught me an even more important lesson that night.

After the show I fought my way to the front of the stage where David Clayton-Thomas was toweling off. Nervously I said, "You were great tonight. You're my favorite singer of all time."

After five long seconds he brushed me aside and said coldly, "Yeah, whatever kid, now quit bothering me."

To make matters worse, he refused to accept the cassette I tried to hand him. I told him that this tape contained a song I had written especially for BS&T called "Don't Write Me Out of Your Life" and a second song The Ides had just worked up. Unfazed, I carried the tape upstairs to the band dressing room and handed it to the guitarist of the band, Steve Katz. Steve couldn't have been nicer, telling me he would be sure to give it a listen.

Recently, I got to sub in for BS&T's current lead singer at a few Midwest shows. I felt a dream coming true as I sang one of my all-time favorites, "You've Made Me So Very Happy." One night back-stage Steve and I compared notes about the time The Ides ran into them at the Atlanta airport the same week "Vehicle" reached number one. I reminded him of the cassette tape I handed him way back in 1970. He said, "You know, I never listened to it until a few weeks ago and had no idea that 'Vehicle' was that second song on that ancient cassette!" He told me, "Next time you hand me a tape—I'm gonna listen!!"

No matter how bad an impression David Clayton-Thomas made on me, I still totally immersed myself in his persona and voice. I even took to holding the mic stand in the air and at an angle like he did onstage.

In the studio that crisp December day in 1969, having already cut the music track to "Vehicle," it was now time to lay down my lead vocal. I got into character and figuratively became David Clayton-Thomas.

After take one Frankie Rand barked through the talkback, "Sing it like Jim Peterik—not David Clayton-Thomas!"

I got all defensive and cried, "I am singing like myself! That's just the way I sound! We must have similar voices." Maybe yes, maybe no, but bottom line is I had every shade and nuance of his voice down cold.

So now, really pissed at Frank, I did take two like I didn't give a rat's ass. The words just kind of tumbled out of my mouth. But somehow my voice had a relaxed authority I had never expressed before. I didn't try too hard as I sang:

I'm the friendly stranger in the black sedan
won't you hop inside my car?
I got pictures, got candy,
I'm a loveable man
And I can take you to the nearest star..."

Copyright 1970 Jim Peterik/Bicycle Music ASCAP

Wait a minute! This relaxed approach was really starting to work. On the words, "my car," I was kind of mimicking a W.C. Fields type of rap, "Come over here, my little chickadee."

The vocal unfolded from there. I added the vernacular of, "If you wants to be a movie star / I can take you to Hollywood." "Wants"? I don't really know where I got that from!

After we got the master vocal take, The Ides went out to get a snack at our favorite dog house, the Grand Deli. When we returned to the studio, a look of despair was plastered on everyone's faces.

Did they stretch the tape like they had all those years ago at MBS? "Even worse," said Bob Destocki. "Rich, our second engineer, pressed the wrong button and erased thirteen seconds from the master take of 'Vehicle.'" Where once was sound was now the sound of silence.

Suddenly our future ground to a halt. We were stunned. After stumbling about the studio for a while, I actually went outside to fill my lungs with some needed oxygen. When I finally returned about two hours later the mood had swung back.

"Check this out!" shouted Rich. With those words, the master take came roaring through the speakers—with the thirteen seconds seamlessly restored. We shook our heads and shouted like a miracle had just taken place. "I spliced that thirteen seconds from take one into the gap, I didn't think it had a prayer of working, but you guys were so consistent in your meter it worked!"

This was in the day before bands routinely played along to a metronomic "click track," which would have made the splice relatively easy. I can hear the spliced section to this day. It starts with the "Great God in Heaven" line in the second verse, and goes all the way up to the very first note of my guitar solo—we almost lost that solo twice!

All was right with the world and our rung on the rock 'n' roll ladder was tight as a Gordian knot; preserved forever.

For some reason, our producers put "Vehicle" last on the demo reel we sent to Warner Brothers Records in early January, 1970. When the news filtered back, CBS "suits" said they really didn't "hear" the first three (record-biz code for "no commercial potential"), but that fourth song was a smash! Exchanging high fives all around, we celebrated at Salerno's that night, finishing off two family-sized pies between the seven of us and emptying four pitchers of Coca-Cola.

The next week, The Ides played The Blue Village in downtown Westmont, Illinois. We had a huge following at this former A&P grocery store, which had been converted into a teen club. The place was lit with black lights that made the girls' white brassieres glow brightly through their sweaters, much to the guys' delight. It also highlighted dandruff on your shoulders as I found out to my embarrassment.

That night, we went through our killer set, which included covers of great songs currently on the chart such as "Celebrate" by Three Dog Night, "For What It's Worth" and "Mr. Soul" by Buffalo Springfield, and a unique jam of The Nashville Teens' "Tobacco Road," which often went as long as twenty minutes.

Of course, we played our originals, like our hit "You Wouldn't Listen" and "I'll Keep Searching"—the flip side of that record. Finally, I announced our soon-to-be-released single. For the first time, I gave the introduction that has followed me around the world every show since: "Strap yourself in, it's gonna be a bumpy ride, and this is the 'Vehicle' that got us here today!"

Then, just like the song's debut at Valley View…*Ba da ba ba dah*—pandemonium. Even though the song had not yet hit the airwaves, it seemed to have "smash hit" imprinted somewhere in its dynamic DNA.

After the show, as usual, we raced to Salerno's Pizza in North Berwyn. No matter where we played in the Midwest, after the show we'd look at each other and say, "If we hurry, we can make it to Salerno's!"

And we always did, even if it meant defying speed limits and stoplights. It was (and still is!) the best pizza in Chicago. Thick crust (but not pan pizza) covered with the highest-grade Wisconsin cheese, spicy Italian sausage, and the tangiest tomato sauce we'd ever tasted! Two pieces would fill up a mortal man. The Ides must have been immortal. We would roll out of there after scarfing down two extra-large pies.

On this day, we walked into the restaurant and the place was buzzing with some news. One guy there had been "looking for Jimbo." That was the day I got my nickname. He said that he wanted "to fill me in."

It turns out that we were already big news; WLS radio had just premiered "Vehicle" on the Art Roberts show. We had already felt the rush that comes from receiving airplay with the release of our first single back in '66, but this felt different—electrifying. People were raving about this song, calling it a smash, calling it their favorite song.

Art Roberts built us up in the pre-sell, using even more hyperbole than usual. "This song, by Chicago's own Ides of March, is destined to go number one. You heard it here first!"

Art had a little something to prove. Bob and Frank had hand-carried the acetate of "Vehicle" over to WLS a few weeks earlier to get his reaction. He had told them that he loved the record, but strongly recommended that we add vocal answers after each "Love you" (love you) and "Need you" (need you).

This idea, which now seems like such an obvious one, was definitely generated by Art, and to this day, we are grateful. Excitedly, we rushed back to CBS to sing and record our new responses, but when we got there, we found out that there was a big problem. We were completely out of tracks. We had used up all sixteen!

The only way around this, according to Dick Dearborn, was to record the vocals onto a second two-track recorder. That version would then become the master. For this reason, there are slightly different vocals on the mono and the stereo mix, because there actually were two different performances. This is also why you don't hear these "response" parts in movies that use "Vehicle," such as Stallone's 1990 release, *Lock Up*. These parts don't exist on the sixteen-track master.

On my way home, I tuned in to WLS and suddenly heard "the riff," which introduced my growling vocal. The oval speaker in the dashboard of my Valiant was pulsing with sound as I jacked the volume higher and higher. I thought about the girl who inspired the song and the journey we had taken together. I didn't know what the future would hold for us. All I knew is this song was kicking ass on one of the most powerful stations in America. Millions of radio listeners were hearing the little ditty I wrote about my limousine days with my ex-girlfriend. My foot hit the pedal and didn't let up. I became that "friendly stranger" as I barreled down Cermak Road at sixty miles an hour past the savings and loans and bakeries. As I drove I only prayed that Karen would hear the song and reconsider.

Our managers hustled us into the studio to do an album to support that explosive single. We had a whopping two weeks to select songs, record, mix, and master the entire record. We had a few things "in the can" already, songs that we had presented to Warner Brothers earlier that year: "The Sky Is Falling," "Lead Me Home, Gently," and our first Warner Brothers single from 1969, "One Woman Man," which I had written for my "Berwyn Girl" on my parents' Formica dinette.

The rest we pulled from our live show, including "Symphony for Eleanor" (our ten-minute-plus show-stopping version of the Beatles' "Eleanor Rigby"). To that we added our mash-up of "Dharma for One" (based on the Jethro Tull version but substituting brass for Ian Anderson's flute) with "Wooden Ships" by our current heroes Crosby, Stills and Nash. To that we added hastily cut tracks such as our tribute to the sound of Creedence Clearwater Revival, "Factory Band" and our since departed trumpet player's song contribution, "Time for Thinking." One song stood out like the jewel it was. It was called "Aire of Good Feeling." (To this day, The Ides often open with this song.) It started out with my fast-strumming acoustic guitar and then went into a very original-sounding solo trumpet line. Then

Mike's drums hit in and the whole song took flight. "Hey Marie, why can't you see, aire of good feeling coming over me. Hip hooray, strike up the day, aire of good feeling coming- coming- coming my way!" "Sounds like the perfect follow-up to 'Vehicle'!" said Destocki. We all agreed.

Every morning during recording I would wake up with a huge smile on my face knowing that later that day we would be in the studio capturing our magic on tape. Ever since that first session at MBS, I lived in anticipation of the next opportunity to stand in front of those fine German mics and throw down the sounds I heard in my head. We would joke around and cavort around that studio like the Beatles in *A Hard Day's Night*. We were living the dream—big time!

We were all on summer break from high school and junior college so we could get down to CBS studios on Fairbanks in Chicago by around 1:30 p.m. and rock until the key engineer, Dick Dearborn, had to put on his hat and walk out the door at 6 p.m.—sometimes even during a final take!

Soon the album started to take shape as we gathered around the huge Altec Lansing "Voice of the Theater" speakers, relishing every good stretch of song and lamenting loudly the parts that were out of time, out of tune, stiffly played, or all of the above. But we had a deadline to meet and a hot single rapidly climbing the charts.

Finally the album was finished and was received warmly by the head cheeses of Warner Brothers Records.

Now it was their turn to deliver and we waited on pins and needles as we anticipated the fantastic cover art we so expected. We'd recently had an epic session with one of the great Chicago photographers and couldn't wait to see our handsome, young, sexy images splashed on the cover of our first album.

On that fateful night Bob Destocki and Frank Rand entered The Ides of March rock cave in Larry Millas's basement. They had smiles on their faces but their body language told a much different tale, and I could sense it.

They unveiled the album cover from a large brown paper envelope with the words, "Well here it is guys! I hope you love it, cuz it's already in print."

When we saw it there was an audible gasp and then an "Oh shit! This stinks!" We wondered out loud what some perverted "genius" was thinking when on the cover of our life's work he put an image of a naked baby doll abandoned carelessly in a field with an ominous black sedan lurking in the background.

At first we took it as a joke. "Very funny, guys," I intoned. Rand chimed in, "Pretty brilliant, huh. But it's no joke. This cover is a part of your whole promotional campaign!"

We were apoplectic. I went to the washroom to gather my thoughts and possibly puke: All that work to be marginalized by the most literal and perverted of all translations.

We walked out of our rehearsal room shell-shocked and scorched. Our first, but not our last encounter with the scourges of the music business.

It was such an offensive cover that the biggest record retailer in the nation, E.J. Korvette, refused to even stock it due to the certain repercussions. That tasteless cover cost us thousands in sales.

But even this graphic setback could not dampen our spirit. We still believed that the power of the music would override the careless choice of marketing material.

It was the spring of 1970. What a glorious year to have a hit record! In the next few months, we would play alongside some of our favorite artists, earning the respect of our heroes.

"Strap yourself in"—indeed!

From the Backstreets to the City

THOSE LAST FOUR YEARS saw a marked change in me. The kid who got bullied in seventh grade was now confident and walked with an easy swagger. The same girls who sat on the cafeteria stage no longer looked untouchable (which I discovered firsthand), and the jocks were a little jealous of this band that had a chart-breaking record.

In fact, the whole band looked a hell of a lot cooler. When "You Wouldn't Listen" hit, I was still wearing Dockers, black horn-rimmed glasses, and a peacoat hoodie. Now it was tight jeans and yellow-tinted aviator frames.

Larry was a shade cooler than before, starting to perfect his John Lennon look. Bob weighed in at about a trim 145 pounds and was all taut muscle. (He was a team swimmer.) Mike changed the most of all. Before the record hit he was the AV (audio visual) guy you would see wheeling the clunky projector cart through the hallway with a pocket protector carrying about a dozen pens, slide rules, tools, and gadgets. Now he was sporting a hip white-boy afro, a red satin shirt, and American flag pants.

By the time "Vehicle" hit the charts, I was attending Morton (Junior) College, the community college of the area, the companion school to my high school, Morton West. I could have been accepted anywhere. I had all straight A's throughout high school, except for a C in algebra with my dreaded teacher, Mrs. Buddeke. As a senior, I was voted the most likely to succeed.

I chose a community college because my band was really the only thing I cared about. I didn't need the social strata of Greek honor societies or college dorms. I had my social universe right here in The Ides. I roamed the halls of the decrepit school armed with my Gibson J50 acoustic guitar, looking for opportunities to perform.

People still come up to me and say they saw me performing in C hall for anyone who would listen. One woman reported she would watch me play in the smokers' lounge on the second floor while she was enjoying a butt. No place was too humble, cramped, or inappropriate for me to break out my guitar and play "Leaving on a Jet Plane" by Peter, Paul and Mary, or "Chelsea Morning" by my favorite, Joni Mitchell, or try out one of my new originals such as "Rock and Roll Man" or one called "Someone to Give It All To."

As "Vehicle" hit the Top 10 all over the country, I was on summer break. I went from strumming in C hall (picture the nerdy Stephen Bishop playing on the dormitory stairs in the film *Animal House*) and packing 45s into envelopes at MS, the local record distributor (one of the 45s we got to ship was our own record "Vehicle" to WLS and WCFL to play!) to playing to 20,000 in Winnipeg on a bill with The Youngbloods, Iron Butterfly, and Led Zeppelin. Talk about a change in fortunes.

One day at the studio, Bob Destocki and Frank Rand handed me an envelope. In it was a publishing check for $10,000. I looked at it again and again trying to wrap my head around that figure; it was not 100 dollars, not 1,000 dollars—I counted the zeros again, it was *ten freaking thousand dollars*! I could barely speak. It was more money than I could comprehend. (Today it would be more like $40,000.) The guys were happy for me and knew I deserved it for writing our big hit "Vehicle." At the same time Mike started calling me "Lucky Bucks." Fortunately, no apparent animosity developed over our disparate fortunes.

As "Vehicle" motored up the charts, becoming the fastest-breaking record in Warner Brothers' history, The Ides would go wherever Herb Gronauer would point us. We often, half-jokingly, said that he would throw a dart over his shoulder at a map of the United States and that's where we would play. The routing was that bad.

To get from one show to the next, we often had to drive all night in our twin Ford Econoline vans, one blue, one school-bus yellow, stenciled with "Here Comes The Ides of March!" But because of the ornate lettering, it looked for all the world like "Here Comes The Joes of March!"

When we arrived, we'd catch maybe a two-hour nap and head over to the local radio station to plug the show that night. When you're nineteen, you can do this night after night.

The world at large and especially the South was still not very accommodating to visiting long-haired hippies like us. We were refused rooms at many hotels; we were bullied and razzed at truck stops and restaurants.

We were taunted, "You boys are a disgrace to manhood!"

My quick response was "Thank you!"

The guys loved me for that quick rejoinder. We had a secret code for being hassled. We called it an "E.R. shot" ("E.R." stood for *Easy Rider*). It indicated the kind of treatment seen in the Peter Fonda/ Dennis Hopper classic. The constant E.R. shots eventually took their toll on us. But we stood proud and took on all comers.

One of my favorite memories in the summer of 1970 is playing in Atlantic City, New Jersey, at the famed Steel Pier. This was a big deal for us. Everyone who was anybody had graced the stage in the main ballroom. On the same week engagement, Oliver was also appearing. (Remember the recording artist who sang the hit "Good Morning Starshine" from *Hair, the American Tribal Love-Rock Musical*?)

He, too, sported a shag haircut like mine and wore aviator frames. I would get mistaken for him all week long. The Ides would joke that when the Oliver fans asked me, "Are you Oliver?" I should bellow, "Yeah, I'm Oliver, now get out of my way and leave me the hell alone!" Of course I'd never do anything to sully anyone's reputation, but it was fun to imagine.

We did three shows daily at the ballroom at the end of Steel Pier—3 p.m., 6 p.m., and 9 p.m. Each time, we'd immediately follow the opening act, the legendary diving horse that would jump into a big wooden tub of water from twenty-five feet in the air just outside the ballroom.

We were instructed that as soon as we heard the splash we were to hit the first chord of our opening song—not a second must elapse! We were always poised and ready: *Splash*—"People get ready, there's a train a-coming. You don't need no ticket, you just get on board…" as the slightly damp hordes filed into the ballroom.

We never missed our cue. We ended each show with our hit, "Vehicle," and everyone left happy. One time we even saw Oliver in the audience. We were very glad, at that point, that I hadn't played my little prank. He even invited us to the place he and his partner shared in Los Angeles should we ever come to town. We took him up on his invitation when we hit L.A. a few weeks later and had a home-cooked gourmet dinner in his California-modern ranch overlooking the smoggy Hollywood Hills. Gordon Lightfoot stopped over to see his friend Oliver (Bill Swofford) while we were there. He played us an amazing album of an artist we'd never heard of, the late Kenny Rankin.

About a month later, with "Vehicle" sitting at number one on KHJ (the hottest top 40 station in Los Angeles), we were invited to perform on the popular Mama Cass show. Oh, sure, we would have preferred to perform on the Dick Clark show, but this was a Dick Clark production and they wanted to boost their ratings. "Could The Ides please appear?"

Of course, our management said yes and decided to arrange some shows in L.A. to promote the record and defray the cost of the flights and rooms. I was the only Ide who had ever been to Los Angeles. My Uncle George and Aunt Jenny lived there and my family and I visited often. I loved the palm trees and the pool in their backyard, Knott's Berry Farm, and Disneyland. Wow!

When The Ides got off the plane, we were all pie-eyed with the sights, sounds, and smells: cool restaurants like Ben Franks on Sunset Boulevard, Top Taco on La Brea (our burrito heaven), Pink's Hotdogs, and Barney's Beanery.

We stayed at the infamous Hyatt House on Sunset (famously nicknamed the Riot House by countless TV-smashing rock bands) and thrilled to the super-friendly ladies who would walk down the street, winking and smiling.

We thought we were pretty hot stuff 'til we were informed that these ladies were, in fact, hookers looking for their next john. No matter, we were in heaven. Berwyn seemed, in fact, "light-years away" as I later quoted in my song, "L.A. Goodbye."

We were scheduled to play the Whisky a Go Go in a few days and we could barely contain our excitement. The next day, we were guests of Warner Brothers Records, who took us to Dan Tana's for an expensive lunch. They treated us like their very own Beatles. We were on top of the world.

The day of the Whisky gig we were all on edge. Here we were, seven kids from Berwyn, about to open for the great Tony Joe White, who was just coming off the big hit, "Polk Salad Annie" ("Gator's got your granny—chomp chomp!").

There was also the rumor of a surprise guest to join Tony onstage so anticipation was high. Joe Smith, the very vocal and high-profile president of Warner, was there to greet us. "Do great tonight. The company's all here and counting on you. We expect to see a great show!"

"No problemo, Joe!" I stated, with fabricated confidence. I mean, it was one thing playing the Pink Phink in Chicago or following the diving horse at the Steel Pier, but this was a horse of a different color. The who's who of the Hollywood scene would be in the audience that night. We felt clearly out of our element and it showed in our performance. Instead of the cocksure confidence we'd show onstage in our hometown, suddenly, I couldn't find anything clever to say to the packed house and was blowing chords.

The Ides of March at the Whisky a Go Go.

It didn't really matter. The audience was hardly listening. They were waiting for the star attraction to come on. My teenybopper medley went over like a lead balloon. Our extended version of "Tobacco Road" sounded excruciatingly mundane in this experimental world of the West Coast.

Everyone in the audience seemed as if they were "on something" and way too cool to listen to us kids. Finally, when we hit our closing song, "Vehicle," a few folks roused from their stupor and clapped their hands. We were not asked back for an encore. Joe Smith and a couple of WB suits were waiting dutifully in the dressing room when we got off stage.

"That was…real good, guys…real good. If there's anything you need while you're in town, don't hesitate to let me know."

Now, that is one of those lines everyone says, not really expecting a reply. This time, one of our horn players, John Larson, asked earnestly, "Do you think you can get us a deal on some…some clothes?"

Joe Smith, never one to be lost for words, was for once in his life speechless, finally stammering, "Uh sure, just give me a call tomorrow." With that they were gone. There were no celebrations or high fives.

When Tony Joe White took the stage, we watched from the audience as this pro worked the crowd like the ace he was. After a few songs he announced, "Now I'd like to bring up a special guest—Mr. Stephen Stills!"

Crosby, Stills and Nash could not have been hotter at this point in time and the crowd went bonkers. As it turned out, Stephen hadn't bothered bringing a guitar with him and asked, "Is there a guitar in the house?"

Actually, there was—my Les Paul Goldtop—which I eagerly retrieved from its case and handed to Stephen onstage. There was one problem: The Ides always tuned our guitars a step and a half lower to make it easier to hit the high vocals on some of the hits we covered.

As Tony launched into some blues classic, Stills confidently hit an A minor chord. Then it was your classic "Oh, shit" moment when he realized his guitar was not in concert pitch. He spent the whole song awkwardly trying to put the guitar in tune, but because of the super heavy gauge strings we used, this was not easy.

I have nothing against Stephen Stills, but on that particular night, we thought it was absolutely hilarious as we watched the spectacle from the audience with Stephen red-faced, sweating bullets, and hurling obscenities. It was kind of sweet revenge to the whole Hollywood scene, which had given us a bum's welcome just minutes before.

The next day we drove over to ABC studios to appear on the Mama Cass show. We only saw Ms. Cass Elliot briefly but, suddenly, through the dressing room door, glided a vision—the eternal teenager, Dick Clark, looking even younger in person.

I had cut my baby teeth to this guy as he played "rate a record" ("I'd give this record a 92, it's got a good beat and you can dance to it") and spun the latest payola-fueled hits. Everyone had their own favorite dance couple on the floor. These pairs became celebrities in their own right.

Dick looked tanned and rested when he greeted us warmly. The humiliation of the bad night at the Whisky seemed far away as he chatted us up. "Love the new record, guys! I knew it was a smash the first time I heard it!" He reminded us that he had featured "You Wouldn't Listen" as his spotlight dance a few years previous.

Okay, the vibe was back. Suddenly L.A. didn't seem as evil and foreboding as our chilly reception felt last night at the Whisky. It's not that we didn't put on a decent show. We just weren't tripped out and hip enough for the room. Maybe it was because we weren't doing the same drugs as they were. We took none. In fact, when one cool dude asked me what I took before a show, I replied, "A good shit." It taught us a huge lesson in finding your own niche in the music world: You can only blaze new trails to a willing crowd. Otherwise, preach to the choir.

Dick Clark went on to chat with us about his beloved collection of Mercedes Benz roadsters. He was the king of rock holding court and we were his willing subjects. We hit the soundstage and although we lip-synched our way through "Vehicle," we did such a convincing job with every nuance and syllable that people thought we were playing live.

The next day will forever be a page in "The Ides' Best Moments." We took a boat ride twenty-six miles to Catalina Island to tape the John Byner show, *Something Else*. He was a very clever and beloved comic at the time, famous for his dead-on impersonation of Ed Sullivan, and The Ides were all huge fans. His show was filmed at the Grand Ballroom overlooking the Pacific Ocean, a famous landmark since it was constructed in the '20s.

The venue had seen every popular entertainer through modern history, including Frank Sinatra and all the big bands such as Benny Goodman, Duke Ellington, and Stan Kenton. As Byner said, in our introduction, "And they were big bands!" This became a catchphrase in the expanding book of "Ide-isms" that we would use as a sort of private code. From then on, whenever we would see a well-endowed female, someone would say, "And they were big bands!"

This time out, though, we were still lip-synching to "Vehicle." We gave it all we had. Today, the videotape of this show is one of the few surviving relics of that era of The Ides. We performed like we'd been shaken like a can of Coke and then allowed to spray our contents forcefully all over the room. It was like our careers depended on this two-minute, fifty-seven-second segment. We were electrifying, even after the five takes it took to get it just right.

That night, after a VIP tour of Disneyland (ushered to the front of every line—maybe Joe Smith was good for something after all), we unloaded our equipment at the iconic United Western Studios on Sunset.

I was wild with anticipation, this being the studio (in fact the very room—Studio B) where many of my favorite groups recorded their biggest hits: The Beach Boys, The Mamas and the Papas, Scott McKenzie, and The Association, just to name a few. It was the home of the ace team of session musicians known unofficially as the Wrecking Crew.

We were there for a reason. Warner Brothers was already looking ahead to our follow-up release to "Vehicle." We had intended that to be a great horn-fueled number from our debut album called "Aire of Good Feeling." We started every show with this song.

We would first do a harmony-laden snippet of The Impressions' "People Get Ready," then right into the bracing horn lick of "Aire." The trouble was, this was the era of sound-alike follow-up songs. The Jackson 5 followed up their smash "I Want You Back" with "ABC," which sounded nearly identical to its predecessor. Same thing with

countless others such as The Osmond Brothers and even The Rolling
Stones. "Aire of Good Feeling" was a fresh take on the Ides sound,
not a clone of "Vehicle." WB wanted a clone.

I begrudgingly sat in my room at the "Riot House," sweating out
sparks and trying to inject the magic into a song I had been working
on called "Superman."

> *"Faster than a speeding bullet.*
> *Able to leap the tallest building in a single bound*
> *More powerful than a locomotive*
> *I'm here I'm there—I'm everywhere*
> *I'm always around*
>
> *Chorus:*
> *Well I'll be—your Superman*
> *Give you super loving every chance that I can*
> *Yeah I'll be—your Superman*
> *Take hold of my super hand*
> *I'll take you to ever-ever land*
> *Great Caesar's Ghost I'll be your Superman"*

Copyright 1970 Easy Action/Warner/Chappell Music ASCAP

The arrangement boasted a horn lick that I borrowed from a Cat
Stevens tune called "Matthew and Son" and a downward moving
rhythm guitar part, reminiscent of Jimi Hendrix's version of Dylan's
"All Along the Watchtower." The huge hook in "Vehicle," "Great
God in Heaven" was replaced by "Great Caesar's Ghost"! Clone-y
enough for you, Warner Brothers?

As we tore into take one in the studio, we noticed the members of
the hot new horn group Chase entering the cramped control room.
(They were present because Bob and Frank now managed Chase as
well as The Ides.) This band was led by the superhuman trumpet
player Bill Chase, who had cut his chops as the star trumpeter in
Woody Herman's Thundering Herd Jazz Band. (His arrangement of
"Camel Walk" was legendary in jazz circles.)

No note was too high for Bill. He would part the molecules of the atmosphere with his pure and piercing high notes. He could stun small animals and seduce the hottest women with his tone. He didn't even need to be mic'd onstage. He was plenty loud without a mic.

The Ides were enormous fans of Bill and the four-trumpet attack of his band. Everyone watched intently as I took the mic. I was buzzed on pure adrenaline and black coffee and, at age nineteen and 145 pounds, I was rock 'n' roll fightin' trim. One take was all it took to shred the night.

When I listen to this record today, I can still hear the desperate urgency of a kid ready to take the rock world by storm—and intent on blowing away Bill Chase and his band who were watching slack jawed in the control room. The track bristled with a raw intensity that is palpable even when I listen today. The Ides have recently put it back in our show due to all the requests for it.

When "Superman" came out, Larry Lujack, of WLS, perhaps the first of the so-called shock jocks, played the record. On the back-sell he snidely remarked, "I think that's the same track as 'Vehicle,' only with different words! Nice job guys! Heh heh!" This sarcastic sentiment seemed to be echoed whenever it got played. The record stalled at number 17 on the *Billboard* charts but it stands as a postcard from Los Angeles at a very key time in The Ides' career.

As we boarded the 747 back to Chicago, we were feeling so many warring emotions: the joy of spreading our Berwyn gospel to the exalted reaches of the West Coast, contrasted with the disappointment of having basically bombed at The Whisky, and the feeling that we were the low men on the Warner Brothers totem.

Combine that with the fact that we were coming back to the cradle of our civilization—the comfort of our families, the fans that adored us, Salerno's Pizza, Frielach's Ice Cream Parlor, WLS, and Dick Biondi.

"Familiar" felt good on my skin as we got off the plane at O'Hare Airport. And yet, I had the feeling that the world was a much less secure place than I had thought. I was shaken—and I was stirred.

At that moment, I wrote a song that crystallized all those emotions into one. To many of the true Ides fans, this song is perhaps quintessential—"L.A. Goodbye."

> *"Well my wavelength gets a little longer every time I wave*
> *   goodbye-hi*
> *Sentimental breakdown—you know I break down and lie-hi*
> *Where I'm not supposed to lie my head*
> *Always seemed my softest pillow*
> *And as I board my plane—something inside my brain*
> *Hates to wave L.A. goodbye-hi—L.A. goodbye*
> *Sunset Strip and I field trip over to your hideaway—hey*
> *Sunset princess beckons and we love the night away—hey*
> *And now I feel light-years away*
> *From the West Side of Chicago*
> *And as I board my plane—something inside my brain*
> *Hates to wave L.A. Goodbye—L.A. Goodbye"*

Copyright 1971 Easy Action/Warner/Chappell Music ASCAP

My Wavelength Gets a Little Longer

THROUGHOUT THE SUMMER TOUR of 1970, I communicated with Karen constantly. There were phone calls almost daily, love letters, candy grams, and flowers for different occasions. I would have sent up smoke signals if I could. We were in love. Big time. The guys all knew it. When I'd get off the phone with her, I would sit in the motel room wearing a glazed look of supreme satisfaction on my face.

I had recently won Karen back. Here's how it happened. One night The Ides were playing one of our favorite clubs, The Blue Village, in Westmont, Illinois. I saw Karen in the audience, looking amazing with her honey hair worn back. When I saw her, I convinced myself that I felt nothing. By now I was dating a girl from Morton College named Chris. She looked so similar she could have been Karen's sister. After the set Karen came to the stage and we exchanged niceties.

I finally felt I had put her behind me. When I showed her my wallet photo of Chris I noticed Karen was visibly shaken. Then I told her about the time I took Chris to see Led Zeppelin at The Kinetic Playground and it got so late we watched the sunrise over Lake Michigan.

A few days later I received an artfully decorated letter from Karen. I trembled as I read her words. She explained that she had made a mistake breaking up with me. That she still loved me and wanted to try it again. I calmly got in my 240Z and drove to Chris's house in Cicero and told her it was over between us. Karen had come back. That's how sure I was that our reunion would be a success.

I did not, however, call Karen back to acknowledge the letter. Instead, I went away on a weeklong family vacation to Florida. Every day I re-read the letter just to feel that feeling of joy again and again. I was relishing just letting Karen hang out on the line for a while.

When I got home I called Karen immediately and told her I had gotten her letter and would love to get back together. She told me she was worried when I didn't respond right away—exactly what I wanted! This time our love would last—forty-four years strong as I'm writing this book.

Back on the road I'd sit shotgun in the van with this shit-eating grin on my face.

"I hate it when you're elated!" our drummer Mike would say.

I was elated. But if a phone call to Karen didn't go well or I didn't get an "I miss you" at the conversation's end, I would pout and generally be a drain to be around. I could really poison a room.

One day she called me "repulsive." I asked our manager Frank Rand, in all seriousness, "Frank, am I 'repulsive'?"

He didn't know whether to laugh or cry and just said, "Not particularly."

Some of the more unattached guys were enjoying the fruits of the labor of being a rock star. It was a dirty job, but someone had to do it. One of the band members was even urinating strange, bright colors caused by the meds he was taking to clear up a nasty little STD. Crabs were another unwanted bedfellow in one of the guy's beds. The temptations were out there, no doubt. But my sense of Catholic morals and knowledge that I already had the best waiting back in Berwyn always kept me in check. I even felt guilty when our managers took us to a strip club in Los Angeles. Years later, on the road with Survivor, Jimi Jamison started calling me "Father Jim" because I was always trying to convince various band members and crew not to mess around on their trusting wives and girlfriends, that it was not worth the risk of disease and guilt, advising them to buy a *Hustler* and beat off instead.

When The Ides played in Little Rock, Arkansas, a cute little waif was hanging around after the show at the local high school. Her name was Connie Hamzy. I found out later she had just turned fourteen, but she looked more like eighteen.

She was a brunette, well-endowed (and they were big bands!) with a come-on look that begged attention. I was her focus. I think she was put in my path just to test my loyalty and commitment to my future wife, Karen.

The next day while lounging at the Holiday Inn, a car pulled up. It was Connie and her mother. They were looking for Jimbo (this would be a pattern!). While mom stayed in the car, Connie and I chatted awhile in the room. Next thing you know we were wrestling on the bed, grabbing and groping, kissing and fondling, like the two teenagers we were—one underage, as I later found out!

"Put it...down there!" Connie kept saying. "Down there!"

Well, it was sooo tempting, but I really had no intention of putting it "down there." If she was this available to me I figured it would just be a matter of time before I, too, would be pissing razorblades.

She left unfulfilled and rejected and climbed back into her accomplice mother's waiting car. Of course, Connie went on to fame and misfortune to become, perhaps, the most infamous groupie of all time, immortalized in "We're an American Band" by Grand Funk Railroad: "Sweet sweet Connie—doin' her act."

I ran into Connie back in Little Rock a few years later, this time with Survivor. The years, beers, and tears had taken their toll on her. Outside the tour bus, she gave me a hug and a much too salty kiss, confiding to me that I was the first real "rock star" she had pursued. Whether that was true or not, I enjoyed believing it!

For the next three summers, The Ides of March averaged 200 shows a year crisscrossing the U.S. and Canada. The word got around from promoter to promoter that The Ides "delivered the goods." A few of the groups we opened for, however, refused to play with us again because after our "take no prisoners" set, they found it very difficult to follow us—The Allman Brothers, for one. The Ides lived and breathed The Allman Brothers, who inspired many of our free-form jams onstage.

In one memorable show, when we opened for them at Louisiana State University, Gregg Allman found it necessary to drawl into the mic, "Well, now we ain't no show band. We don't have no brass or nothing fancy [like The Ides!]."

The Byrds, in their country-rock phase, with Roger (don't call me Jim!) McGuinn, and featuring the late, great guitarist, Clarence White, of B-Bender fame, his patented device that, through a clever lever located at the strap button, would simulate the sound of a classic pedal steel guitar, also refused future dates with The Ides.

Their laid-back set, though excellent, just couldn't compete with our thousand-kilowatt attack complete with my teenybopper medley (my monologue satire of bubblegum music), a progressive twenty-minute rendition of "Eleanor Rigby" ("Symphony for Eleanor" from our *Vehicle* LP), and our send-up of '50s rock 'n' roll where we transformed ourselves into Ricky and the Rockets—hair greased back with giant combs doing choreographed dance steps to the strains of Dick Clark's *American Bandstand* theme song.

After one show at a southern university, we were hanging out with The Byrds in our shared locker room/dressing room. I had just taught The Ides a brand-new country rock song I had written called "Carry On." I rodeo-ed Roger into a corner, circled the wagons, and asked him if we could present a new song for The Byrds to record. He squirmed as he nodded his head.

With just my acoustic guitar and The Ides' sweet harmony blend, we started:

"Sarah Jane—she ruined my name—
she left the town last Saturday
And now I feel so blue and alone
Hong Kong flu—my hopes did, too

I don't think I will graduate
In the meantime I'll just carry on"

When we finished, we looked up at Roger. He had been waving his green nylon stage shirt through the air trying to dry the sweat off as we were playing. ("I can wear this baby night after night!" Great, Rog, but how will it smell?)

He stopped waving long enough to say, with a kind of pained expression, "Well, you know guys, I got like Bob Dylan pitching me songs like every week, so ..."

I interrupted him right there and said with a straight face, "Oh Dylan. Like he is so over. This is the future."

It was a true Jimbo moment that the guys will never forget. I pulled the same thing after The Ides opened for Johnny Rivers, playing him my song "Freedom Sweet" after the show. He loved it, but after a huddle with my management he decided that if he couldn't own half of the publishing he wanted no part of it. I was crushed by my managers' inflexibility at the time.

There were so many snapshot moments in these golden days touring with The Ides to promote *Vehicle* and the albums that followed.

There was the time when yours truly escorted a much worse for wear Janis Joplin to her hotel (she couldn't remember which one; I knew she was checked in where we were staying) after we opened for her in Calgary. She couldn't have been sweeter as we walked arm in arm down the streets.

I love the memory of exchanging guitar licks with my hero Duane Allman in the dressing room at the Warehouse in New Orleans. After which I picked up the "perfectly good" strings he had just taken off his Gibson SG Les Paul and wound them up on my own Les Paul to use a few nights later. (I was in the audience when the Allmans took the stage. Duane asked on mic if anyone had any "Coke." I rushed to the refreshment stand and laid a can at his feet. He looked at me bemused as he took a swig. Then he asked again, "Does anyone out there have any coke?")

Another great moment was stopping into the Datsun dealership in Baton Rouge after The Ides' appearance at the Big Swamp fest there in 1970. (We had just brought down the house with our set as Cubby Koda and the rest of Brownsville Station watched in the wings. That started my long friendship with Cubby.) I was on the three-month waiting list in Chicago for Datsun's amazing new entry into the sports car field, the 240Z! Now in Baton Rouge there was a breathtaking British racing green one right in the showroom window. When I walked in with my fringe flying, the slick salesman kind of snickered and drawled, "Don't think you can afford one of these babies, son." With that I walked back to the hotel where Larry gave me nearly $4,000 in cash to buy my dream car and have it flat-bedded back to Chicago. That guy is probably still shaking his head.

But those were fun days for sure. All of us were now in college. Because of our upbringing, dropping out was not even an option. As I look back now, I see how much bigger we could have been if we had devoted all our time to The Ides. We had to pass up many opportunities because of school.

Mike Borch studied architecture at IIT, Bob Bergland was being groomed as an accountant, and Larry Millas was at Roosevelt in the music program. Me—I majored in psychology, which would ultimately provide me with a skill set I would put to good use when dealing with the personalities of my next band.

You see, we bought into the old parental yarn about having something to fall back on when our little music hobby petered out. I think I actually believed that!

When "Vehicle" hit number one, I said, "See, See!"

My mother just shrugged and said, "Okay, now do it again."

Karen and I were now a solid couple, showing up everywhere together including nearly all Ides gigs. She and the soon-to-be "Brides of March" sat cheering in the audience until we launched into our twenty-minute version of "Eleanor Rigby," at which time they all headed to the rest room. To them our "Suite for Eleanor" was a huge snore.

A guilty pleasure for Karen and me was going to a little ice cream parlor in suburban Oak Park called Happiness Is. The gimmick was that you could sit in an old-fashioned carriage and consume your mounds of amazing homemade ice cream. One time, high on our love hormones and butterfat, we looked at each other suddenly and said, "Hey, we could get married!" It was like a revelation. We set a date to get engaged. I surprised Karen by giving her the ring at the entrance to Riverside Brookfield High School, where we first met in line to see The Turtles.

We set the wedding date for September 2, 1972. I asked The Ides for two weeks off to go on our honeymoon in Hawaii. I remember saying good-bye to Karen at her parents' doorstep the day before the wedding. There was a sadness in my eyes. Although I knew marrying Karen was the right thing, I was only twenty-one (Karen was nineteen) and I was kind of mourning the loss of this golden dating period. I did not want to become my parents. It was a bittersweet feeling of transition. It would be years before I fully integrated the married Jim with the carefree "rock star" Jim.

We had a small but beautiful wedding ceremony with The Ides acting as my groomsmen, Mike Borch as my best man. We flew to Hawaii the very day of the ceremony. It was Karen's first flight and she got quite nauseous. When we reached the hotel we were tired, jet-lagged, and in a strange land. Honeymoon night was not the idealized vision we might once have had! We were both virgins on our wedding night so to say we were lacking in certain sexual skills would be an understatement. Fortunately, we were quick learners. When we weren't practicing that skill I spent a lot of time clinging to my former mistress, my Gibson J50 folk guitar, writing what was to become The Ides' next single, "Mother America," on our hotel balcony overlooking the blue Pacific.

When we got back from our honeymoon, I left Karen on her own in our tiny apartment and immediately hit the road with The Ides. Talk about seduced and abandoned. As I toured I was constantly thinking that perhaps it was time to break off on my own and try my way in the world as a solo artist. Karen encouraged this idea, feeling that perhaps The Ides had run its course.

Between 1970 and the day we called it quits, The Ides recorded four albums: two for Warner Brothers—*Vehicle* and *Common Bond*—and two for RCA—*World Woven* and *Midnight Oil*.

The Ides in the studio cutting *World Woven*.

Our musical journey was marked by a constant shifting in focus. Most bands don't get a record deal until their members are in their mid- to late-twenties. By then, they arguably have their direction sorted out.

The Ides, however, did all of their growing in the public eye and ear. We started as a British Invasion, jangly guitar band, then turned into a horn band in the mold of BS&T. Next we moved toward more vocal harmony-based music on our second album, then on to Crosby, Stills and Nash–style arrangements (listen to our hit "L.A. Goodbye"), and finally on to Bakersfield country.

Our third album saw a marked change of sound due to the addition of Dave Arrellano, an amazing blind keyboardist we discovered playing at a hotel bar on our Canadian tour. This guy just had it—a cross between Billy Preston and Stevie Wonder. In a few weeks, he moved his family to a small apartment in the western suburbs of Chicago to be a member of The Ides of March.

Dave's influence was undeniable on The Ides' last two LPs. His gospel stylings were a perfect fit for songs such as "All Join Hands" and

"Diamond Fire." He embellished the song I wrote on my honeymoon in Hawaii, "Mother America," with swirling B3 organ and the then-revolutionary Moog synthesizer. This primordial synth took up nearly the entire back wall of the control room of Universal Studios on Walton in Chicago. It must have had about 1,000 knobs and switches.

Dave was the owner of one of the first Mellotrons in the country. The Ides bought it for him at a whopping six grand! This is the keyboard where every key would trigger a six-and-a-half-foot stretch of audiotape. It contained prerecorded string and flute sounds. It is the slightly wobbly sound you hear on many early albums of The Moody Blues. This was a primitive and extremely fussy piece of gear. It usually broke down when we needed it most, like the big show opening for Sha Na Na at Chicago's Arie Crown Theater.

Meanwhile I was enrolled at the University of Illinois Circle Campus near downtown Chicago. This concrete jungle of cubist, austere buildings was as cold and foreboding as the fierce Chicago winter.

Again I roamed the barren corridors armed with a folk guitar, playing in study halls and poetry classes. I was fearless in everything—everything except the possibility of being drafted into the armed forces at any time. The country was under the lottery system where every U.S. male within a certain age group was given a number. The lower the number the more likely it would be that you would be drafted to serve in Vietnam. I was numero 32.

This death sentence loomed over me as I schemed ways to be ineligible. The school deferment no longer was in action. I visited the university shrink and told him that my anxiety to be called was ruining my school concentration, hoping for a letter of exemption. No dice.

Finally three short days before the end of 1972 my dear mother read an article in the *Tribune* that stated that if you signed up for an "assigned risk" pool before the end of the year you would get an automatic 1Y deferment if you were not called in the first three months of the next year. They made it clear that you had a much greater chance of being called in that time.

My letter was postmarked December 30. Then I bit my fingernails and waited. It was the longest three months of my life 'til one day in April I received my 1Y deferment. If my mother never gave me a single gift in my life, her quick thinking, which may have saved my life, would have been enough.

The final Ides of March album, *Midnight Oil,* was heavily influenced by our growing infatuation with country rock. Having just toured with The Byrds and having recorded in the same studio (RCA on Sunset) next to Poco (Richie Furay was one hell of a Ping-Pong player—I should know!), we stretched our geographical and musical boundaries and headed south. By this time, our management had convinced us to drop the horns ("Clive Davis says brass is passé."). We had the sad duty of telling John Larson that he was out of the band. Chuck Soumar stayed because besides playing trumpet he was a good singer and percussionist. We never had to fire anyone before and it was as hard on us as it was on John.

Larry had taken to playing some bottleneck slide work and I affected a bit of a southern drawl onstage, a cadence I lifted from an amazing country rock band we used to play with called Mason Proffit ("Two Hangmen" was their mid-charting hit).

The LP contained "Lay Back" and "Roadie Ode," which featured the superb pedal steel work of Rusty Young of Poco (also one hell of a Ping-Pongist!). It rocked out with the first single, "Hot Water," which is still a stage staple for The Ides. But overall, our audience had become "much more selective" (to quote a line from the movie *Spinal Tap*) and we had trouble making much of an impact in the country or any other market for that matter.

I was enamored with Cat Stevens, Paul Simon, and Elton John, feeling I could easily fit that mold. It was all leading up to that life-changing meeting in the summer of 1973.

I gave my notice one day in Larry's basement. "I want to see what else is out there in this world of music," I said. But what I really wanted to say was, "My success with you guys is not nearly as big as my ego. I have heard—time after time—that I alone am The Ides of March, and I'm starting to believe it! What's Paul Simon, Elton John, and Cat Stevens got that I don't? Nothin'!" But I didn't say that, and I only recently realized just how arrogant I had become. The guys stood there shell-shocked by my rash decision but accepted it after Larry gave it his best shot at changing my mind.

"Why don't you just take a break from The Ides and do your own album?" It was a sage suggestion, but one that fell on my deaf ears. In my mind I had to make a full commitment to the solo thing. Somehow I knew I would not lose this band of brothers as friends. We had too much shared history—too much skin in the game. Most of us were buddies even before we had a band. I was correct. We all stayed close through the years.

Also, certain members seemed ready to pack it in as rock stars. Bob was ready to join a large accounting company. Chuck was ready to take over his recently deceased father's upholstery shop, and Larry was looking to do more behind the scenes in the recording world. Mike was ready to take the band MS Funk up on their offer to join. Soon Mike would be onstage with that great band, which was fronted by a very young Tommy Shaw, who soon after went on to become a lynchpin of Styx.

We had Herb Gronauer book a final concert at our alma mater, Morton West in Berwyn, for a few months from then—November 8, 1973. We did shows leading up to that with the knowledge that this was about to end. We put on our game face and played our asses off 'til the end.

On that fateful day, our co-manager Bob Destocki's voice quivered as he introduced the band: "And now—for the last time anywhere— The Ides of March." A lump rises in my throat every time I hear the recording of that moment. We played the show of our career and left everyone shaking their heads that this couldn't possibly be the end of The Ides. I didn't know exactly where I was going, but fate was at the wheel and I was its Vehicle—baby.

The Ides marched out in style.

Time to Trade Those Dreams

SO THE WONDERFUL SAGA of The Ides of March was over for now. It would take twenty-three years and a thousand victories and heartaches to once again unite onstage with my brothers in arms.

It was now down to Karen and me in our three-room apartment in Riverside, Illinois, the town just west of Berwyn. Our first home together was one of those handsome apartment buildings built in the 1930s with about twenty units on three floors, located at 32 Lawton Road, just across the street from the fire department and the Riverside Recreation Center. We still drive past it to reminisce.

When we moved in, Karen saw only the potential of this fairly dilapidated place.

"Okay, we'll paint the walls white. I'll make curtains for the windows and build a valance to cover the rods. Let's paper the back wall of our bedroom with a floral print, put up faux wooden beams, and I'll sew pillows for the living room!"

That last sentence became one of our favorite in-jokes. Karen's voice rose with such childlike exuberance that now, whenever she gets an idea that particularly catches her fancy, I cry, "I'll sew pillows for the living room!"

But to us, this apartment was a penthouse suite. We loved our little love nest. It was our monument to young independence. We converted the pantry into an eating nook by taking the door off and constructing a narrow table. The space was so tiny that when we sat across from each other, our knees would touch, but we didn't mind one bit. We'd even pack two additional adults into this area when we had company.

We made love in practically every area of the place—on the lush, shag carpet in the living room, on the bathroom floor during the Ides Christmas Party, and against the sink in the kitchen—pretty much everywhere except that boring old brass bed.

Karen and I went on pilgrimages to St. Charles and Geneva, Illinois, in search of antiques. I'd borrow one of The Ides' Ford Econoline vans and we'd come back with a mother lode of church pews, hall trees, Parsons tables, Tiffany lamps, packing chests, footstools, and armchairs.

We'd haul our trash and treasures over to my parents' basement and spend countless afternoons stripping off old varnish and applying transparent Danish oil. It was so fulfilling watching the deep grain of the wood coming to life after years of suffering, hidden under gobs of ghastly dark varnish or gaudy paint.

When we got hungry, we got pizza from Salerno's and found that we could polish off an entire medium-sized pie while inhaling the intoxicating perfume of furniture polish mixed with the scent of dank basement mold. As Karen's late brother, Andy, would say, "Hey, when you're in love, it don't matter."

When The Ides were still together and touring, Karen and I didn't have the time we had now to express our inner Ralph Lauren at the apartment. Now we were like kids in a candy store; making these three rooms our heaven on earth.

Early married days in the apartment.

During this era I was employed as a songwriter for Warner/ Chappell Music. My manager, Frank Rand, who I inherited from the Ides days, believed strongly in my talents as a songwriter. His goal was to secure me a publishing deal. He was convinced that once other artists heard my songs they would be lining up to cut them.

We flew to L.A. and met with one of the biggest publishers in the world: Warner/Chappell. I have to give Frank Rand and Bob Destocki big points for going to the top company immediately. I nervously played CEO Chuck Kay a sample case of some of my new ones and ended with my hat trick song: "Vehicle." He signed me that very day.

I had to quickly get accustomed to the mentality of writing for other artists. I had only written for myself, or for an entire band, previously. I was then put on a salary (actually a draw against future royalties) of about $400 per week. It was a wild undertaking. It was like I had to put out for the company. At first, to be honest, I didn't really take well to it.

But I struggled on and every once in a while I would get "the call." It would be short and sweet and go something like this: "Frankie Valli is looking for a song." So, at that time, I submitted one called "Ramona, Won't You Stay?" Warner/Chappell liked it, but Frankie Valli turned it down. I had to get accustomed to rejection like never before in my career.

One thing that steadied me as I got more used to my new position, was that I had a backlog of songs that had already been written. One of them was "San Pedro's Children."

I really, really liked that song and I was excited that the powers-that-be were pitching it, quite enthusiastically, to their roster of artists. Tony Orlando had it on hold. What that means is that the artist can consider using the song, for, say, a three-month period. They get an exclusive on it; if they record it, they get the first rights to release it. But Tony Orlando decided not to cut it, so it became available for the world.

At that point, it was pitched to Johnny Rivers. He was a mellow singer who had been looking to revive his career when he first heard my song in 1977. He thought it was perfect. He loved the song, so he went into the studio to cut it.

One part of the lyric is a chant that should sound like an echo from a distant cathedral. It's supposed to be the sound of little Mexican children singing. However, I didn't know enough Spanish to really do it right. So I made up a bunch of words that sounded "Spanishy." The phrase I conjured up was something like, "*Viva el Diablo en todo en la noche felice.*" But to tell you the truth, I didn't really know what it meant.

Meanwhile, all of the session musicians (most of the Wrecking Crew) had been selected and hired. The time was ticking by at the most expensive studio in L.A., A&M Studios. They were already in the process of cutting the song when Johnny started singing, "*Vive el Diablo en la noche,*" and one of the studio assistants, who was Spanish-speaking, and of Mexican descent, caught Johnny's eye.

"Dude," he says. "Do you know what you're singing? You're basically singing, 'Long live the devil.'"

Johnny was furious. He stormed into the control room and shouted over the phone to Mike Sandoval, my agent at Warner/Chappell, "What the fuck are you doing? You sent me a religious song that says, 'Long live the devil!'"

Mike, in turn, frantically called me up and said, "Dude, did you know what you were saying?" Sheepishly, I answered, "No, I didn't know what those words meant." Mike told me that I had to change this chant immediately. I began to panic. I didn't know anyone who spoke Spanish in town, so I finally called the Mexican Consulate in Chicago and told them what I needed. I asked them how to say "Praise to God" in Spanish. I waited and waited.

Finally, after about four hours, a gentleman called me from the Consulate. He gave me enough suggestions so that I could rewrite the chant and make it more conducive to the original meaning of the song.

Ultimately, Johnny cooled down and cut the record using the right lyric. But it's a miracle I survived the day when Johnny Rivers was threatening to kill me!

That incident was especially ironic because my heart had been in the right place when I wrote the song. "San Pedro's Children" was about orphans who worshipped at the village cathedral every day; the chant was designed so that you could imagine their tiny voices resonating over the distant hills. I still consider it a gorgeous song, despite the humiliation of Johnny Rivers' tirade.

> "From a run-down cathedral that stood on the edge of the city
> On Sundays, came a sound, I will always recall
> It was sweet and complete and it flowed through the cold-
>   hearted city
> And it sends me a heavenly shiver to think of it now.
> To hear the voices of San Pedro's children fill the air—oh oh
> Singing out His gospel for the world to share—oh oh
> And how the city would ring- when San Pedro's children
>   would sing
> You'd hear them going—la la la la la"

Copyright 1974 Easy Action/Warner/Chappell Music ASCAP

My "songwriter for hire" status also got me in touch with singer David Hasselhoff, who, many years after that incident, cut his own version of "San Pedro's Children." David was a big star in Germany at that time.

I also became friends with audio engineer Bruce Swedien, who produced David. Bruce frequently collaborated with producer Quincy Jones. I had met this handlebar-mustachioed audio genius when I wandered into Studio A at Chicago's Universal Studios one day while he was recording the number one hit "Have You Seen Her" for The Chi-Lites. That day set a new bar for me regarding audio excellence.

Our connection continues: I recently sent Bruce some of my son Colin's material, which he loved. Colin and I went down to Florida with my engineer Larry Millas, Khari Parker (drums), Jeff Lantz (keyboards), and Bobby Lizik (bass), in early 2012, to cut some tracks with the master in his studio. The walls were covered with platinum records and signed accolades from artists as diverse as Frank Sinatra to The Motels. Bruce's artistry was apparent while we watched him strategically place the microphones. The first thing Bruce did was to sit us down in the control room and play us (at 120 db—loud!) the master two-track of one of Bruce's greatest feats of engineering: "Billie Jean" by Michael Jackson. The sound was breathtaking—beyond anything I'd ever heard before or since. He then played us Michael's heartbreaking version of Charlie Chaplin's great song "Smile." There was not a dry eye in the control room, especially because Michael Jackson had recently passed away.

My songwriting has taken me in many unexpected directions. Warner/Chappell pitched a song I had recently completed called "Indelibly Blue" to Reba McEntire. "The Queen of Country" loved it and included it on her 1981 album, *Heart to Heart*. It was funny that, with all of the celebrated songwriters in Nashville, a kid from Berwyn got one of her key cuts. Maybe all that listening to Johnny Cash as a child was starting to pay dividends.

"Lost in the city
Deserted and Cold
Watching the cars passing by

What a classy couple, mother and dad, Alice and Jim Peterik, freshly wed and looking like movie stars in front of Alice's family's butcher shop in Hawthorne, Illinois.

Me toddling down Wesley Avenue, Berwyn, IL, happy to be anywhere, already a tastemaker in my trendy cardigan sweater.

Jimbo in the works in front of St. Odilo's Church with Alice, Jim, Alice Anne, and Janice. I was so convinced I had my look just right, I refused to remove my hat in church.

The Hi-Hatters in our living room on Oak Park Avenue. Al Tobias far left, Dad second from right, me in front on alto sax, practically levitating with pride.

The Shondels' first publicity photo. Early 1964, with our first drummer, Bob Erhart in his parents' living room. Left to right: Bob Bergland, me, Erhart, and Larry Millas. Skinny ties and all!

The Shondels, "getting down" on the gymnasium floor at an after-basketball sock hop.

1966: The Ides of March through the studio glass at the famous Sound Studios on Michigan Avenue. Visible is the back of engineering great Stu Black.

The other side of the glass—same day, cutting "Roller Coaster," our follow up to "You Wouldn't Listen." Left to right: Larry Millas, Mike Borch, me, Bob Bergland. Larry uses this Epiphone Riviera to this day.

Me with my prized, jacked-up, air-shocked, mag-wheeled
time machine: my '64 Plymouth Valiant—my Vehicle, baby!

The day after doing the Mama Cass show on the Warner Brothers movie set; first trip
to the West Coast to promote our top ten hit "Vehicle." Left to right: John Larson,
Larry Millas, Mike Borch, Bob Bergland, Chuck Soumar, me, and Ray Herr.
We were on top of the world.

The search is over—on the steps of St. Mary's—September 2, 1972, me and the new Karen Peterik, the love of my life. I could see forever.

The newlyweds in Kauai for our honeymoon. At ages twenty-one and nineteen, we had so much to learn. Together.

Me and the alluring Karen Peterik. Outtake from the photo shoot for my solo album on Epic, *Don't Fight the Feeling*, on our antique brass bed—the only place we *didn't* make love.

Publicity photo after I changed my name to Chalmers Garseny. What was I thinking?

The original Survivor lineup. Left to right: Dennis Johnson, Gary Smith, Frankie Sullivan, me, and Dave Bickler. This early publicity shot includes my "desperate hand" logo idea executed by Barb Weigand.

Me and my partner in a team of rivals—the one and only Frankie Sullivan—in the iso room at Right Track recorders, NYC cutting *Too Hot to Sleep*.

On the platform of the Chicago subway in our alternate personas for Survivor's "I Can't Hold Back" video. Left to right: Jimi Jamison, Frankie Sullivan, Marc Droubay, Stephen Ellis (nun with Heineken!), and James Peterik attorney at law. Our best video I'd say.

The scene onstage at Survivor's sold-out show at the Greek Theater—double platinum celebration for *Vital Signs*. Standing with us are many of the architects of our success, including the Scotti Brothers, Johnny Musso, manager John Baruck, and Cliff O'Sullivan of Epic Records.

Me and KP at the first famed Music and Tennis Festival in San Diego, 1984, with Jimi Jamison and our dear friend Theresa Clarke. My doubles partner was Alan Parsons.

The honorable Jim and Karen Peterik enjoying our favorite Japanese specialty: shabu shabu prepared for us in our room in Kyoto after the second Survivor tour of Japan, 1986.

1990: the first publicity shot of the newly reunited Ides Of March. Top: Dave Southern, Larry Millas, John Larson, Scott May. Bottom: Mike Borch, Jim Peterik, Chuck Soumar, Bob Bergland.

Whee! One sure way to get a smile out of a young Colin Peterik—in our backyard in Burr Ridge.

Colin observing from above the chording prowess of Jeff Carlisi of 38 Special. In my studio.

My favorite moment of every show: The Ides bow to the royalty, the audience.
Left to right: Dave Stahlberg, John Larson, Chuck Soumar, Mike Borch, Larry Millas, me, Bob Bergland, and Scott May.

Jimbo and the amazing and "saxy" Mindi Abair performing one of our co-writes, "Slither" at World Stage 2011.

"The Big Bow"—just one of many memorable World Stage concerts. From left to right: Ed Breckenfeld, drums; me; Lisa McClowry, vocals; Jack Blades, Night Ranger; Dave Bickler, Survivor; Bun E. Carlos, Cheap Trick.

Me with one of my finest collaborators, Don Barnes, lead vocalist/guitarist of 38 Special. World Stage 2009— shiver me timbers!

It's my honor getting to share the stage with the amazing singer/songwriter/keyboardist/producer Colin Peterik—World Stage 2014.

Guitars that followed me home—honest Karen! In the foyer of Lennon's Den studio, a nice sampling showing an original '58 Gibson Flying V, a mint condition '58 Les Paul Custom, and one of my custom painted Minarik Bad Ass Bees.

The team at the FF/FF Friends Forever Fergie Frederiksen fundraiser in Excelsior, Michigan—July 18, 2010. The proceeds from this show sent Fergie and his family on a vacation to California. Left to right: Mark Hoyt, John Cafferty, Kevin Chalfant, Alex Ligertwood, Char Frederiksen, Mike Woodley, Pamela McNeill, Tris Klohn, Fergie Frederiksen, Jeff Dunn, Jimi Jamison, Barry Dunaway, Barry Goodreau, Kenny Haaland, Fran Cosmo. Back row: me, Mike Reno, Mark Reuter, Jim Caughlin, Dave Coyle. Bless you Fergie—you're in our hearts!

With my lifelong friend and recording engineer and musician extraordinaire Larry Millas—at the console. Makin' hits.

Jimbo turns the pages of desire mining through past notebooks searching for uncut diamonds.

Home Avenue in Berwyn is now Ides of March Way. 2012—Receiving the honor at our alma mater Morton West High School. Left to right: Bob Bergland, Mike Borch, me, Larry Millas, and Berwyn mayor Robert Lovero. Thanks to Rich Brom for spearheading the naming.

Me in full mentor mode with Ariel, Zoey and Eli. This frame is from an episode of *Steal the Show*, our new reality show currently being shown all over America on the Cozi NBC affiliate and other outlets. Their talented dad Matt Engelbert is behind the camera.

2014 Ides of March publicity shot for our 50th anniversary boxed set and tour, Last Band Standing. Left to right: Mike Borch, Scott May, Dave Stahlberg, me, Tim Bales, Larry Millas, Bob Bergland.

A full circle moment. In Times Square for the premier of Tony-nominated *Rocky Broadway*. A day I will never forget.

They're all going places
That we used to go
And it's driving me out of my mind...
And it's making me blue
Indelibly blue
Can't shake the memory of me and you
Oh- indelibly blue"

Copyright 1974 Easy Action/Warner/Chappell Music ASCAP

She sang it from the heart like only Reba can. This ballad is not only on that album, but it also landed on one of Reba's Greatest Hits compilations and it holds special significance for me because it was my very first crack at writing a country tune.

Yet as much as I enjoyed placing songs with amazing artists like Reba and Johnny Rivers, I would sometimes feel aimless. As a song-writer-for-hire, I would invariably end up with material that was in limbo; songs without a home. Still, I worked hard on creating these "homeless" songs, despite the distinct possibility that they might end up stacked with the thousands of dusty quarter-inch tape boxes.

Warner/Chappell had done me the great service of getting my songs to Reba, Tony Orlando, Johnny Rivers, and David Hasselhoff, and I was grateful, because otherwise many of these gems might have remained on that shelf. Still, it would take some time before I would enjoy the social interaction that comes with writing directly with another performer or songwriter. Ultimately, my biggest songs were written while under that initial contract with Warner/Chappell. Our partnership began in 1975 and continues to this day.

Around the same time that I got my publishing deal with Warner/Chappell, I had also started singing jingles downtown. Again, my manager, Frank Rand, was the one to hook me up with this lucrative source of musical revenue.

In the next five years, I would go on to sing more than 100 national commercial "spots." My first jingle was for Dick Boyell, one of the three jingle "Dicks" in the biz—I think that particular first name was required! There was also Dick Reynolds and, of course, the biggest of all (so to speak!) Dick Marx. At nearly every Dick Marx session, I would notice a cute, dimpled little blond boy, who was no more than eleven years old, drinking in every last drop of the musical action. That little kid grew up to become Top 40 hit-maker and songwriter Richard Marx.

Dick Boyell threw me in the deep water by asking me to sing a final, as opposed to a "demo," version of a spot for Old Style beer.

"When it's funky in the summer and you just can't escape the heat... It's smooth goin' down—Old Style from 'God's country.'"

Dick asked for my "Vehicle" persona—tough and swaggering with R&B overtones. I nailed it and soon the word got around. I became the proverbial "new kid in town," supplanting many singers who were used to monopolizing the market.

Because of my diplomatic style, I made sure I fit right in with the old order folks (Bob Bowker, Bonnie Herman, Len Dresslar [the bottom octave guy of "Valley of the Jolly Green Giant—Ho Ho Ho" fame] and Ruth Marx), showing the great respect I had for them. Soon, the other Dicks started calling, leaving urgent messages with my answering service (remember those?).

In a three-year period, I sang for McDonalds in the "You deserve a break today" era, and Schlitz Malt Liquor ("Look out for the Bull, look out for that Schlitz Malt Liquor Beer. Nobody makes malt liquor like Schlitz. Nobody."). This one was big bucks because I was the lead singer on it and also because it was a national radio and television buy. Remember the bull tearing ass through the china shop?

I also helped sell V8 tomato juice: "Now that you've had a drink—oh, what a time to think—I should have had a V8!" I used my friendly voice on that one, not my beer and tires growl! Also, United Airlines: "The friendly skies of your land—United Airlines."

But the biggest of all was Sunkist orange soda, running and casting off "blue money," which was the code name we'd all use for the blue Talent and Residual checks that seemed to breed in my mailbox, for seven—count 'em, seven!—years. I got to sing lead on The Beach Boys classic, "Good Vibrations": "I'm drinking up good vibrations, Sunkist orange soda taste sensation." (Recently I said apologetically to Brian Wilson, "Don't shoot me, Brian, I was just the jingle singer!")

Very significantly, there was one session where I sang across the microphone from an amazing tenor vocalist named Dave Bickler. His fine-grade sandpaper voice evoked some of the great rock 'n' roll singers of all time—Lou Gramm of Foreigner and Sam Cooke, come to mind.

On breaks you could see Dave in a quiet corner reading books by Isaac Asimov and other science fiction authors. It wouldn't be too long until I'd be giving him a call to sing background vocals on my soon-to-be-released solo album, *Don't Fight the Feeling*.

Our voices just seemed to blend magically. Dave sang the retorts on the long fade out on the album's big power ballad, "Let There Be Song."

I knew how to play the jingle game and was not offended when a client would say, "Jim, can you put more smile into it? A Rice Krispy would not sound like that."

But eventually the routine got old. I happen to remember the exact line I had to speak at my last jingle session ever. My part in the session was saying, with great, forced brio, "The meat, fish group!" for a cat food commercial.

When I said that line, suddenly the room started flexing. Bob Bowker, one of the great jingle singers of our time, was transformed into a cartoon elf as he pumped his arms vigorously from side to side, and the beautiful Bonnie Herman (first-call female) began to undulate and then melt slowly. I had never taken acid so I knew it couldn't be that. My heart was racing and my hands were numb. I finished my cat food line and staggered out not even filling out the W-4 government form.

This was my final session. I knew suddenly that this money machine was breaking down. I felt clearly that this was not a part of my life's game plan. It was fun while it lasted, though, and it funded many hours of studio time demoing songs for what would become my first album as a solo artist, *Don't Fight the Feeling*.

The jingles were really just a means to an end—the end being a record deal for myself on my own. In between the jingles I was doing every gig that came my way. It should have been a total downer to be playing for fifty people at the Marco Polo in Myrtle Beach after playing to thousands opening up for Zeppelin and wowing huge college crowds with our own headline shows. But I had tunnel vision. I was on an independent mission and I convinced myself that these shows were the stepping stones to solo success.

I wrote furiously in our cramped apartment on the five-foot grand piano I had bought for $250 at an antique shop in Berwyn. It was a nasty instrument that never stayed in tune, but this ornately carved keyboard from the 1920s was good enough to pound out some potential hits. Sometimes I would play 'til 4 a.m., confounding my landlord/janitor, old Mr. Markendorf.

He didn't like me and my habits much. Once, he politely knocked on our door to see what the racket was. He looked just past me and saw the four-man soul act I produced, Essence, doing a complete choreographed dance routine to a song I wrote and produced for them, "Chicago Blues," in full matching DayGlo polyester suits. With a slightly frightened look on his face he just muttered, "Could you boys please keep it down?" and left without another sound. We dissolved into laughter imagining the way it all must have looked to this kindly Old World gent.[4]

When I felt I had the right songs for a strong presentation to the various record companies, I booked time at the great Paragon Studios on Ohio Street in the near-north section of Chicago.

Paragon was the standard-bearer for me. From out of this tiny room came some of the best-sounding records ever: "Fire" by the Ohio Players, albums by the late, great Steve Goodman ("City of New Orleans"), folksinger John Prine ("Hello in There"), and, most significantly, Styx. (*The Grand Illusion* was just one of the amazing records Styx recorded at Paragon.)

But what made this studio so special? Oh sure, the custom-built Flickinger console was sweet, their mic closet one of the best, and their outboard gear was up to date. But, the real secret weapon at Paragon was a wiry little guy with long, curly hair, wire-rim glasses,

---

[4] As I watched those intricate dance steps in our tiny apartment I should have guessed that stand-out hoofer and Essence lead singer Marzette Griffith would one day break out to become Chicagoland's number one stepper in competitions five years running in the '90s.

and a wry sense of humor: Barry Mraz. He defined the word "genius" in the field of sound recording.

When it came time to make my demo, Barry was my only choice. Everyone else was tied for second. Sadly, Barry had a congenital heart defect made even worse by a fierce cocaine habit. He passed away in 1989 at a very young age with many of his audio secrets dying with him.

The demos I made with Barry Mraz eventually got me signed to Epic Records by Lennie Petze, one of their top A&R (artist and repertoire) men. After hearing my demos, Petze came out to see me perform at my ground zero, Orphans Pub, a tiny club located on Lincoln Avenue. He would later sign a quirky, redhead singer named Cyndi Lauper.

He had to hear for himself that the sound on those demos with songs such as the stately "Let There Be Song" (with Dave Bickler), "Daphne with the Laughing Eyes," and what would become my debut's title track, "Don't Fight the Feeling," was not just a studio creation. The joint was packed the night Petze came to see me, and along with my band, Shy Rhythm, we could do no wrong. I was doing my whole dog and pony show, singing up a storm, revving up the crowd, and playing my Les Paul behind my head. Though it was always a surefire crowd pleaser, this stunt is the reason for the collapsed vertebrae in my neck and chronic pain in that area later in life.

I was signed to Epic the next day and assigned to a producer named Toxie French (you can't make up a name like that), who was still basking in the reflected glow of producing the Top 10 hit by one-hit wonder artist Chi Coltrane, "Thunder and Lightning."

I begged Lennie to let me stay with Barry Mraz at the helm, but Barry, instead, became the engineer underneath Toxie ("Toxic") French. The sessions became a pissing contest for control with me caught in the crossfire.

Unhappy sessions create unhappy vibes and bad vibes create a lifeless album. That pretty much describes this, my first solo venture. Epic tried to promote it even though it was in direct competition with some label mates (another Petze signing) whose album came out the very same week as mine—you may remember a little combo by the name of Boston.

I opened for Boston on their second show ever, here in my hometown at the north side Uptown Theater. Shy Rhythm and I did a powerful set, featuring songs from the new album and ending with a bluesy retread of my Ides of March smash, "Vehicle."

Near the end of the song, I finally did what I had wanted to do since my eyes fell upon it at sound check—I jumped into the orchestra pit, sending the packed house into a frenzy.

Brad Delp, lead singer of Boston, was a basket case just before their set. "Jim, Jim, I can't go on. I'm scared shitless! I can't do what you just did out there. You're a veteran, what do I do?"

As I forcibly shoved him onstage, I said, "Get the fuck up there, take a deep breath, and sing your ass off! Just doooo it!" With that, he sailed up to his mic, and as the set wore on he seemed to get more and more into this star thing.

By the end of the set, he had transformed himself into a cross between Robert Plant and Sammy Davis Jr. As he came off stage, he hugged me and said, "Thanks, Jim, I couldn't have done it without you!"

The very next day I opened the entertainment section of the *Chicago Sun-Times*. The headline screamed, "Boston Rocks, But Hometown Rock Tops!" I couldn't believe my eyes. And this was us performing without our keyboard player, Terry Fryer, who had decided to quit that afternoon!

There was a photo of me in the orchestra pit with the crowd gathered around me. I felt I had died and gone to heaven. The reporter, Cynthia Dagnal, became my champion for many years after that.

We went on to open up for many great acts that year, most memorably label mates Heart, Boston, and John Hiatt. The album managed sales of only about 30,000, even with my promotional video that comically documented me ordering and consuming fifty White Castle hamburgers, while the hairnet-wearing counter ladies feigned horror—all to the strains of "Don't Fight the Feeling." This marketing tour de force was the result of me telling Lennie Petze about my serious slider habit. I actually ate twenty-six burgers that day and was on the mug practically nonstop for three days after that.

While touring constantly to promote this album, I developed a nasty cold, which just wouldn't go away. Finally, the hacking cough was racking me with pain. I could barely get through the set vocally and my energy was gone. I was sweating profusely. Finally, at a club in Waukegan, Illinois, called The Night Gallery, I boinked. I couldn't sing a damn note. I croaked out the songs in a kind of talk-sing style. I knew this was serious.

The next day, the X-rays proved that out. I had contracted severe pneumonia in both lobes of my lungs. The congestion was also way up high in the lungs making it even harder to reach with antibiotics and physical therapy. It was as if God had hit the reboot button to force me to stop my tireless pace and sit back and reevaluate my life.

I ended up at La Grange Memorial hospital for three long weeks. The only fun of it was when Karen and my family visited and brought me Italian beef sandwiches from Carms after I was finally well enough to keep food down, and, of course, there were those pretty nurses who would come in to pound my chest every day to help loosen up the phlegm.

It was in that hospital room, a bit light-headed on codeine, that I started concocting my next plan of action: the ultimate rock band comprised of the hottest musicians I could find. My pen jotted furiously as I made my short list to present to my manager, Frank Rand:

"Dennis Johnson: incredible bass player, formerly with the group you co-managed, Chase. This guy's chops and groove are undeniable."

"Gary Smith: monster drummer, also of Chase. This guy's fills are like machine gun fire."

"Dave Bickler: Every time I do a jingle session with this guy, we blend like magic. Maybe we could have two lead singers in this group—me and Dave!"

"Lead guitar: I could handle the chores or maybe find some good-looking hotshot kid to do the real flashy stuff."

The seeds were planted. The roller coaster ride was about to begin. The group that started as my hospital fever dream would one day become one of the biggest groups in the world.

My solo days and fascination with introspective artists such as Cat Stevens and Paul Simon were coming to a close. I was ready to get serious—"There Goes Rhymin' Peterik." He'd soon return in full rocker's garb.

Two Worlds Collide

BY THE TIME I had my dance with mortality—
the doctors said this strain of pneumonia had killed weaker victims
in the past—Karen and I had stabbed westward to the western suburb of La Grange, Illinois.

We found a very hip little ranch home at 823 South Stone Avenue
that had our name written all over it. It was one of those 1960s modern designs with a pitched roofline that created cathedral ceilings in
nearly every room. Against Frank Rand's advice that I couldn't afford
it, I plunked down the down payment on the $89,000 asking price.
Gulp! Now I had better land the next Schlitz Beer national spot! (I
did.)

The front room of the house overlooked the tree-lined street and
was home to my high-gloss walnut Ibach piano. I had deep-sixed
that ornate piece of junk piano, selling it to some poor bloke who,

The Jungle Room.

just like me, was seduced by its good looks. (Actually, it was to a great guy, Bill Syniar, who is a dear friend and the bass player on Survivor's *Too Hot to Sleep* album—he loves it!)

I adorned the brick wall of my front music room with my growing collection of gold records and started hanging vintage guitars on the walls like so many shrunken heads—proof of my conquests. (Hence, I called it "The Jungle Room" in homage to Elvis's den at Graceland.)

The neighborhood kids started coming out in droves for what seemed like "rock-star field trips," walking by to gawk at the gold and platinum records on the walls or catch a glimpse of me composing a new song or the future Survivor, woodshedding for a show. Sometimes they would stop me as I was mowing the lawn or shoveling snow. They sometimes even knocked sheepishly at the door for an autograph or a playback of the new Survivor acetate. (One of those young teens was none other than Joe Vana, who used to ride up on his bicycle to hear new Survivor acetates. Flash forward to 2001 and I'm producing him as co-lead singer along with Fergie Frederiksen for the Frontiers Records debut of the group Mecca.)

It was from this launching pad that my dreams of creating the ultimate band took flight.

My ex-manager and friend, Bob Destocki, was producing a local band called Mariah. It was kind of an off-shoot from Dave Bickler's early band, the Jamestown Massacre, who charted with a pop gem called "Summer Sun." He convinced me to come to a show to check out not only the band but also its two lead guitarists as possible candidates for my new group.

As they launched into a great set, I heard the three songs of mine that the band recorded for their Destocki-produced debut album on United Artists. The songs, "Reunion," "Nomad Man," and "How You Gonna Keep 'em Down on Broadway (After They've Seen the Farm)," never sounded better. The one guitarist, the rotund Lenny Fogerty, kind of disappeared as I noticed an engine of a guitarist named Frankie Sullivan running and jumping around the stage, basically provoking the audience into a reaction. I recognized him as a guy who kept showing up at Jim Peterik Band shows, usually with a friend of mine, Rick Weigand. He would come in various personas—most recently with his blond locks permed, looking for all the world like a younger Peter Frampton. He always watched my band respectfully, never introducing himself. Now I saw this person onstage and it all made sense. He was the star guitarist I had been hoping to find for my new, world-beating band.

Rick Weigand started calling me, asking if he could bring Frankie over. Finally the day was right. I was in the mood to meet this guy, who would someday co-write with me one of the biggest songs in rock history.

He stood somewhat tentatively at my door at 823 South Stone with his black Les Paul case—no Rick Weigand in tow. Cool: not joined at the hip. We exchanged hellos and I invited him in. I told Frankie that he had blown me away at the Mariah show a few weeks earlier. I tried to put him at ease as we made small talk about our favorite groups of the era. We both agreed on our love for Journey, Thin Lizzy, and Boston. He lent me the *Burn* album by Deep Purple.

It didn't take me long to realize his taste for the harder, edgier rock of the day and I was wide open.

He carefully took out his 1976 tobacco sunburst Gibson Les Paul, which would later be rechristened "Firewood" after it fell off its stand at a preproduction rehearsal with Ron Nevison, and had its headstock broken clean off! When it was repaired, the instrument sounded better than ever! We chatted about the guitar, which he had purchased from Kenny Hoffman at Associated Music, where I too did business.

As soon as he sat down at the now storied counter in my airy kitchen, he started casually strumming the intro lick to "Somewhere in America," a new song I had just introduced into my show. This was the one that the crowd started responding to and requesting, as if it had already been a hit. I was impressed, to say the least, not only because Frankie played it flawlessly, but also because he had taken the initiative to learn it. We repaired to the Jungle Room where we continued bouncing riffs off each other in a kind of rock 'n' roll Ping-Pong game. It was magic! I knew that very day that Frankie was the guy I was looking for. He came off as nice, caring, and unpretentious.

The very next day I called up Gary Smith and Dennis Johnson. I had been fantasizing about playing with these guys since I sat in with their former group, Chase. These guys were chops city. I was eager to find out how those intricate power jazz chops would translate to the rock genre.

I flew Dennis and Gary in from Phoenix and the four of us revved up a sound with balls and passion. It was clicking, with Dennis whipping his long blond mane from side to side as he played, his bass sitting way up high and his feet moving constantly. Gary was businessman sharp in neatly trimmed hair, a manicured mustache, a banker's vest, and a cruel yet hilarious sense of humor. I could tell they were having as much fun as Frankie and I were, whipping through "Somewhere in America" and a new one called "Love Has Got Me." I was especially impressed with Dennis's thumb-slapping technique on "Love Has Got Me." It gave the song a huge sonic kick in the ass. We exchanged high fives and schemed to get them relocated to Chi-Town ASAP.

When Dennis and Gary left, Frankie stayed. "Do you think we need another singer, Frankie?" I wondered out loud. I was already looking toward Frankie as a partner in the decision making.

"I don't think so, Jim, I think you can handle it all." (Note that, at this point, we were called "The Jim Peterik Band.")

I told him about this super singer I had been sharing the mic with for hamburger jingles, named Dave Bickler. Despite his previous statement, Frankie was more than open to the idea of a co-singer.

The day Dave came by was a game-changer. He entered my house with a sci-fi book tucked under his arm, and a shy smile. He was wearing his soon-to-be-signature black beret.

After some small talk, I grabbed my Gibson J50 acoustic guitar and showed Dave and Frankie a new song I had just written. This bittersweet song told the story of a greaser I knew whose nickname was "Pepperhead," who could not let go of the past. Even in the '70s and '80s, you could see him around town with his ducktail hairdo, high-water workies, and a pack of Lucky Strike cigarettes tucked into the rolled-up sleeve of his white T-shirt.

The song called for tight, three-part harmony à la Crosby, Stills and Nash. As Dave and Frankie learned the melody and lyrics, the vocal parts started to fall into place, with me at the bottom, Dave in the middle on the melody, and Frankie's clarion call sitting a third above.

Ron Nevison used to say, "Frankie, your voice sounds like a trumpet! I love it!" Indeed, it did.

We took a deep breath and, for the first time together, sang in three-part harmony:

> "He'd drive his blue Desoto down the main drag at dark.
> He'd wear his leather jacket like a Purple Heart.
> 'Cause he's living back in 1959
> They call him Pepperhead—he's a friend of mine."

Copyright 1979 Jim Peterik Music/Warner/Chappell Music/Bicycle Music ASCAP

Ooooh, weeee! Hell, yeah! The hair is standing up on my arm right now as I'm writing this—just as it did way back then on that fateful day. The blend was pure twenty-four-carat gold with the three voices becoming a fourth voice with a distinctive character all its own. We looked around at each other and kind of gave that knowing smirk. We knew we had caught lightning in a bottle with this mixture.

At that very moment we saw the future.

The Child Is Born a Survivor

BANDS. KAREN AND I used to say that they all suck, because aside from The Ides we never witnessed one that wasn't bickering and in-fighting and filled with huge yet fragile egos. However, when a band is right, there is nothing like the power-front it can create. Sometimes a group can actually harness the negative energy, internal tension, and creative differences to make magic. As time progressed that described Survivor.

Frankie was the brash rock 'n' roll kid from Franklin Park; I was the already-successful guitarist/songwriter, who had, years before, made an impact on the charts. Dave was a gifted jingle singer and a former member (one of two vocalists along with V.J. Comforte) of the 1970s rock band, Jamestown Massacre. Dennis and Gary brought their own cache of success, chops, and bravado into the mix from the fusion-rock horn band, Chase.

This was the original recipe of Survivor. Karen and I had endless talks about entering the arena of rock bands again. The Ides of March was a dream team, with everyone getting along, each man playing his own distinctive role, and supporting each other like family. This stew was different—and yet, I knew it was something special.

By adding Frankie, suddenly, there was a vibe and a buzz going around town. This kid just "had it": the look, the talent, and the spark of rock 'n' roll. Suddenly, Barry Mraz, who declined to produce my second solo album (which never materialized), was calling me, begging to be involved. Doors opened magically. The combination of my credibility and songwriting talents, Frankie's aura and rock-star good looks, and Dave's flexible, soulful voice was irresistible.

I realized, at about the third rehearsal, that this ensemble could no longer be called The Jim Peterik Band. Although I sang roughly half of the songs and we featured "Vehicle" and "L.A. Goodbye" in our live set, this was a brand-new entity that needed a fresh moniker.

Many names were tossed about: "Electric Warrior" and "Peterik" to name just a few. The latter, suggested by former Styx manager Derek Sutton, caused Frankie to effectively deep-six him from the management sweepstakes. Then I thought of a very strong word that I first saw in the opening line on Jim Charne's liner notes on the back of my *Don't Fight the Feeling* solo album: "Jim Peterik is a survivor." He was referring to my fighting the "rock wars" since age fifteen, and still standing strong.

A tragic subtext was that I was very nearly on the flight that killed Bill Chase and most of his band, Chase, just a few years earlier. That year, I was doing guest spots with Chase to promote his *Pure Music* album, where I wrote and sang two cuts, "Run Back to Mama" and "Love Is on the Way." (On Chase's debut album I contributed "Boys and Girls Together.")

I was scheduled to be on what became their final show, when I realized I had a prior show commitment with the Jim Peterik Band. Hence, I was not on that doomed flight in the same Twin Beech aircraft, with the same pilot, "Dirty Dan," that had flown The Ides to countless destinations.

Dan was in the habit of taking enormous chances to get us in and out of town in order to make shows. Once he even had all of the college staff (and a few students) line up their cars at the end of the runway with their brights on, to cut through the night fog and to mark the runway's end at the small town airport.

It was a terrible loss to the music world. I have many fond memories of working with Bill Chase. At one of our writing sessions he came to me with a fantastic horn riff. "It was written by a bird," he said with a straight face. "Okay, I'll play along, Bill." "Well you see I was camping up in the Canadian Rockies and I was awoken in my tent one morning by an insistent bird tweeting the coolest riff I'd ever heard—over and over and over. Finally I shook myself out of slumber, got out a piece of staff paper, and charted it out." The result was the fantastic song we wrote that day, "Run Back to Mama," which became the first single from Bill's final album *Pure Music*. I joked back then that the writing royalties should be shared with the Audubon Society.

At another session Bill said with a straight face, "The next thing I want to write with you, Jim. I want to score the orgasm: the buildup— the rise—the climax—the fall—the detumescence—the slumber."

"Count me in," I said quickly.

I performed with Bill a mere week before his fatal plane crash at Faces, a great club on Chicago's famed Rush Street. In the now popular bootleg video of that night, after performing "Run Back to Mama" and "Love Is on the Way" with Bill and his dynamite band, as I'm leaving the stage Bill says into the mic, "Me and Jim are gonna be doing a lot together." Well, Bill—maybe in the next life.

So the name Survivor had many layers and was dense with personal meaning.

We rehearsed in a warehouse in Franklin Park at first. I brought many new songs to the party: "Travelin' Music," "Press On," "Kid Dynamite," "Chancy," "Music Machine" (which became "Boys with Guitars"), "Slipping Away," and "Love Has Got Me."

Rick Weigand, our soundman and crew chief, recorded these songs at rehearsal with the help of Joe Stopka and Larry Millas. These primitive two-track demos were our first recorded material.

But we still had not played out. In late 1978, I got a call from Rocko Reedy, a new acquaintance from the Pick Stop, the La Grange music shop where I bought strings and accessories. He and Tim Rozner, members of the student council at Lyons Township High School, asked me if the Jim Peterik Band would be interested in playing two shows in one day at the Reeber Center at L.T. They would pay us $1,500 for the two shows. I grabbed the chance immediately. Rocko went on to become Survivor's stage manager in our glory days, then became U2's tour manager to this day. Tim Rozner became one of the biggest rock show promoters in the country.

Here was an opportunity to introduce to the world (well, La Grange anyway!) this new juggernaut called Survivor. The posters screamed, *Appearing this Saturday for two big shows, Survivor! (formerly the Jim Peterik Band)*. I had the talented graphic artist Barb Weigand, Rick's sister, come up with our first logo, which featured my idea of a desperate hand reaching up on the letter "I."

Playbills were all over town. Still, all the glitz only encouraged about thirty-five people to come out to the three o'clock matinee. Nonetheless, we played our hearts out as if we were doing Madison Square Garden.

The eight o'clock show was markedly better with an audience of around a hundred. Frankie and I brought our "A" game, with a guitar duel from hell leading into the song "Music Machine." The harmony blend of me, Frankie, and Dave sounded like honey and the music chops of Dennis and Gary were dialed all the way up. The crowd went nuts. It's amazing how many people come up to me to this day and say, "I saw you guys at the Reeber Center and you were amazing!" I must have heard that from all 135 people since that day!

We were chuffed, off and running. With the confidence of that gig in my back pocket, I confidently booked time at Chicago Recording Company (CRC) to record our first real demo. This was to be our entry to a big label deal—the better the demo, the bigger the deal. I used my financial resources from my Schlitz Malt Liquor jingle to pay for the sessions.

At the engineering helm was Hank Neuberger, who was second engineer on my solo album. He learned just about every trick and technique Barry Mraz had to offer. His studio chops were sharp, having just recorded albums with Steve Goodman (*Banana Republic*) and John Prine (his famous *Bruised Orange* album).

We recorded the songs we felt strongest about: "Kid Dynamite," "Chancy," "Love Has Got Me," and the very song Frankie had so impressed me with by knowing it the first time he came over to my house, "Somewhere in America."

The sound was punchy, clear, and huge! It sounded like a master recording and we all knew it. I gave the mixed demo to my old co-manager, Bob Destocki, to "shop" to major labels. Unfortunately he soon had to get earplugs to dampen the sound of record company doors slamming coast to coast. It seemed no one wanted this Foreigner-wannabe rock band from Chicago. Even my old manager and producer, Frank Rand, over at Epic, saw no potential and "passed."

We continued polishing our live act to a fine luster at clubs such as Haymakers, in Wheeling, Illinois; Point East—just over the border in Indiana; Camel's Hump in Hanover Park; The Brat Stop in Kenosha, Wisconsin; The Thirsty Whale in Villa Park, Illinois; and, of course, perhaps the club where most people fell in love with Survivor, Studio One in Downers Grove.

We were building a big and boisterous following. We knew if we got a nibble from a label on our demo, that when they came in to see the band, our live act would seal the deal.

One day I received a call from Craig Aristei. Craig was my responsible agent at Warner/Chappell Publishing and a good friend and ally. He knew that the songs I'd write for Survivor would ultimately end up in Warner Brothers' pocket as publishing income and he would get to keep his high-paying position.

I had sent him the Survivor demo a few weeks earlier. He played it for a friend of his, a music-biz wannabe named John Simmonds, who had a direct connection with John Kalodner, the very high-profile A&R man for Atlantic Records. Kalodner's white suits, flowing beard, and nasal voice were already legendary even before his iconic appearance in the Aerosmith video for "Dude (Looks like a Lady)" where he appears in a full wedding dress. I remembered John

Survivor.

as the guy assisting the famous Jerry Greenberg at Atlantic Records back in '74 when I was in his office as Frank Rand presented me as Chalmers Garseny. (I had chosen that as my stage name and used it for one publicity shot and about five gigs before I realized I just wasn't a "Chalmers.")

Craig was looking for permission to "shop the tape" to labels on Survivor's behalf in exchange for an undisclosed finder's fee should he and his partner in crime, John Simmonds, land a deal. We took Bob Destocki off the case and put our faith in the new team.

It was then that I learned a lesson that I have never forgotten: It's not only the quality of the product that's being sold, it's who is selling it and how much urgency he can create that makes the difference between getting signed and total apathy. John Simmonds and Craig had this dog and pony show down to a high art.

After sending the tape to Kalodner, Simmonds created a feeding frenzy between two other labels to sign the band. Kalodner was first out of the gate, flying to Chicago to see Survivor live at the Studio

Instrument Rental's (S.I.R.) rehearsal studio on the near-north side of Chicago.

John arrived in the bitter cold Chicago winter and couldn't believe human beings actually lived there.

We had been rehearsing all week for his arrival. John Simmonds advised us to start the audition with Kalodner's favorite song on the tape, "Somewhere in America." I felt we needed one more undeniable song that was not on the tape to show him that we had even more goods than he had already heard. I had my hands full the day before John was to arrive, trying to convince the band to learn a new one that I had just written, "20/20."

"We got enough," said Frankie.

Everyone else nodded in total agreement.

I was my usual, persistent self. "Just give it a try, guys! What do we have to lose?"

Pulling teeth would have been easier, but gradually the band learned the song, kicking and screaming into the night. Frankie even added a very cool counterpart on rhythm guitar that fit like a puzzle piece into the chorus. When John arrived, he was limoed over to S.I.R. and stood before us like the judge and the jury.

After stiff introductions, we dutifully launched into "Somewhere in America." We could see his flowing beard nodding up and down in rhythm, making us suddenly much more at ease. Next we played "Love Has Got Me," which, like the first song, featured the co-singing of Dave Bickler and me. This time he almost smiled.

Next we did our epic, "Music Machine," which he didn't seem to react to in the same way. At this point, he said, "Well that's all fine, but I've heard all those on your demo. Do you have anything new?"

I looked around the room with a kind of "I told you so" expression on my face. We tentatively, but convincingly, played him "20/20." This time his beard was bopping, his face was aglow, and he actually stood up, and very awkwardly started dancing. The word "dancing" is a bit generous, as it looked more like a cross between a flail and a seizure.

When we finished the song, without letting a beat go by, he said, "Play it again." When we finished, he said, "Now play it again." It went on this way for five repetitions. After the fifth, he looked into the future and said, calmly, in that nasal whine, "I'm signing this band."

We were celebratory, slapping high fives all around and whooping and hollering. It was one of the greatest and most memorable moments of my life. We couldn't believe it. Our demo was passed over for six months. We really thought we didn't stand a chance. Now we are being signed by freakin' Atlantic Records—by the guy who signed our rock-and-role models, Foreigner!

"I'm taking you to Nick's Fish Market to celebrate!" Nick's, at the time, was the ultimate high-toned hang for the connected and wealthy. We cabbed it over and sat at a long table. I was positioned next to Kalodner. Dom Pérignon champagne was ordered (at $250 a bottle) and consumed by all except me and John Kalodner (so we bonded on that level, too).

I was sitting on a pile of equipment in the back of the van as we drove home, my head spinning from what had just taken place. Thoughts filled my head of whether I could handle the life that was up the road for me: the touring, the buses, the missing home, the sleep deprivation. I'd been there/done that and wondered, suddenly, what I was getting myself into again. But my overriding feeling was joy that my little fever dream had caught the attention of the biggest guy in the business—the star maker, John Kalodner.

With that thought filling my head, suddenly, a musical mood crept into my subconscious. I heard a lone acoustic, twelve-string guitar playing to no one through the night.

"On my own, with the moon and the stars in my eyes, I am blind. Can't recall where I am or what I did last night, though I try and I try—nothing can shake me from your love—it's true . . ."

"This is something," I said to myself. "I'm not sure what—but, boy, it sure has a vibe." This song, "Nothing Can Shake Me (From Your Love)," would wind up as one of the most played FM cuts from our soon-to-be-recorded debut album.

John called me a few days later to say the contracts were in the mail. He was signing us to a new label, a subsidiary of Atlantic Records called Scotti Brothers. At first, I was disappointed that we weren't joining the imprint of so many great artists on Atlantic: Aretha Franklin, Led Zeppelin, The Young Rascals, and many more.

But then he explained that Survivor would have a much better chance of breaking through on Scotti Brothers. He went on to say that for the last ten or so years, the Scotti brothers ran the number-one independent record promotion company in the world. These were the guys that all the labels went to, if they had enough cash, to make damn sure their records got on the radio.

Radio was king in those days and the Scottis, through their "connections" and often strong-arm techniques, could really get the job done. Now with their own label, they had a vested interest to go to the wall for their artists.

Kalodner had us convinced that we were doing the right thing by signing with the Scottis. Plus, we had the giant Atlantic network of distribution, which rivaled any other label. We confidently got together and signed the deal. Now began our search for the perfect producer to capture the sound that captured Kalodner. As it turned out, that would not be easy.

The Man behind the Music

IT WAS JANUARY 1978. Karen and I were cautiously excited as she kissed me and put me on the plane to Los Angeles. Kalodner had set up the West Coast wing of our auditions for various record producers who would be entrusted to capture the sound of his freshly minted rock stars.

Just the week before, we were sent to New York City to do a showcase at S.I.R. in Manhattan to play for iconic producer Tom Dowd (Allman Brothers, Aretha Franklin, Rascals).

Frankie and I also attended a session to meet Jimmy Douglass, who had just struck double platinum with Foreigner. This guy was bouncing off the walls—blowing out three sets of speakers in the three hours we observed, with distorted, ear-shattering playbacks. Not a fit.

There were other producers, as well, who paraded in and out of the cavernous soundstage—most of whom I knew only from having

8'-80

John Kalodner and Karen.

seen their names in album credits. We'd play three presentations of our five anchor tunes and shake hands, hoping to come off like we were cool rockers, but serious about what we did.

Los Angeles, though, was even more important to us. Frankie and I were holding court for two of our hero producers: Ron Nevison and Roy Thomas Baker.

Nevison was fresh off huge successes with Bad Company, The Babys, UFO, Led Zeppelin, and The Who. Roy Thomas Baker was gilded in platinum, having recently produced The Cars and Queen.

Yikes! It was unclear to me just who was auditioning for whom in these showcases, but for these two producers, I felt that we were truly the ones on trial. We were fresh meat on the auction block just trying to impress.

Ron pulled up in his pristine, cocoa brown Rolls-Royce. He was low-key, tanned, and conservatively dressed. He was good-looking and very articulate. He provided a stark contrast to his English counterpart.

Roy Thomas Baker floated in at around 3 p.m. with full entourage, dressed in a fluffy mohair sweater and a flowing scarf. "Where's my Dom Pérignon? I must have my Dom Pérignon!" were the first words out of his mouth. We shook his fey hand and hit the bandstand.

All the while, John Kalodner was mentally documenting the action with a studiedly detached demeanor; John never missed a thing. He was notating chemistry, musical comments and suggestions, and the overall attitude of the band toward the producer.

John had recently fired our first producer, Barry Mraz, when he came to rehearsal at my house a few weeks earlier and saw a distinct lack of progress in the songs. In fact, he thought Barry was well on the way to ruining what we already had (and I think he was right). Barry was overly and anally concerned about the little things—small word changes, tiny musical variations—that hardly mattered against the big picture of a major rock 'n' roll band. I remember John hanging up from a phone call in my La Grange living room, intoning calmly, but his eyes gleaming with a glint of maniacal power, "Mr. Mraz … is a memory."

There were also a few excruciating days at CRC when John Simmonds decided he was the only one who could produce the band. We would run through songs such as "Youngblood" and "Somewhere in America" as he cavorted though the studio hissing, "Come on, guys, make it sexxxxy!" through his nicotine-stained lips. Hopefully no one will ever hear the horrific results of these sessions.

At the producers' showcase Survivor went through the show complete with Rock Moves 101 and manufactured passion—real passion is in short supply at 3 p.m. in a sterile, gymnasium-sized room with thirteen industry suits in attendance. Still, a rugged determination shone deep in our eyes.

We started with "Somewhere in America," then "Love Has Got Me," "20/20," "Boys with Guitars," and finally "Rockin' into the Night." We played like our career depended on every riff—and maybe it did!

After the set we split up and worked the room, meeting and greeting the producers. John Alcock was also in attendance, fresh from Thin Lizzy fame, but we didn't really connect with him totally.

Roy Thomas seemed barely coherent and not all that into the best of what the Chicago suburbs had to offer, although he seemed to take a special interest in Frankie. It was Ron Nevison who caught our attention, most likely because we caught his attention—big time!

We huddled with Ron and Kalodner and talked songs, image, studios, and the future. We all clicked right away and Kalodner made the deal for Ron to produce our first album right then and there.

Having no ride to the hotel, Nevison volunteered to take me himself in his Rolls. Actually, I'm sure John had carefully engineered this to happen. This kind of thing—when I was singled out by someone in power as the head of this operation—planted the seeds of rebellion in Frankie's mind. These feelings were only to grow out of control as time went on.

We made small talk, and finally, in my typical Peterik earnestness I asked, "So what kind of sound do you hear for Survivor?"

He thought for a long second, then said, "Big."

Finally, back in La Grange, I told Karen that we had found the producer of our dreams and would be going to Los Angeles in two weeks to cut our first album. The Scotti brothers had rented us a house near Redondo Beach about a half block from the ocean. It would be about a forty-five-minute drive each day to the Record Plant Studios on 3rd and La Cienega. They also secured for us a broken-down Toyota to cram into. We would be getting a salary of $450 a week. Life was good. We smelled the big time and its scent was sweet. We couldn't wait to get started.

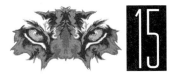

The Dream Gets Changed
on Its Way to Reality

WHEN I GOT HOME FROM L.A., I was brimming with enthusiasm and tales from the rock 'n' roll front. When I laid out my future to Karen, she looked at me sadly and said, "Jim, do you know what this band is going to do to us? You are entering into a five-way marriage. How can ours survive?"

She had a point. I assured her that nothing would change, that she would always be number one and that our relationship was strong enough to withstand long periods apart as I made records or toured.

"Besides, Karen, you have your interior design job to keep you occupied and inspired," I said. Karen had recently graduated from the top-rated Ray Vogue School of Design, and soon after landed a position at an established Park Ridge, Illinois, business.

Still, she really made me think. I could continue making a good living singing jingles and collecting royalties from the dwindling sales and airplay on "Vehicle." Easy, peasy—right?

Wrong. Something else was beckoning. I felt a fire in my belly to create something brand-new, a band that actually had staying power and would not splinter after one or two albums. It was as if I needed to make up for disbanding The Ides of March, perhaps prematurely. I had something to prove to myself. My ambition never rests—that was true even back then.

"Besides, Karen, you can always take off work and come visit me in Los Angeles or wherever we are recording or touring." She reminded me that she did not fit the mold of the clingy female whose main identity was as an appendage to her rock-star hubby.

She left me off at O'Hare airport as I began my three-month stint to make the first self-titled Survivor album. This was the one with actress Kim Basinger on the front cover wearing a wonderfully too-tight U.S. Air Force uniform, and us on the album's back, looking soiled and battered, as we posed in front of the smoking remains of a fighter jet.

Suddenly, Survivor was five very different people living under one roof on a miscellaneous beach in southern California. Damn. We really hardly knew each other. It was kind of like a blind date with destiny.

Added to that stew was Rick Weigand, our road manager and sound guy; the fella who brought Frankie and me together in the first place. Also around at that time was the mustachioed Sal Francese, Frankie's brother-in-law, who was our auxiliary guy for everything and anything that Rick couldn't or refused to cover, and Kevin Sullivan, Frankie's easygoing brother.

Throughout his years with us, Sal would cook us gourmet meals in the studio such as his amazing shrimp limone as well as doing jobs nobody else wanted.

We did preproduction at S.I.R. in Hollywood. We would arrive at around 11 a.m. and run through material. Ron Nevison would roll in with Mike Clink, his assistant and second engineer, at three. The first day I arrived with a bottle of rock and rye whiskey to nurse a sore throat. Later on Clink told me that, at the time, he and Ron saw that bottle and said, "He's gonna be the problem." Instead I turned out to be the sober one!

Ron would listen carefully to our material and make sage and constructive suggestions. He also knew when to leave a song alone, his ego not tied to how much he contributed. For instance, on "Youngblood" all he did was ask us to add two extra measures to set up the out-chorus. It was all that was needed.

On other numbers like "Can't Getcha Offa My Mind," he would turn a song upside down and inside out as together we explored practically every arrangement option possible.

I would be recording the very next week in one of the greatest studios ever with Bad Company's engineer at the helm. I was on a songwriting roll with the immediacy of this prospect.

When I would get back to the band house after preproduction, I would hit the Wurlitzer electric piano and try to extrude whatever I had been hearing in my head all day long. Many of the songs that were ultimately recorded for our debut album came about from this process: "Whatever It Takes," "As Soon as Love Finds Me," and "Whole Town's Talkin'." These are some of my favorites from the album, partly because we were all so excited and in the moment.

I actually presented "Whole Town's Talkin'" to Kalodner at a photo shoot. I sang it to him a cappella, but with such passion that I got the whole thing across. I remember Frankie shaking his head, not believing I had the balls to do this, much less selling the shit out of it—alone.

It was a fertile and creative time for the band. A powerful rocker that Dennis Johnson brought to the table for us to finish, "Freelance" was the first song we recorded when we finally moved our equipment into the Record Plant on 3rd Street.

This place was rock 'n' roll mecca complete with a hot tub room and other creative spaces specifically designed for orgies and drug use. Each recording console was equipped with razor blades for chopping cocaine and at least three boxes of Kleenex.

There was a pinball room frequented by The Eagles and Robin Williams (who always smelled as if he slept in the bowling shirt he always wore). The sky-lit corridors were inviting, as we'd listen to the strains of Blue Öyster Cult, who were recording in Studio B. I was in heaven!

When Ron asked us to come into the control room to hear the first playback of "Freelance," we could not have imagined the power and ear-shattering clarity of the sound that emanated from the giant Westlake monitor speakers.

The drums and bass were thundering. Our twin Marshall-powered guitars shredded the air, and Dave's scratch vocal sounded ragged, but right. Ron ran the playback at about 135 decibels, which is roughly the volume of a Boeing 747 taking off. Goose bumps doesn't cover what we were all feeling—it was more like a full-body eargasm.

That was the only track we cut that day, partially because Ron had taken time to do a shootout between the stalwart 3M analogue twenty-four-track tape transport and the newest innovation in audio, the 3M thirty-two-track digital recorder. It was the first of its breed and didn't even have all the bugs out of it yet. The differences were subtle but real.

The digital playback was crystal clear and as hard as a brick wall. The analogue version of the same performance was cushy, gushy, and gorgeous. We unanimously opted for the latter.

To this day, I prefer the sound of magnetic tape to the sterile precision of digital recording. It's like the difference between film and videotape, the film being a three-dimensional and romanticized illusion of life, while videotape bears the cold, sterile stamp of reality.

I would start each day the same way, getting up around 8 a.m. and heading down to the beach to jog along the Pacific Ocean, music and lyrics floating through my head as the beach girls and boys began to populate the sidewalks along the shore. There were roller skaters, cyclists, and other joggers jockeying for position against the diamond-encrusted sea.

At around 11 a.m., we all piled into the Toyota and drove down to "The Plant." After that first day, we would record two songs per day. At the end of each day at around 6 p.m., Ron would ritualistically

Ron Nevison at the board with Dennis Johnson
and Dave Bickler in the background.

line us up in front of the control room window and administer a
little wake-up snort of coke from his tiny silver spoon for the long
ride home.

Though I never partook, I noticed a certain camaraderie between
the guys as we battled freeway traffic. This was another case of my
not quite fitting in with the others. I was the odd man out. I remember one member saying that, once he had the money, he'd have coke
with him at all times. Unfortunately he was true to his word.

Kalodner would visit about twice a week to monitor our progress.
At first, he was very enthusiastic about the playbacks. He smiled
and rocked to and fro. He would always ask Ron for a rough mix of
whatever song we were working on that day and Ron, begrudgingly,
would usually acquiesce.

After a while, though, Kalodner seemed to get a bug up his ass
about the mixes he was taking home. He would present Ron with

numbered lists of mostly impossible requests such as: "On 'Free-lance' delete cymbal bell," which can't be done because the cymbals leak into every mic on the drum kit.

On John's naive suggestion, I added the incongruous, electric twelve-string intro on "Whole Town's Talkin'." He became very disenchanted with the drum sound, saying constantly, "Too much cymbals!" Indeed, there were a lot of cymbals, but this came part and parcel with the amazing live drum sound Ron was capturing. When Ron stopped listening, it became his kiss of death on this project. Now he could do no right.

When it came time for mixing the record, the record company sent everyone home except Frankie and me. Ron moved into one of the Record Plant's tiny mixing suites. Suddenly the sound seemed to shrink in proportion to the room size. I was a little freaked out.

By trying to give Kalodner what he was after, Ron seemed to be playing down the drum ambience tracks (the sound of the drums bouncing against Studio C's wonderful, live walls), while favoring the close mics on the drums. Suddenly the expansive sound turned claustrophobic. Frankie noticed it, too. It seemed as though Kalodner's meddling had finally taken its toll on Ron.

One lesson I learned in that period is: Don't give nontechnical people what they think they want. They often can't express what they are really looking for. Trust your own gut. At least then you have a fighting chance.

The new mixes pleased no one even though Ron gave John exactly what he was after. One afternoon, the axe came down and Ron was fired. We huddled with Kalodner as he told us he was entrusting the mixes to Bruce Fairbairn, the hot new producer who, along with super engineer, Bob Rock, was doing some amazing work from their Little Mountain Sound Studios in beautiful Vancouver, the very international city in British Columbia. This was well before Bruce's groundbreaking work with Aerosmith and Loverboy, but since his work with a Canadian group called Prism and Scotti Brothers' own Ian Lloyd, the good word was on the street.

We had to go along with the game plan, but neither Frankie nor I were happy. We had a loyalty and belief in Ron and felt he was being dealt a bad hand. If only he had been left alone we felt it could have been a monumental album.

John's first instructions to the Record Plant were to do a twenty-four-track to twenty-four-track transfer making an exact duplication of the multitrack. But… he had them erase (!) the ambience tracks in order to make two open tracks for any overdubs Fairbairn saw fit to do. Erasing ambience tracks is like drum castration. We were appalled at this plan to cut off the balls of our sound. Still, we had little to say about it. John was the boss.

The real nail in the coffin came when Kalodner announced that only I would be flying up to Vancouver to help with the final mixes. This further exacerbated the growing fissure between Frankie and me, and put a lot of undue pressure on me to deliver great mixes on a flawed multitrack.

I got along great with Bruce and Bob Rock. Fairbairn was one of the most organized producers I had ever met, with an erasable board where he would post each day's objectives in different colored markers. It's no wonder that many drugged-out rock bands came to rely on him for the only shred of order in their lives.

We would complete one mix a day. The stuff was sounding pretty good, but far from the sound of the supersonic playbacks when we were cutting the tracks. With no drum ambience, the drums sounded tiny and artificial. Bob tried to gussy it up with reverb and echo, even triggering the snare drum with white noise to add the missing sizzle, but nothing could replace the precious sounds that were lost.

I came home with an acetate of the mixes, after which the firing squad (the rest of the band) filled my living room for the playback session. Scowls and silence were all I saw and heard. Dennis provided the only glimmer of positivity, saying he thought all of it was passable except for "Let It Be Now."

On this mix Bruce tried out a brand-new digital delay unit and, instead of using it on just one or two instruments, he put it on the entire two-track mix! It sounded really bad.

This ill-advised mission became the first real conflict in the band. Suddenly I was villainized as the guy who ruined our first album— Kalodner's little brown-nosed yes-man.

Hell, without my songwriting, funding, and connections, there wouldn't have been a first album! Cut me some slack, Jack! It seemed like the end was coming before we even had a chance to begin. My authority and credibility suffered a blow that I don't think I ever quite recovered from in Frankie's eyes. I found out at that time that there is a very fine line between a hero and a bum.

16

Living for a Dream

BACK HOME, KP seemed to be holding her own, busy with her job at the interior design firm. I would update her practically daily from a phone booth near the band house. But extended separation like this is nobody's friend and she was drawing closer and closer to her work partner. They did everything together mostly by job description. This worried me a bit, but I was on a mission, so I ignored any threats to the sanctity of our marriage. Plus, I thought (incorrectly) that he was gay.

After what seemed like forever, approximately four months after its completion, the album was released in January of 1980. Talk about the quintessential '80s band! Sitting in my infamous kitchen I suddenly heard, "You're listening to WLUP-The Loop here in Chicago. Here is the brand-new one from our local favorites. You may have heard this one already at one of the clubs. Survivor, with 'Somewhere in America.'"

I can't say this moment ranks with hearing "Vehicle" on the radio for the first time on I-55 back in '70, but it was pretty damn cool. The mix didn't sound half as bad as I feared. Maybe now I'd be vindicated.

Our first promotional date was playing the gigantic Loop Fest at the now defunct Chicago Amphitheater. We were headlining with local support by many up-and-coming Chicago acts including the soon-to-be-knighted (by Kalodner) Off Broadway.

That band was a stick up my ass ever since the tale drifted down that lead singer, Cliff Johnson had said, in the *Illinois Entertainer* (we called it the "Illinois Exaggerator"), that we were just an over-commercialized pop confection—not the real thing.

We killed that night. The whole Scotti Brothers team was there: Ben and Tony Scotti, label manager, Johnny Musso, and a cast of others. They took me and Frankie out to a posh Italian dinner before the show (the table looked like a Cosa Nostra farewell party). We were "their boys"—part of "the family" (wink wink!). They told us they would kill for us. This turned out to be a very real possibility.

We felt secure and totally valued. I must say it was a good feeling, no matter what side of the law the Scottis were on. Tales abounded about the former professional quarterback Ben Scotti holding one legendary radio programmer out of a high-rise window by his ankles until he agreed to add the latest Alan O'Day single. Most of these urban legends were true—and now the Scottis were ours! How could we lose? Their methods went against my personal ethics, but after years of being the low man on the totem pole with Warner Brothers and RCA Records, I was more than happy to go along with any method the Scottis employed for getting Survivor on the radio…as long as I didn't have to do the dirty work myself—kind of like hiring a "hit man" (pun intended).

We rocked for the Chicago faithful that night—the legions of fans that had suffered in long lines to see us in some shithole 18 bar in Kenosha (thus called because eighteen was the legal drinking age in Wisconsin). This show was for those who were starting to jam the Loop-line with requests for "Somewhere in America" and "20/20."

Popular shock jock Mitch Michaels (he liked to say, on-air, "I want you to chug an entire six-pack of beer, right now, and blow lunch!") gave us the big show introduction: "And now, Loop fans, the band you've all been waiting for, give it up for Chicago's own: Survivor!"

The place went up for grabs. The Rolling Stones couldn't have generated more excitement. We were Chicago's sons, the city with big shoulders' personal creation. In the audiences' mind, they had made us—and maybe they were right.

We started with the stately, flanged guitar intro to "Boys with Guitars" with Frankie wailing lead. The lights swirled and tension mounted, soon leading to the Aerosmith-ian guitar riff I'd play at the top of the actual song. These tunes, though unknown to most of the country, were all familiar to this crowd, who reacted to them as if they were already double platinum. Not bad for stage morale!

Finally, we ended with the local radio hit, "Somewhere in America," as the entire audience swayed and sang along with the chorus: "Somewhere in America—somewhere cross the sea—uh oh—Somewhere in America—she waits for me-ee!" Bickler was really screaming on key that night!

That show was a total triumph for Survivor. We flew off stage into the waiting arms of the Scotti brothers who hugged us hard and assured us they would take us all the way, no matter what it took; that they would stay with us for the long haul. At that moment, we were made men.

That year, 1980, was really all about building the Survivor brand. We were pretty much out of the clubs—at least for the time being (except for a promotional club run supported by the label on the East Coast)—doing opening slots for Kansas, Triumph, and Jefferson Starship.

By this time, 38 Special was starting their ride up the charts with a song originally meant for the first Survivor album, "Rockin' into the Night." At one session for our album, Kalodner begged Ron Nevison for a rough board mix of the song we had been working on that day: "Rockin' into the Night." This song had been a staple in our live show and one that really got the audience revved up.

A few weeks later, Nevison decided that the song did not really fit the rest of the material on the album, being a bit too bluesy—too southern. With that cue, John Kalodner slipped the rough cassette to his pal, Mark Spector, who managed an up-and-coming group out of Jacksonville. They were named 38 Special, after the caliber of the gun.

After they had just mastered their third album, Spector dropped off this song with them. He asked them to listen to it, and to consider stopping the presses and cutting this song for the already completed album.

They cut the shit out of it, using our rough cassette as their road map. Lead singer, Don Barnes, even got some of the words wrong due to the vocal being buried in the mix on the Survivor take.

The lyric leading up to the solo should have been, "And in the morning light we'll be rolling," but for time and tide it will always be "And it's more than that, yeah, it's more than that." Instead of the correct "and we went rocking into the night," it became "and we were…"

So here we were on the road, fighting for a hit, watching the song that should have been ours rocking up the hit parade. Somehow, I was held accountable by the band, perhaps because of my close relationship with John Kalodner. I'm sure Frankie thought that I colluded with him to get the tape to Spector. Truth is, I knew nothing about it 'til I heard it on the radio.

I will never forget the night we opened for the Starship in Springfield, Missouri. The auditorium was packed and the audience started demanding an encore after our high-energy set.

At the side of the stage I said, "Let's do 'Rockin' into the Night.'" This song had been our standard encore.

Frankie flat-out refused. "No way I'm playing that fucking 38 Special song."

Now that it was a hit for 38 Special, I'm sure he felt we would be promoting them, not us. But this was no time for rumination and speculation. The crowd wanted more. Unfortunately, except for "Rockin'," we were out of songs. Except for one.

We had just worked up a new song of mine called "Rebel Girl." This one just dropped down from heaven, and I somehow convinced the band to learn it as the possible flagship song for our next album.

Survivor rocks around the dock at Chicagofest.

From the downbeat it felt like a hit. (Gary Smith received a writer's credit for suggesting the title, "Rebel Girls." Frankie received a credit for changing "Rebel Girls" to the singular.)

As we huddled in the wings, I shouted, "Let's do that new one, 'Rebel Girl.'" No one resisted, so we took the stage and exploded with it. "Out on the edge of night—in any city you can name—there rides the Rebel Girl—the wild one no one dared to tame—and the light—in her eyes—is a fire."

The Springfield crowd rocked to "Rebel Girl" like it was already a hit. We came off stage, sweaty and triumphant. Waiting for us, backstage, was a promo man from Atlantic Records, the label that distributed Scotti Brothers product.

"Man, that last song rocks! Why isn't that one on the album?" I told him we had just written it and that it would go on the next one.

The next day I get a call from the big man himself, Tony Scotti. "I heard about that song you encored with last night. I want you guys in the studio tomorrow to cut it. If it's as strong as this guy says, I want to re-press the album and include it."

What? That sounded pretty crazy, even to me, but two days later we dutifully dragged our gear over to Pumkin Studios to lay it down. I originally sang the verses, thinking it was too low for Dave. After we cut the track, Frankie suggested, "Dave, why don't you try the lead vocal on the verse?" Well I had to admit he sounded fantastic. But this sort of thing started a trend where I'd be aced out of vocal after vocal to suit Frankie's vision of the band. Kalodner was always disappointed, too, at these decisions, envisioning a band with two lead singers.

We sent the mixed acetate to the Scottis. They flipped over the song, but felt it needed help in the production and editing department. They flew us to Los Angeles to work with some fey joker named Robie Porter who had a bunch of big hits in his native Australia.

He proceeded to line the floor of the studio control room with miles of two-inch tape as he attempted various edits of the song. We hated every minute of this process. He made Frankie put on some corny extra leads. He had Bickler rasp the screaming high notes that lead into every chorus. (Actually that was kinda cool.)

When it was done, "Rebel Girl" was two minutes, thirty-five seconds, of super compressed, over the top, pop and roll. I'm not sure what it was, but, boy was it ever wired, wacky, and weird.

Chicago was on it immediately, of course. The Loop was playing the song every two hours. The phones were lighting up. Every girl in town felt that she and she alone was the Rebel Girl. We had struck a major chord. Popular jock Steve Dahl started spinning it constantly at his 50,000-watt Detroit station. Other stations started to follow suit. One problem—it wasn't on the album!

The Scottis hastily pressed up singles and made plans to re-press the debut album to include this one. The trouble was that Scotti Brothers Records was changing record distributors after a dispute with Atlantic and was making a new deal with Epic.

Well, certainly, Atlantic wasn't going to press up and distribute records if they were no longer involved, and Epic was not yet in place.

"Rebel Girl" died on the vine. It never became the hit that everyone had predicted. The 45 and especially the big twelve-inch single became instant collector's items. I wish I had a nickel for every time someone says, "'Rebel Girl' is my all-time favorite Survivor song. Where can I find a copy?"

Eventually, the song was included in the Japanese pressing of the first album, but most significantly both "Rebel Girl" and the original rough mix of "Rockin' into the Night" were finally rescued from the vaults, remastered, and included on the *Ultimate Survivor* compilation released in 2004. I am forever grateful to Jeremy Holiday of Sony Legacy, who spearheaded that release and did the interviews for the comprehensive liner notes. For the first time, fans got to hear the Survivor version of "Rockin' into the Night," the very song that started the hemorrhage of bad blood between me and Frankie.

The Currency of Love Changes Hands

NOW WITH SURVIVOR'S debut album in stores and on the radio, it wasn't long before we were doing shows coast to coast, opening up for Jefferson Starship, featuring a guy that would go on to become a good friend and sing background vocals on *Vital Signs*, Mickey Thomas. We were in awe of his clear, soulful tenor voice. I realized then that this was the voice we all heard on Elvin Bishop's hit "Fooled Around and Fell in Love" a few years earlier. It wasn't Elvin singing after all!

We also opened for Triumph, always noticing that the drummer and bass player acted more like managers than rock stars. It was on these shows that I started an enduring friendship with their lead guitarist, Rik Emmett, who is now a frequent guest at my World Stage shows, as is Mickey.

But for me the road was a place to nurture new songs. We were renting a horrible bus. This thing had to have been from the '40s. The bunks were like little coffins. My way of coping with it all was to immerse myself in the creative process. It has always been that way for me; when my parents were fighting, I would hide in a song. I truly believe if it wasn't for my ability to escape into songwriting I'd have become hooked on drugs or in some loony bin weaving baskets. It was and is that much of an oasis from the barren world of the road and a better high than any cheap euphoria.

One afternoon on the bus en route to a show, Frankie complained to me, "Jim, you're always so damn happy. What's with you? Can't you see the shit we are going through right now?" I told him that the superficial stuff really didn't matter to me. I had my faith in God, my wife back home, and my songs to keep me warm. I don't know if it got through to him at the time, but I'll bet he gets it now.

Though we were receiving airplay on a few of the tracks, most notably "Somewhere in America," "20/20," and "Nothing Can Shake Me (From Your Love)," the album, in part due to the "Rebel Girl" fiasco, suffered from a failure to launch. A third single was never issued and soon we were back playing at the Thirsty Whale, B'ginnings, The Night Gallery, and Haymakers in our hometown.

The good news was that while other bands had to scrape together songs for their sophomore album, I had already written a bunch for the next Survivor record. This was a time when groups would often put out two albums a year.

Before we knew it, John Kalodner had us in rehearsals for our second album. It was not yet the carpet warehouse where we'd later shed for the *Eye of the Tiger* and *Vital Signs* albums; it was another nondescript warehouse in Franklin Park. It was here that I showed the band a new one I had started at the Journey show I attended with Karen and Kalodner a few weeks earlier. When the pocket lighters came out while they played their song "Lights," as I was basking in the reflected glow of Bics and admiration, I grabbed my pocket cassette recorder and sung the chorus to what became "Light of a Thousand Smiles." It's moments like these that have always spawned my best songs—the spontaneous combustion of circumstance meeting creativity.

It was in this warehouse that Frankie very tentatively showed me a verse for a song he was writing called "Summer Nights." I was unaccustomed to Frankie offering songs in such a well-formed state; usually he contributed riffs and grooves. I really dug this song seed and as I drove home that day a huge chorus just popped into my head. This idea I came up with worked so well both lyrically and musically because the key of the song shifted upward when the chorus hit, lifting it big time.

I excitedly called Frankie when I got home. When I really believe in an idea I am never at a loss for powerful adjectives and descriptions. "Dude, you know that verse you showed me? Well I got the chorus of a lifetime to go with it. This could be our first number one!" I sang it over the phone: "I still remember those—summer nights—all night- dancing in the light of love—summer night—so right—couldn't last beyond September … "

"Cool, man," said Sullivan nonchalantly. "I'll come over tomorrow."

In spite of his casual tone, I could tell he was as excited as I was.

I had some extra motivation to write some great new songs that would put Survivor on the charts. Here was 38 Special having success with a song meant for our band. Even though I had nothing to feel guilty about, I was determined to exonerate myself in the band's eyes by creating some hits for Survivor.

When John Kalodner came into town to hear the new crop of songs for the next Survivor record we had a few good ones ready to play: "Light of a Thousand Smiles," "Summer Nights," "Missing Persons," "Live with Me Tonight," and one that Frankie wrote on his own and sang himself, "Sweet Candy."

John was particularly taken with "Light of a Thousand Smiles" and "Summer Nights" and sent us to CRC to record demos of these songs the following week. Hank Neuberger was again in the engineer's chair with Frankie taking a more and more active role right next to him at the console.

As we recorded, Frankie and I did our best to guide our rhythm section into a more streamlined rock groove. The trouble with musicians with jazz roots is that they actually play too much. Gary Smith would add complex drum fills to nearly every break. Dennis Johnson, although a gifted player, refused to just "lay it down" simply and in support of the song. I told Dennis to "play every other note." In addition, Frankie seemed to hold something personally against Gary (I never found out just what it was) and wanted him gone for reasons other than musical.

At the next band meeting at 823 Stone, it fell to me to wield the hatchet. "We have decided to move forward without the both of you" was the way I worded it. Gary and Dennis showed very little emotion, almost as if they had been expecting it.

When they left, Frankie and I looked at each other with a sense of relief. This look soon turned to panic when we realized the daunting task ahead of us of finding a game-changing rhythm section to take their place.

Dave Bickler, Frankie Sullivan, Sal Francese, and I headed out to Los Angeles the following week to find and audition players to fill Dennis and Gary's shoes. Kalodner had come up with a bass player he thought might fit the bill—Bruce Turgon, longtime crony of Lou Gramm. But when we jammed at S.I.R. the magic just wasn't there. We tried out different combinations of bassists and drummers for a few days with nothing that felt or sounded remotely like a fit.

Finally, exhausted, our good friend and Chicago expatriate Fergie Frederiksen (a rock veteran of Trillion, Probe, and, one day, Toto), suggested we just chill out one evening and hang this whole audition thing out to dry for the night. "I'm gonna take you guys over to Flipper's Roller Disco. It's this crazy place on the corner of Santa Monica and La Cienega where you can watch all these babes skate around in their little short skirts—maybe even pick something up for yourself." Soon we were jammed into Fergie's jalopy, riding over to Flipper's.

I have to admit, it was a wild scene full of hot girls in tiny skirts. But ever the realist, what I noticed immediately was a rock band playing in the middle of the rink. They were called Baxter and they were playing some really solid original music. The bass player was a standout: he had a good rock look, played a Fender P-Bass, and more importantly he was just "laying it down." Nothing fancy, just solid slabs of stringy, edgy bass. I also noticed he played with a pick and was obviously influenced by Chris Squire of Yes.

Frankie turns to me and says, "That's the kind of bass player we need."

My rejoinder was, "How 'bout that very bass player?"

I waited for the band to take a break, then I dodged, bobbed, and wove through the rushing, skating bodies 'til I got to the center. "I like your playing!" I said to the bass man, who introduced himself as Stephan Ellis. "I know you're in a band but would you consider coming down to S.I.R. tomorrow morning to audition for my band, Survivor?"

Stephan looked at me blankly. I don't think he had ever heard of the band, but he said he would be there. I told him we had a record deal with Atlantic Records. This really got his attention. He mentioned that he had just auditioned for The Babys but there was not enough "pixie dust" for him to get the gig. I added that Marc Droubay, a drummer that Frankie had jammed with in Chicago a few years back, would be auditioning as well. But I didn't mention that when Frankie contacted him a few weeks earlier, Marc answered the phone in his telemarketer persona, which had been his job at the time.

Everyone showed up promptly at 9:30 a.m. at the Studio Instruments Rental in Hollywood. I met Marc for the first time and felt comfortable with his easygoing personality from the get-go. When I shook Stephan Ellis's hand, though, I couldn't help but notice the distinct smell of beer on his breath. *Kind of early for that*, I thought to myself. I made a mental note of that as we set up our gear.

The song that we used to test the new players' mettle was a new one I wrote called "Hearts of Stone." When we tried it with other rhythm sections over the last few days, the song just lay there in a soggy heap. I started to question whether this song really had what it took.

So tight—so hot—so right... Survivor hits the stage
with Stephan Ellis and Marc Droubay.

Today was different. *D—A—G—*"Hearts of stone—ba- ba- ba- are the first to crumble." I looked at Frankie—Frankie looked at Dave—holy shit—it was so tight—so hot—so right.

That very day our new best friends were making plans to move to Chicago to be members of Survivor. On the ride back to our hotel Frankie and I were quiet and reflective, kind of like "Okay, here we go. Don't know where this ride is taking us but we're in it for the long haul so hold on tight." It felt like the proposed title of our soon-to-be-recorded album, *Premonition*. We saw the good to come but we also saw the pain and struggles ahead of us. I personally saw my original power base slipping further away as Frankie's old pal Marc Droubay took the place of my Chase buddy Gary Smith. But the sound of what I had just heard at S.I.R. made every potential doubt disappear. The band sounded right. We had found the engine that would propel us to the top of the charts. Against all odds we decided we were ready to take on every challenge.

In that moment Survivor as the world came to know it was born.

Don't Lose Your Grip

"MY HENCHMAN." That's what Scotti Brothers label manager Tony Scotti called Johnny Musso—and for good reason.

Johnny was a believer in Survivor and even more specifically in Jim Peterik, to the core—so much so that he decided to let Frankie and me produce our second album, *Premonition*. Bless his heart.

Having "the lunatics run the asylum" was practically unheard of at that time. Power was usually shifted to one of the heavy-hitter producers, such as those we had held court for not even a year earlier.

Johnny loved our demos. He actually preferred our demo version of "Somewhere in America" to the committee-produced version that finally got released.

Frankie and I were like two kids let loose in a musical candy store once we discovered all the great Los Angeles studios we could choose from. We finally settled on a fairly new complex in the sleepy L.A.

suburb of Canoga Park called Rumbo, which was owned by the Captain (Darryl Dragon) of Captain and Tennille (Toni Tennille)—the married duo that made famous the Neil Sedaka/Howard Greenfield tune, "Love Will Keep Us Together."

We were impressed by Studio A's sheer size and the vintage Neve 8088 console. Knobs and faders and blond maple stretched for twenty feet leading to twin Studer A800 multitrack machines synchronized to create forty-eight wonderfully warm and dimensional analogue tracks. This was and, perhaps, still is the best-sounding recording console ever produced.

The walls were covered in exotic woods and a nautical theme ran throughout, complete with a diving bell isolation booth to cater to "the Captain's" taste.

Unfortunately, on the first day we were to record, Frankie, the late Phil Bonanno (the engineer we had brought from Chicago, who had cut many of our previous demos), and I discovered that the cavernous studio "A" recording room was an acoustically dead environment.

Me and Phil Bonanno.

Rather than renege on the sweet deal we had made with Rumbo, we walked around the spacious premises banging on a snare drum, like two madmen on parade, hoping to find a space that resonated with the ambience we required for the sound we heard in our heads.

It had to go *Bang-Snap!*—like a bullet ricocheting off of an abandoned building, not *Bang-Plop*—like a spoon hitting your morning oatmeal.

Frankie and I were both greatly influenced by the drum sounds on the Led Zeppelin albums, which were heavy with ambience and compression. And we also loved the drum sound that Ron Nevison got on Bad Company's debut disc, specifically on the cut "Can't Get Enough of Your Love."

Our banging quest led us to two areas: the long, narrow hallway that led from the front door to the studio itself, and to the wood-clad kitchen.

The Captain was none too thrilled, though, when we informed him we would not be recording drums in his "acoustically perfect" studio, but instead impeding day-to-day business in the hallway and kitchen.

The first day of tracking we set up the drums at the very end of the hallway facing the outside door. The snare sounded like a cannon—in other words, just right! Marc's kit barely fit width-wise. When you listen to the first song we cut, "Runway Lights," you can hear that magical hallway.

But the next day, the studio personnel put their foot down. "People have to be able to enter the front door!" crowed the Captain. We moved the drums into the kitchen, positioning them back against the massive stove and brushed aluminum hood. The sound was even better here than in the hall: crisp, cracking with a woody ambience that was pure, unadulterated rock 'n' roll (if there is such a thing).

The drum sound we achieved defined the overall mood of *Premonition*, coloring the sound of all the other instruments. It was raw and right. We were breaking the mold and we didn't care. This was not going to be a slick, Hollywood studio sound. This was destined to be "refined garage."

In the previous weeks before we hit Rumbo, we rehearsed at S.I.R. We were right down the hall from Tom Petty and the Heartbreakers, becoming fast friends with them all, especially the late Howie Epstein.

It was a creative environment, to say the least, with our driving new rhythm section kicking our asses to come up with the toughest rock of our careers.

Out of that hard-rock petri dish came "Love Is on My Side," "Take You on a Saturday," "Chevy Nights," and the song that very soon would catch the ear of Sylvester Stallone, "Poor Man's Son."

Much like the transformation of "Chevy Nights," which went from singer/songwriter fare to hard rock due to Frankie's guitar riff and arranging skills, Dave's urgent rasp, and Marc and Steph's attack, "Poor Man's Son" became something much tougher than I had originally envisioned. This was a band working on all cylinders with a turbo charger bolted on for good measure.

The tracking went smoothly; we typically nailed a track or two a day. When the recording was done and it was time to mix, the Scottis called a meeting. They told us we had to mix at their studio on Pico Boulevard. We rolled our eyes in unison. Although not a hole in the wall, the studio was still a far cry from the divinity that was Rumbo.

Begrudgingly we relocated to the rundown section of Santa Monica. The Scottis had booked us into a motel frequented by drug dealers and hookers. There were literally gunshot holes in the walls and a colony of deceased locusts around the picture tube of the black-and-white television. To make matters worse, in the studio we were assigned the Scotti Brothers' staff engineer, Tony Papa.

Tony was a decent engineer for the likes of other acts on the Scotti roster: Susan Anton, The Cuff Links, and someone who was to enter the picture soon, Frank Stallone. But Survivor bore no resemblance to any of these acts. We were from the mean streets of Chicago—full of spit and grit.

Finally, after two days of fruitless mixing and our nonstop bitching, the Scottis relented and we were reinstalled cross town once again at Rumbo. We felt like newly freed convicts as we blasted our new music through the giant Westlake speakers.

I came back to Chi-Town exhausted, but triumphant. We had created a brand with this record, leaps and bounds over the tentative steps of the first one.

Survivor went back to the clubs and waited and waited...and waited for the record to come out. I'd speak to Johnny Musso every week. "Johnny—Jimbo. When's this thing coming out? Is it even coming out?" He would assure me that their deal was still being set up with Epic Records, their new distributor.

Then one day, Johnny called and I detected a different tone in his voice. "Some of the new guard over at Epic aren't thrilled with the record. They are calling for a remix. We have two guys ready to help you, Artie Kornfeld and Artie Ripp. You'll be mixing at Ripp's Fidelity Studio in the valley. It's really state of the art with an MCI console and..."

By this time, I was not listening. My mind whirled like a Rolodex gone wild as I scrolled through my memory banks as to why the invocation of these two Artie's names set my hair on fire.

As Johnny prattled on, I suddenly recalled an exposé I had recently seen on CBS's award-winning news magazine, *60 Minutes*. The piece was about a Hollywood mogul/artist manager who had just been accused of ripping off singer/songwriter Billy Joel for millions of dollars of publishing money.

The man's name was Dickensian: Artie Ripp. The footage showed an uncomfortable interview with the silk-ascotted, sunglassed Ripp, sartorially perched behind the wheel of his cream-and-red Excalibur Cabriolet replica, spouting phrases like "No comment. Speak to my counsel." And, "I did nothing illegal. I made Billy who he is today. If it wasn't for me..."

As Johnny continued, I thought of another interview I'd recently seen featuring one of the founding fathers of the Woodstock music festival: Artie Kornfeld. It was on the anniversary of that particular festival of peace and love that Artie got to ramble on about how he had made it all happen. His frizzed-out hair and ragged vintage tie-dye T-shirt were sheer acid-casualty chic. "Yeah man, I did Woodstock, man! I'm a star today," he murmured, his eyes darting like a pinball machine gone mad.

As I put the phone down, I realized that we were putting our sacred songs, hell, our future, into the hands of these two characters. When Johnny went on to suggest that they would also like to manage Survivor, I felt trapped. I felt like we had to cooperate with our record company's plan. Fidelity turned out to be basically a rundown hole in the wall, but with the expert help of Phil Bonanno, Frankie and I did the final mixes that you hear today on *Premonition*.

Karen had long since stopped counseling me in business matters, but she couldn't help but notice my increasingly skittish behavior around the house. I was boarding a runaway train and I could see no way of getting off.

Storm upon the Skyline

WHEN FRANKIE AND I worked together toward a common goal, we were an unstoppable force. But when we pulled in opposite directions, it was a nightmare. This particular era saw both sides of the duality of Peterik-Sullivan in play.

Frankie and I had talked the two Arties out of their first promo idea for *Premonition*. Artie Kornfeld, in his extreme Brooklynese accent, called me on the phone one day. "Me and Tony Scotti have been talking. You guys are going on a tour of high schools across the country. The slogan will be 'Put your heart and can on the line!' It's for the poor, get it? The kids bring a can of food to gain entrance to the Survivor concert. Brilliant! Right?"

I was speechless. My dream was to tour the world with a major recording act playing sheds and stadiums—not to collect cans in high school cafeterias.

We had gone from the frying pan into the fire. The band had just gotten out of our first, disastrous management deal with John Simmonds, who brought Kalodner into the picture and helped make our record deal with the Scotti Brothers—we would eventually pay him sixty grand to go away. We had been coerced into signing that contract on a Sunday without benefit of legal counsel.

Now we were with the Arties. Again, label pressure made us feel we were beholden to sign with these bozos. Now we were supposed to "Put our heart and can on the line!"

We finally talked them out of the "can" idea and soon we were out on the road opening for Kansas, Triumph, and Cheap Trick. I was mainly relegated to playing keyboards for the first time in my career. I considered myself a guitarist, a lead singer, and a front man with a knack for revving up the crowd. With The Ides of March, this had always been my role and that role defined me.

Part of my new role on keys had to do with the new route our songwriting had taken. Perhaps influenced by the keyboard-heavy sound of the times I was composing more and more on the keyboard.

But there were other reasons for my instrument shift. In subtle and some not-so-subtle ways, Survivor was being molded into Frankie's vision of the band. "Uh, ya know that intro part you do on 'Missing Persons'? It would sound like way better on keyboard." Though John Kalodner had signed us in part because of our two-guitar, two-lead-singer concept, Frankie wanted none of this. And now that his buddy Marc Droubay had been installed on drums, my seat of power was drifting even further and further away.

I would get withering and angry glances from Frank if I moved around too much or stood too close to the front of the stage. I didn't dare come near him on the few songs that I still played guitar on. There could only be one star guitarist, and it sure wasn't me.

When I'd come into the control room, I'd catch Frankie entertaining the rest of the band with a disrespectful caricature of me singing "Vehicle."

One day, before Marc's total brainwashing by Frank, I saw him humorously writing: *Pete—Trick—Pete—Trick—Pete—Trick* on the dressing room's chalkboard to mimic the Cheap Trick logo gimmick. I loved it! This was too cozy for Frank; he angrily erased the lettering.

So there I was: the guy who named the band, paid for the logo design, and financed all the demos that got us signed.

I was the guy with the connections, the guy who already had a million seller, and I was virtually under the thumb of this brash kid from Franklin Park! If I spoke too long setting up a song, Frankie would say sternly, into the mic, "Peterik, shut the fuck up and play the song!" How did I let this happen? People shake their heads and wonder—I wonder sometimes myself.

All I can say, in my personal defense, is that a guy like me can only take so much negative reinforcement before he starts to modify his own behavior. I wanted peace in the band. I craved success. I caved to Frankie because I knew it was the only way it could possibly work. It was the only way to keep him from stalking out of the room, as he liked to do when he didn't approve of the conversation.

It was either: *can* Frankie or live with Frankie. I knew I could not fire him. We had an unmistakable magic that we somehow created together (a team of rivals, as it were). Because he was so hard to please, he became my challenge—the person I most wanted to please. So I contorted my personality to fit.

I could see Frankie already had Marc wrapped around his little finger. Stephan just kind of went along in his Carlo Rossi haze, and Dave Bickler was too busy romancing girls on the road to care much about band politics.

Dave didn't just get laid. He'd actually fall in love with someone new every night, walking hand in hand with her blissfully through the hotel lobby the morning after the night before.

Stephan, on the other hand, would send his one night stand "out for ice" after the deed was done and then lock her out of the room when she returned with the bucket. "Out for ice" became band code for getting rid of an unwanted guest.

I would try and keep Karen in the loop of my musical life, but no matter how hard I tried, it seemed as if she and I were drifting further and further apart.

As I prepared for the upcoming tour to promote *Premonition*, she, again, wondered why I couldn't just stay home and sing jingles for a living. She was also starting to lose respect for me. Karen felt I was weak for letting Frankie, in essence, take over the band.

"Frankie's got you in his back pocket, Jim! What happened to you?"

I was no longer the confident band leader she first met and fell in love with. Frankie was hurting my position both in the band and at home. I was even losing respect for myself, too. Suddenly I didn't feel supported by either my band or my wife, which made it easier for Frankie to wear me down.

Karen was spending practically her whole week working side by side with her co-designer at the interior design firm. They had lunches together—sometimes dinners, after working late.

On weekends, I was playing shows, but I had little time to ponder this disconnect. I also had a career to run.

Meanwhile, in my new role as wooden Indian on keyboards, I made the most of my diminished stage presence by pouring myself further into the songwriting process. While the others were skirt chasing or freebasing (some of the guys graduated from doing a few lines of blow to pulling all-nighters smoking cocaine), I was on reconnaissance missions in the cool sections of whatever town we were in, after the show, equipped with my notebook and pocket cassette, just documenting life.

I also learned early on that unless I included Frankie in the writing of a song, it hardly stood a chance of being worked out by the band. But if Frankie was involved in any way with a song, he would rally behind it and market it to the other guys like Procter & Gamble.

I got Frankie involved in the writing process of countless songs that I could have easily finished on my own. This is not to say that he didn't bring his own sensibility and rock intensity to everything we worked on together. The best thing he brought to the writing table was a fairly infallible barometer of uncool and cool, commercial and uncommercial. If one of my chord changes was too unconventional, it was homogenized.

From left to right: Larry Stessel, Cliff O'Sullivan, Frankie Sullivan, me, Marc Droubay, and Artie Ripp.

Today when people ask me how I let this kid take over the band, I tell them the truth: For better or for worse, this is how the cards were dealt and the way it had to be—even the way it was meant to be.

The first single from *Premonition*, "Summer Nights," was Top 5 in Chicago, but stalled at 62 on the *Billboard* chart. The second single, "Poor Man's Son," did considerably better.

But that song did much more than graze the *Billboard* Hot 100. It opened up the ears of Sylvester Stallone when he heard our raw, honest sound.

The following Survivor album could not have happened without the setup of *Premonition*. Everything that had happened up to that point was merely setting the stage for what was to follow: the recording of one of the most powerful and motivational songs of our time—"Eye of the Tiger."

Keeper of the Flame

"WHY DO WE EVEN have to call the album *Eye of the Tiger*? We could call it, for instance, 'The One That Really Matters!'" I said to Cliff O'Sullivan, our product manager with Epic Records, the Scotti Brothers' parent company.

Cliff looked at me like I was out of my mind. I really just wanted to elicit a response and to make the point that there were plenty of other great songs on this record. It was clear that both labels were putting all their eggs in the *Rocky* basket, and I just didn't want "Eye" to eclipse the fact that we were a band, not a Stallone product.

At the time I actually valued some of the other songs more on this album. Sometimes when a song comes as easy as did "Eye of the Tiger," I have the tendency to underestimate it. I did that with my other number one, "Vehicle," years before and here I was doing it again.

I had just co-written two songs for *Rocky III* when I met up with my father for what turned out to be the second to the last time I would see him alive. The songs were "Eye of the Tiger" and "Ever Since the World Began." The latter was the big ballad, which was also commissioned by Stallone for *Rocky III*. Ultimately Sly could not talk the director into finding a place for it, though he used it a few years later in his movie, *Lock Up*. It was the end title and sung by Jimi Jamison.

I sat my father down in the living room of my La Grange ranch house and played him the acetate of "Ever Since the World Began." I chose this one, not only because I considered it, at the time, the best song I'd ever written (way better than "Eye of the Tiger," ha!), but also because my father had just suffered a heart attack and his mortality informed this song.

"Still we walk this road together
we try and go as far as we can
and we have waited for this moment in time
ever since the world began."

Copyright 1982 Easy Action/Warner/Chappell Music ASCAP /Rude Music BMI/Sony/ATV Melody BMI/Three Wise Boys Music LLC BMI

It was a moment for both of us with my normally stoic dad taking his glasses off to wipe away the tears with his initialed, white hankie. I told him there was another one called "Eye of the Tiger" that was pretty good, too.

Before I left for L.A. to record, I visited my father one last time—this time at McNeil Memorial Hospital in my old hometown of Berwyn, Illinois. He had suffered another heart attack and was there for recovery and observation. At his bedside, I noticed how frail he looked, though his eyes were still full of music.

When I told him I was off to make an album that just could make my career, I added casually, "I'll see you in a couple of weeks when I take a few days off!" Then I saw the look in his eyes that spoke volumes. He already knew somehow that I would not see him alive again. It was all conveyed in his last glance as I said good-bye—for the last time. That certain, hard-to-define look on his face is one I will never forget.

I will always believe that somehow my father heard my most popular song ever, "Eye of the Tiger," on some cosmic network station. In fact, I attribute the gargantuan success of that song, in part, as my father's final gift to me—his only son, blood of his blood and fellow music journeyman.

Back at Rumbo, as Dave Bickler sang his final vocal on "Tiger," I'm sure he felt the pressure of not only giving the performance of a lifetime, but also living up to or surpassing the amazing vocal he had performed on the demo.

We have a phrase in the biz: "Chasing the demo." When a band makes a demo, they are generally relaxed, knowing it's not "the final thing." That relaxation usually shows itself in a smooth and natural performance enhanced by the excitement of recording what is usually a fresh, new tune. It's the feeling of discovery.

On the final recording of "Tiger" we were definitely chasing the fantastic demo we had done back in Chicago a month and a half earlier. In fact, I was the odd man out in favor of actually taking the demo and remixing it through the superior equipment at Rumbo.

Frankie's decision was to start from scratch. What would have been my call, one short year ago, was now solely his.

A song that took two days to record and mix the first time around took a full month to recapture in its final form. If you want to hear the original demo version, just watch *Rocky III*. This is due to the fact that Stallone and the movie release schedule could not wait for the album final to be completed.

The two versions are extremely similar and very few people actually realize there are two distinct versions. The version you hear in the movie is a bit more raw, a bit sloppier, and has a lot more vibe in my opinion.

Of course, I love the sonically superior final as well. It's just that we nearly killed ourselves trying to beat ourselves at our own game. But when the album finally wrapped I could visualize our records turning from black to gold—and then to pure platinum.

One evening after a long vocal session, I was relaxing at the Oak-wood apartments in Reseda when I got an urgent call from Karen.

"You'd better book a flight to Chicago in the morning. Dad is touch and go. I think you should come in. It could go either way."

After booking my flight and informing the band, I entered into a fitful sleep. At exactly 4:15 a.m. I was jolted awake by a most violent pounding in my chest beyond anything I had ever felt. I was gasping for air as I stumbled out the door to the parking lot. There I got down on all fours and fought for my life with every breath... Gradually I settled down and felt somehow strangely peaceful as I got back into bed.

Throughout the whole plane flight home, I was wracked with worry and wonder at what I would find when I landed.

Karen was there at the curb in baggage claim. I noticed she was in the brand-new, black Toyota Supra that had apparently arrived; we had ordered it a month ago. I took this as a good sign, thinking Karen wouldn't have chosen to pick me up in this shiny new car if she had bad news to deliver about my dad.

I opened the passenger door with a tentative smile, "Well, is Dad okay?"

Karen hesitated for a long second, then said, "He didn't make it."

Stunned, I said, "Really? Are you sure?"

"Yes, he suffered a massive heart attack at six-fifteen this morn-ing," she said—precisely the moment that, on West Coast time, my own heart was leaping out of my own chest!

My world was starting to spin. I realized I'd never get to see my wonderful, musical, funny dad again...and I started sobbing as we traveled south down I-294, back to my parents' house in Berwyn, where everyone had congregated. Karen clutched my hand and cried, too. Only seventy years old—I'm certain he would have sur-vived with today's medical technology.

All I could think of at the wake, as I played the song, "Ever Since the World Began," which I wrote for him, were all the things I never got to tell him, all the questions I never got around to asking him, and the stories of his youth that he never got to tell.

A Peterik family tradition, a sing-along featuring me,
my dear dad on the sax, and my nephew
Doug McCabe on bass—1979.

These stories died with him. But his spirit has been with me ever since, and it has been a constant source of musical and spiritual inspiration. This was the guy who helped us lug equipment into dance halls, and who played tambourine on "No Two Ways about It," my first recording. No two ways about it, this man will always be my Hero.

Oceans between Us

WHEN I RETURNED from my dad's funeral I walked into the control room at Rumbo to hear the playback of the final mix of "Eye of the Tiger." I think everyone thought I'd be in grieving mode as they offered their heartfelt condolences.

The truth was that I had done my grieving in Chicago. I got a strong signal from my dad through the cosmos to get back to work and carry on with life—to make the most of the opportunity at hand.

I missed him every day, but I knew he was just fine on the other side. He came to me in a dream a few days after his passing. I saw his kind, handsome face with an expression that conveyed the perfect peace that he had found. He uttered one word in an intonation that was only his, saying it all in a single word: "James." I mentally play back that moment whenever I'm feeling lost or untethered in my life.

The mixes of the new album sounded massive coming through the giant Westlake speakers mounted in the wall of Studio A. Frankie Sullivan was aided by engineers Phil Bonanno and Mike Clink (who went on to multiplatinum success as producer of Guns N' Roses) so I knew the album was in good hands.

My role as co-producer had gradually diminished over the last few years; my main input became writing the songs, supervising the rehearsals, vocal production, musical arrangements, and overview perspective all along the way. It was ironic that it was I who gave Frankie his first chance behind the console and now there was very little room for me next to him. However, similar to the intangibles Frankie added to my songs, I was definitely the X factor in the production team.

The results I heard upon my return from Chicago were stunning, however. The clarity and punch of the sound was etched in steel. The balance was even and the harmonies glistened. I recall Cliff O'Sullivan coming in with a few members of the Epic team; they were blown away by the playbacks, especially a new epic called "I'm Not That Man Anymore." I came back to Chicago feeling that this was indeed the album that would be Survivor's defining moment.

The Scotti brothers requested we do a music video for "Eye of the Tiger" due to the emergence of MTV as a major engine of promotion. They wisely chose feature filmmaker Bill Dear to direct. His idea was to intercut scenes of our staged performance of the song with key scenes from the movie itself. Sounded good to me.

But Frankie, ever the contrarian, had different ideas. "That just ties us to that damn movie! We should do a video about the making of a rock band—our story."

I felt this concept had potential, though I secretly mourned losing the opportunity to use that soon-to-be-iconic footage. I presented the idea to Bill Dear and lo and behold he went for it and wrote an alternate storyboard just one day prior to the first day of our shoot.

I'll never forget shooting that first scene: the band walking badass down the sleaziest street we could find in the hookers-and-drugs district of San Francisco. Cliff O'Sullivan, our product manager, was there wearing this funky white sweatshirt. He looked smashing in it.

I asked if I could borrow it for the video. He said, "Sure." Bad idea. At the video preview I watched in horror as I saw myself marching down the street looking huge in this white sweatshirt. I looked nothing like the good-looking Cliff O'Sullivan. I looked like "Fatboy" from days of yore. Note to my overweight friends: Don't wear white in a video, and never think you'll look like the model who wore it first.

We did some pretty cool scenes in a funky rehearsal warehouse and of course the finale of us on a soundstage wrapped in black Hefty bags being drenched in water as we played. But I cringe every time I see this video, which, by the way, seems to be viewed more now than in 1982.

A few weeks after the album hit the stores, *Rocky III* hit the screens. The week before, Survivor had been invited to the premiere screening of *Rocky III* at the Hollywood Palladium. It was a glittery and star-studded event with every major player in attendance. Cameras flashed and videos whirled as we, a humble Chicago rock band, walked the red carpet in our rented tuxedos.

The movie sounded as fantastic as it looked. The jaded Hollywood audience sat on their hands as our song blasted through the giant theater speakers, but I could feel the tension building. At the end of the film the audience stood up and cheered—it was a true Rocky moment for real.

When I got back to Chicago to prepare for our upcoming tour with REO Speedwagon, Karen and I snuck into the tiny, neighborhood La Grange Theater and sat inconspicuously in the back row. The house was packed with excited locals waiting to see the just-released *Rocky III*. I wanted to see just how the average Joe and Jane would react to the movie.

It didn't take long to assess. When my telegraphic guitar part hit, it was like Morse code cuing them to start cheering wildly. The place went up for grabs as Frankie's guitar slashed the night. This was beyond Hollywood. This was small-town America and they were eating it up.

It seems like it's always the little slices of life that mean the most to me. Early in the REO/Survivor tour as the song was approaching the

Top 10, I went to a Shakey's pizza parlor before the show—just like always, a fly on the wall with a notebook. From the jukebox came the first strains of "Eye of the Tiger." At that very moment, a little blonde girl, not more than four or five, dashed to the tiny parquet dance floor and started spinning around, shouting, "Mommy, Daddy, they're playing my song!"

It was at that moment that I realized just how many lives and how many generations this song would go on to touch.

On the road we were relegated to a forty-five-minute opening slot for REO. Kevin Cronin, Gary Richrath, and the boys certainly had their share of success up until then, and now they had what would become their biggest-selling album to date, *Hi Infidelity*.

REO made around $75,000 every night. Survivor was paid $7,500. This was the price of getting the opportunity to play in front of 20,000 people a night and spread our own brand of music. What we didn't know at the time is that, because of the popularity of "Eye of the Tiger," Survivor was responsible for bringing in much of the crowd!

Our shows were strong with Dave's tenor rasp at its most feral and Frankie's tobacco sunburst Les Paul searing the night like a hot blade through butter. But further seeds of internal unrest were planted around this time with our very own rebel son not showing up for our ritual vocal warm-up before shows and refusing to perform certain songs. (Much later in the band's career he inexplicably refused to put "Burning Heart" into the set list on our first visit to Japan despite the shouted requests from the audience and the fact that it was currently in that country's top ten.)

There were also incidents created by Frankie's often idealistic standard of star treatment—like when he gave orders to Sal Francese not to allow the host disc jockeys of WLUP access to the restroom located in our dressing room, forcing the very people responsible for debuting "Eye of the Tiger" to battle through the heavy crowds at Poplar Creek Amphitheater to get to the public john. After that the station tried to pull the single from their playlist but due to the public's clamor for that song they could not. It was my idea the following Monday for the group to visit The Loop, portable toilet seat in hand, and apologize in person for our lack of goodwill. Damage control became a very big part of what we had to do because of some of Frankie's overly idealistic ideas of what it means to "make it."

REO treated us like equals. I had known Kevin Cronin for many years. In fact, when he was head of the student council at Oak Lawn High School, he had once hired The Ides of March for their school prom!

Soon after that, we would play the same coffeehouse circuit when we were both trying to be the next Cat Stevens—dark, smoky places like Chances R in Champaign, in downstate Illinois, and Like Young, in Chicago's Old Town district. We always got along great and being on the road together was no exception.

The sad truth is that I probably hung out more with some of the REO guys than with my own band. The key issue that caused my alienation from Survivor was the success of 38 Special with songs I helped them write.

At first, Marc, Dave, and Steph were happy for me, feeling that somehow my success as a songwriter would enhance the success of Survivor—a theory that I support to this day.

I used Lennon and McCartney as my template. Contributing songs to other artists such as Billy J. Kramer and the Dakotas, Peter and Gordon, and others, only raised their value as members of their own band.

Frankie didn't buy into this line of thinking, though, and did everything he could to make the rest of the band turn against me and feel like I was hurting Survivor's chances by creating competition.

After the success of 38's first hit, "Rockin' into the Night," which was co-written with Frankie, John Kalodner put me together with their lead singer/guitarist Don Barnes and guitarist Jeff Carlisi to write songs for their follow-up album.

At the very first session at the kitchen counter of my house at 823 South Stone, we came up with the song that became, perhaps, the signature song of their career, "Hold on Loosely."

After that, Frankie started demanding his own dressing room away from me and shot me daggers onstage every chance he got. Now it was time for 38's follow-up album and again Jeff and Don came into Chicago to write.

Jeff, Don, and I would cloister ourselves in my mother's basement in fear of Frankie stopping by my own house for a visit. These great, uplifting melodies and lyrics were all written in a dank Berwyn basement by three rock 'n' roll exiles.

In recent months John Kalodner (or "Old Clog Ears" as Roy Thomas Baker called him at our showcase) had also put me together with Sammy Hagar, fresh out of Montrose and ready to kick ass on his first solo album for John's new label, Geffen. I was flattered of course to be asked but I also worried about repercussions from Frankie similar to the 38 Special debacle. John was very convincing though and I felt obligated to do it since he had signed my band just a year earlier.

Sammy picked me up at the San Francisco airport in his brand-new blazing hot Ferrari Daytona convertible. "Nice country, America—right Jimbo?" I had to agree as we proceeded to wind through the wilds of San Fran en route to his spread in the foothills of Mill Valley. As we entered the business district of this picturesque little town we were regaled with, "Hey Sammy! You rock Sammy!" from countless townsfolk. He was a hero even then. We stopped at his favorite coffee shop and ground a pound of the highest octane bean I've ever tasted. Later that day those beans came in handy as we hunkered down in his basement studio to write.

I found out that this was Sammy's first songwriting collaboration. "You got my cherry, Peterik!" Sammy quipped. At first we kind of sat and stared at each other, guitars at the ready, making small talk and waiting for lightning to strike. Finally sensing his insecurity I said, "Look, Sammy, we're like two lions ready to strike but afraid we may offend the other. Even though you and I have hit records under our belts doesn't mean we're not gonna have some really dumb ideas and suggest some really bad lines. Let's not be afraid to suck!" With that Sammy laughed out loud and the freshman jinx was broken.

Loosening up he said, "Ya know, my manager, Eddie Leffler, just told me there's a new sci-fi animation called *Heavy Metal* that needs a title cut. Wanna give it a go?"

"Is the pope Catholic?" was my oft-used rejoinder.

Riff followed lyric followed riff as we mined our natural chemistry to paint a 3-D image of a couple of metalheads at a rock show, wild with anticipation for the spectacle to begin. "Sammy, I don't know about you, but for me the most electric part of a rock show is anticipating what's about to happen—the buildup of tension knowing that you're about to be blown away."

Sammy started, "Headbangers in leather." I parried with "Sparks flying in the dead of the night." Sam: "It all comes together when they turn out the lights." JP: "How 'bout 'Shoot out the lights.'" Hell Yeah!!! "Fifty-thousand watts of power—and it's pushing overload. The Beast is ready to devour—all the metal it can hold." We gave each other that "How the hell did we come up with all that cool shit" look. On and on it went 'til 'round tequila time at D'Angelo's restaurant, at which time we had a finished song and a crude but rude eight-track demo made on Sammy's primitive Tascam multitrack cassette recorder.

It's not as if I was giving away ideas I should have been saving for Survivor. As I would with any good collaboration, I pooled the best ideas in the room and helped create a synergistic sum of the parts. That's one of my strong suits—bringing everyone's unique strengths to the foreground.

For instance, in "Hold on Loosely," the opening riff, which created the chord progression of the verse, was contributed by Jeff. The title was Don's. Let it be known for the first time anywhere that Don heard the phrase "Hold on Loosely" uttered by none other than Dinah Shore when, on her afternoon talk show, she described the way one particular guest was giving her husband the space he needed to save their relationship. "In other words, hold on loosely, right?" Dinah said.

Now, as "Eye of the Tiger" was climbing the charts, so was 38 Special's latest Peterik co-written hit, "Caught Up in You." Again, if Survivor could have embraced my success as a songwriter, it could have been an additional band asset.

Instead, Frankie turned the radio off indignantly if a 38 song came on the air. If an interviewer asked a question about 38, he would clam up or storm out of the room. I was more accustomed to seeing Frankie's backside leaving than his front! I was ostracized from dressing rooms and ignored at parties. Dave was his own person and didn't buy into this mentality, but Frankie and Marc put up a formidable resistance.

One fact also revealed here for the first time is that Frankie's name is listed as co-writer on "Caught Up in You," the 1982 hit by 38 Special, because he claimed I had borrowed the chord progression of the chorus from another song I had been working on, with him, called "Take it All," and he was ready to take us all to court. Even though there was no solid evidence to the similarity, I got 38 to agree to cut him in to the copyright just to avoid a lawsuit.

This was the climate on the road promoting the number one song in America, "Eye of the Tiger." People always say, "Jim, those had to be some of the best times of your life." I usually nod and smile. If they only knew how miserable I was, they would never have believed it.

That 38 album was the last one for many years that would include a Peterik co-write, which killed me and that band. We had a successful format combining my pop sensibilities with their gritty, southern rock style. But I could not take the heat from Frankie one minute longer.

Not that the vibes got any better when I stopped writing with them; in fact, never again would I feel the goodwill I had felt in the hungry years when it was just us against the odds.

Now, even though I wanted desperately to sing lead or duet with Dave and jam out on guitar, I didn't have the credibility to even make my case. I was the odd man out. In fact, at one meeting at my house, Frankie suggested that I exit the band—that I had lost the "Eye of the Tiger." Dave said nothing. Frankie's guy, Marc, nodded in agreement, and Stephan just nodded out.

My relationship with Karen was good on the surface, but I felt her resentment. The band took me away from her for months at a time and robbed me of my individuality. She was frustrated at my inability to stand up for myself with Frankie, and her respect for me was waning.

When I'd finally come home, I was a stranger in her world, a place she learned to manage quite well on her own, "Thank you very much!"

All of these elements came into play when Karen and I were sitting in the audience on Oscar night. "Eye of the Tiger" had been nominated for Best Original Song. Our manager, John Baruck, had to beg Frankie to show up. "You'll regret it forever if you don't go, Frank!" This should have been the night of our life. Instead, it was a bad B movie.

A few weeks earlier, Frank had refused to go to the Grammy Award ceremonies where "Eye" was up for Best Rock Performance by a Duo or Group. The nomination was for Frankie and me as the song's producers. The Grammy foundation limited the event and plane tickets to only Frankie and me, so he refused to attend in a misguided nod to band solidarity. The band was totally fine with us going without them, but had to agree with Frankie that they were "getting seriously screwed!" If I had gone alone, I'd never have heard the end of it.

I'll never forget the empty feeling I had watching the Grammy Awards alone on my tiny, portable TV set in the kitchen as they announced our victory while Karen was working late. The day I had waited for my entire life had arrived and I was eating a frozen pizza by the flickering light of a picture tube.

The famous kitchen counter and TV at 823 South Stone.

So there we were at the Oscars; Frankie and his wife, Gloria, and Karen and me. Frankie and I did not say a word to each other, sitting stony and feeling miles apart. The girls hardly knew each other, so they shared no common bond. The crippling silence could not have felt more awkward and dysfunctional.

We shared a cringe as the Temptations performed an ersatz soul version of "Eye of the Tiger" complete with bad choreography and trashy dancers dressed in tiger suits.

Then came the moment when the Best Original Song award was announced. Noted Chicago film critics, Gene Siskel and Roger Ebert predicted our clear victory over the other four nominated songs: "Up Where We Belong" from *An Officer and a Gentleman*, "How Do You Keep the Music Playing?" from *Best Friends*, *Tootsie*'s "It Might Be You," and "If We Were in Love" from *Yes, Giorgio*.

I always wondered what it would feel like to be the guy on the split screen with the egg on his face and a forced smile. Now I knew firsthand. I was watching it all, hovering over the scene like in a near-death experience, which indeed it was at the time.

"...And the winner is 'Up Where We Belong,' music by Jack Nitzsche and Buffy Sainte-Marie, lyrics by Will Jennings."

The slightly nerdy-looking guy that was sitting immediately to my left kissed the woman next to him and wriggled down the row to the aisle. In a flash, Jack grandly accepted his award as I crumpled my prepared notes into a ball and stuffed them into my rented tux.

At the afterparty I spotted Steven Spielberg. I said, "Frankie, let's go over there and introduce ourselves!"

"I'm not gonna do that. You go, dude, if you want to." I could sense from his sarcastic tone what he was probably thinking: If I wanted to go over there and kiss Spielberg's ass, I'd do it alone. I wonder how many movies we could have written for if that meeting had taken place. Taking a piss next to Dudley Moore was, perhaps, the high point of the night.

Soon thereafter, we attended The People's Choice Awards, where "Eye of the Tiger" had won the category of "The Most Popular Song." Karen and I had a table next to actress/health advocate Jane Fonda.

We were huge fans. We loved her movies and worked out to her exercise video every chance we got.

At that moment I thought of my father. Once he went right up to comedian George Gobel, who was walking down Chicago's State Street, near the Palmer House, when we spotted him. I was only about nine years old. My dad tipped his hat and said confidently, "Good afternoon, Mr. Gobel." George twinkled his hello and we all floated off down the street. I loved my dad for having the balls to approach a big star like that.

This time, I went over to Jane Fonda and said, "Excuse me, Jane, my wife and I are big fans of yours and work out to your video all the time!"

"That's really cool, 'cause I work out to 'Eye of the Tiger!'" she responded with a twinkle in her translucent eyes.

The band had everything—everything except happiness. We had the world by the Tiger's tail. As Ron Nevison used to say about us, "If we knew what a blessing was, we'd know how to count them." Unfortunately, it took a long, long while to learn how to count.

Mean Streets, Blind Alleys

THE TOUR WITH REO crisscrossed the nation, doing sellout shows in every town. Fifteen to twenty thousand fans went crazy for this sample case of good old-fashioned Midwestern rock 'n' roll, night after night. Survivor was doing double duty, holding court for prospective managers to take over for the doddering Arties. The who's who of management teams came out to see us including Irv Azoff (appearing out of nowhere at the Meadowlands in New Jersey), known as the "Poison Dwarf," named for his diminutive size and toxic style. "Lies are a necessary part of the business of rock 'n' roll," he would preach.

We ended up going with REO's manager, John Baruck, and his partners, Tom Consolo and Alex Kochan, who already believed in us enough to have put us on the REO bill. It felt good to be a part of a truly professional team.

A big part of the profits of any tour is band merchandise. Early in the tour we were splitting hundreds of dollars in undeclared cash after each show from the massive sales of T-shirts emblazoned with the Survivor logo and all different images of tigers: white ones, gold ones, tigers on mountains, and tigers in packs. These were some awesome shirts with really cool artwork—all good until Frankie made the executive decision one day that "the tiger" took the glory away from the band concept and, again, linked us to the *Rocky* franchise. Overnight the shirts were changed to an image of us five jamokes standing like wooden Indians, and the logo. Sales dried up significantly, immediately. Frankie may have had the right motives but from a sales point of view, that tiger image was what everyone wanted.

The last show of the REO tour in Cleveland, the whole REO band and crew punked us by running up onstage as we played our final song, "Eye of the Tiger," dressed in cartoon drag. We're talking giant rubber boobs, huge oversized hats, strap-on latex dildos, and full makeup complete with fake eyelashes. As we tried to play and keep reasonably straight faces, Cronin and the crew nuzzled us and flirted like a seduction from hell. It was hilarious. I don't think the Heartland crowd knew quite what to make of it, but it was something I will never forget.

After the last show, we all repaired to "The Dungeon." In every hotel, REO would christen one suite this way and it became the den of iniquity for mingling, booze, drugs, and hooking up. I was a stranger to "The Dungeon" most nights, but after the last show I decided to come up. It was like a replay of the party in the penthouse after the Led Zeppelin show when I was with The Ides of March. I was fifteen years older now, but the strippers performing sex acts that night still seemed as foreign as they did then. All I could think of was how sad their mothers and fathers would have been to see their daughters ending up like this. I guess I think way too much.

We were all noticing that Dave's voice was starting to sound a bit ragged. The high notes that were so clear in the past were just not ringing. His personal party habits may have been contributing to this. We figured this was to be expected in the flow of a grueling tour.

Back home in La Grange, it was now time for the inevitable transition to civilian life, which was never easy. Karen had only come out once during the whole tour, when we played New Orleans. We had a great time exploring the French Quarter and eating Creole food and those deep-fried, powder-sugared wonders called beignets. Karen was not the rock-star appendage type; she never was. She has always been a very purpose-driven individual with her own agenda. Coming on the road just to hang on my arm never appealed to her.

Epic Records threw us a big, congratulatory dinner at a famous restaurant in the French Quarter the day "Tiger" went to number one. At the dinner, the head Epic honcho, Gordy Anderson, stood up and proposed a toast to "the man who made it all possible"—Jim Peterik.

At that moment, Frankie made a quick and dramatic exit. I really can't blame him. He was in the trenches with me from the beginning and took up the slack when my father died and basically finished the *Tiger* record alone.

I regret to this day that I didn't stand up and say thanks, and then acknowledge that I couldn't have done it without Frankie and all the members of the band, who had worked so hard to get to that night. After that dinner, the fissure between the band and me got even deeper.

"American Heartbeat" was released as the second single from the *Eye of the Tiger* album. We could have picked almost any song from that album, and it would have suffered equally dire consequences, mainly because it is practically impossible to follow an iconic song like "Eye of the Tiger."

It stalled on the *Billboard* charts at number 17. The proposed video for the song was deep-sixed when Frankie convinced the band that the concept "sucked," and he refused to get on the plane to the West Coast to make it. The $75,000 that was already spent on its development became a figure on Survivor's ever-mounting debt sheet to the record company. It would take until 1996 to get into the black with Epic/Scotti Brothers, meaning that no one had the chance of making dime one on record sales until then. The decision to abort the video pleased our product manager, Cliff O'Sullivan, not one bit and deepened the rift between the label and us.

A similar Frankie audible caused another major shit storm when he decided that the band should not be merely the opening act for Bryan Adams in our hometown of Chicago. He felt we would not be given enough room on stage because we were forced to set up in front of the headliner's equipment, and that we would not be given enough time to play (forty-five minutes). This came after the contract was already signed and all the advertising had gone out. We canceled at the last minute! We sat at home as the concert went on without us and thousands of Survivor fans went home without seeing half the reason they bought tickets in the first place. It caused bad blood between our fans and us in Chicago for years to come.

As always, I escaped the nonsense by committing myself to the daunting task of writing new material to follow up an album that was now rounding the double-platinum mark. Frankie decided that this time around he would be the sole producer and that Mike Clink would handle the engineering slot, leaving Phil Bonanno behind. I was given the token title of "Production Assistant"—to me that was akin to "piss boy." I just did not have the will to fight for my rightful position as co-producer.

The Scotti Brothers contract had recently been renegotiated by John Baruck and yielded the band a cool million bucks. Unfortunately most of this money went to pay off the numerous accounts and prior managers, most of which were threatening legal action. After Frankie negotiated $100,000 for himself for his role as co-producer of the *Eye of the Tiger* album (I received zero), each band member bitterly accepted a "whopping" thirty grand.

I was demoing songs at the local garage studio called Tanglewood in suburban Brookfield, operated by my lifelong buddy and fellow Ide of March, Larry Millas. It was there that I laid down the seeds for "Ready for the Real Thing," "What Do You Really Think," and a song that never saw the light of day called "The Fighter."

"Too *Rocky*-ish," griped Frankie. "The Fighter" was also a finished song before Frankie got to add his input. As I mentioned earlier, I came to learn that if I wanted his support on a song, I had better include him in the songwriting.

I will say though, that when Frankie and I did get together to write for what became our fourth record, *Caught in the Game*, he showed up at my house with a virtual straw hat and cane—his attitude as positive and guileless as the kid who came over that first day he played me the guitar part for "Somewhere in America" at my kitchen counter.

This was the Frankie I liked best. All I can figure is that he knew what side his bread was buttered on—that songwriting was where the real "bread" was and that he'd better put on his game face. To be fair, I'm sure he really enjoyed the creative process as well, and he always extracted the best out of me. He was a great editor, especially of my lyrics, which could tend to be overblown at times or "too quick to live," "not mainstream enough," or "too intellectual."

Whatever his motivation was, we had a blast fine-tuning songs such as "I Never Stopped Loving You" (although I still mourn the loss of a killer bridge that he decided was over the top), "Santa Ana Winds," "Jackie Don't Go," "Half-Life," and, of course, the title track—the song that is driven by perhaps the most powerful and enduring riff Frankie ever devised—"Caught in the Game."

When we hit Rumbo Studios and the spring of 1983, however, nothing felt as good as it had when we were making the last two records there. Something had changed. Maybe it was the high expectations set by the platinum sales of the last record, which made Frankie overly careful about every last detail, or maybe it was the bad blood on the tracks from the months of dressing room disconnect. Whatever it was, the climate in the control room was icy.

We now had a cool half-million-dollar budget to make this album. And damn it if Frankie didn't seem hell-bent on spending every last dime as he worked day after day, endlessly experimenting with snare drum sounds and other minutiae. He would work straight through the weekends, not realizing just how burnt out he was getting. He even bowed out of a wonderful dinner party thrown for us by Don Felder of Eagles fame, who was recording in Studio B at Rumbo.

Dave Bickler and me.

Mike Clink and I would often grab a beer after the session and commiserate on the time being wasted in the studio and the lack of stellar results even in the face of the time and money spent.

Then there was Dave Bickler's voice. At the end of the last tour he was a shred of his former tenor. Now in the studio, Frankie worked tirelessly trying to elicit strong vocals from Dave, but to this day I can hear the strain in his nodule-riddled voice.

As a songwriter I had come to count on the abilities of the lead singer to inspire me to write my finest songs, including the soaring melodies that had become my trademark. Enunciation of lyrics also became an issue. If the audience can't understand the words, it's difficult for them to grasp the meaning and emotion I was trying to convey. In the end, it was not just about Dave's abilities, but also about my abilities as a songwriter for the band that forced Dave's exit.

While surfing the numbing boredom of making *Caught in the Game* I decided to break the monotony of gazing at the four barren walls of the Oakwood Apartments by taking a few tokes on a joint that I had stashed in my wallet some weeks ago. The only previous encounter that I had with this herb was during the making of the first Survivor album when a few of us, including our head henchman Rick Weigand decided it would be a blast to visit the King Richard's Renaissance Faire in L.A. County. On the trek there a "J" was passed around and the world started to look more beautiful by the second. By the time we reached the fairgrounds everything we said seemed hilarious and I had developed a hunger like I had never known. As I ate my way through the event (giant turkey leg, skewers of deep-fried veggies, funnel cakes [plural], and of course plenty of rotgut red wine) suddenly the gaily appointed men in tights and saucy wenches seemed just downright hysterical. They tell me I tried jousting.

Now at the Oakwood I was eager to see what would happen if I tried to write a song in this altered state. After a few drags I got out my Gibson J200, hit "Record" on my trusty Sony recorder (moving up from my Radio Shack model), and for the next four or five hours laid down a song cycle to beat all song cycles. The ideas were flying out of my distorted head. When I finally came up for air it was 1:30 in the morning, and I hit the sack with the inner peace that I had perhaps just written the next *Sgt. Pepper* or at least the next two or three Survivor albums.

When I woke up that day I shook myself out of slumber and eagerly went over to my tape deck and hit "Rewind." To my utter and disbelieving horror all that greeted me was the loud hiss of tape noise whirring past the playback heads. I turned the tape over and rewound—that same nauseating sound greeted me.

I'm not a good recording tech to begin with but in my blissed-out state I had pressed "Play" instead of "Record." Were the ideas really as good as I thought? Probably not, but the world and I will never know for sure.

After we wrapped up this record, Dave had surgery to remove the nodes that had developed on his ravaged cords. This canceled our plans to tour behind the release of *Caught in the Game* and prompted our co-manager, Alex Kochan, to print up "hilarious" T-shirts that read "Survivor—*Caught in the Game*—the Non-Tour." No one, least of all myself, was amused. It was just sad.

The album came out with a thud, fueled by an unintentionally camp video for the first single, "Caught in the Game," depicting the band caught in a giant video game of craps. It was cheese at its cheesiest. We all looked as bad as we felt making it.

After Dave Bickler came out of throat surgery, he was told he should not sing for a year. This was one year longer than we felt we had to pick up the momentum we had lost on this release.

Dave seemed to be his usual distant self, at least to me. I'm sure he was upset about his impending dismissal, but we had very little communication about it.

Frankie and I started to weigh our options. We secretly asked around to all of our acquaintances if they knew of any lead singers who could possibly fill the shoes of the once mighty Dave Bickler. Many names were bandied about, but one rose to the top. My former manager, Frank Rand, who was now a big honcho at Epic Records (yes, the same guy who passed on Survivor, four years earlier), told me of a guy who sang lead for a soon-to-be-defunct Epic act called Cobra. His name was Jimi Jamison. We could not have known how prominently this name would figure into the resurgence of our once proud moniker. Would this be the new voice of survival? We could only hope—and pray.

It's the Singer Not the Song

CIVILIAN LIFE AT HOME with Karen and our two cats, Rocky and Cher, was typically typical. We would go out to dinner but we seemed to have very little spark. Much of what drew us together had disappeared.

As far as the band, for me and Frankie it was déjà vu all over again—only this time we were searching for a new lead singer, not a new rhythm section. We knew it was rare for a group to withstand a head transplant like this. The new voice would have to be a bit reminiscent of the original singer but also bring something fresh to the party. We wondered how the Dave Bickler fans out there would handle a new lead singer. To this day there seems to be a "Dave Camp" and a "Jimi Camp," each one passionate that theirs is the golden era of Survivor. The "Dave Camp" seems to be male dominated, by the way!

We put the APB out to all our friends, but on the down-low so it didn't turn into a cattle call. Henry Paul suggested one guy who came in and tried his best but he was about forty pounds overweight and his vibe was just too southern rock to fit the bill.

I called up Kevin Chalfant, whom I had known for years. We always shared a laugh when we crossed paths at a recording studio or gig. He was between bands at the time, having just exited 707.

When he appeared at the carpet warehouse, the vibe was good at first. He sang the Survivor material great and seemed like a team player. Frankie and I exchanged positive glances as he sang. We thought we might have found our man.

In further interchanges over the next few days he was very vocal about his ideas for the band and wanting to be an integral part of the songwriting team. Usually ambition like this is rewarded. But in this case, Frankie and I had a pretty pat formula and great chemistry in our composing team and we felt that Kevin would not be happy sitting on the sidelines.

A few days later, Frank Rand sent us a VHS tape of a guy named Jimi Jamison performing with his group Cobra. He had the look, the moves, and he had the voice. He had that "thing," the "it" factor that was undeniable even on this poor-quality video. I recall he touched his crotch on this video long before Michael Jackson discovered that part of his anatomy.

But could he deliver in person? We were soon to find out. He arrived at the carpet warehouse the perfect Southern gentleman. His understated and polite demeanor reminded me of a young Elvis Presley. After pleasantries we got right down to business. Frankie and I had been developing a song called "Broken Promises." I sang the song to Jimi and like a human tape recording he sang it back to me in my ear.

"Holy shit, Jimi, have you heard this song before?" I asked him.

No one had ever been that quick of a study. The sound I heard as he sang at point blank range was like no voice I had ever heard before. It was sweet, yet urgent. It had all that fidelity on the top end and a rich bottom end as well. He infused the lyric with an immediate relatability that elevated and communicated every line we had

Being blown away by Jimi Jamison.

written. When he stepped up to the mic, though, that was when we were completely blown away.

We had been using a very inadequate PA system that sounded weak with every other singer we had auditioned. Suddenly it was as if Jimi plugged in an extra power amp and three more banks of speakers—that's how loud and strong he sounded.

Next I taught him a new one called "The Search Is Over." Frankie and I had written the song in E flat on the Ibach piano in my house in La Grange. Actually, I wrote this song almost entirely in my head as I drove down the highway one day. When I hit the piano I realized I was singing in E flat.

On our first run through, Jimi's voice cracked on the high note of the chorus—on the word "eyes." I immediately stopped playing, turned to Frankie, and said, "Well I guess we better put the song in D."

At which point, Jimi uttered the now legendary line, "Hey, give half a man a chance!"

We tried it again in the original key and he hit every note clearly. That dedication and determination was Jimi's MO.

Marc and Steph and I gathered in the kitchen of the warehouse and decided Jimi was our man. Frank was curiously absent when we told Jimi, as if he knew bringing him in was the obvious and inevitable choice, but couldn't bear to officially ordain him.

One week later, Ron Nevison came to town to hear songs and the new singer. It was great to have Ron back. I was glad that he could put the nightmare of the first album behind him. He had refused to even have his name on that record after he was fired. Regardless of the disaster of the first album, Frankie and I were eager to bring Ron back into the fold, this time unencumbered by the often meddlesome input of John Kalodner. Plus, we were blown away by his production of "Jane" for the Jefferson Starship. Fortunately, Ron did not hold Kalodner firing him against us; rather he correctly pointed his finger at John. We knew that Ron was the best there is and desperately wanted him back.

He was all smiles as he listened to and commented on the new cargo, songs like "Broken Promises," and "The Search Is Over," about which Ron said, "That's a number one." There was "Cry of the Wild Heart"—to this day I believe that Frankie talked Ron out of cutting this gem, perhaps because he had no writing credit on it; the Frankie riff-fueled pop confection "High on You" (my favorite line: "The kinda face that starts a fight"); "I See You in Everyone," a song I started after seeing Kim Novak in the Alfred Hitchcock gem *Vertigo*; "Popular Girl;" and a few good ones that never saw the light of day: "I Just Can't Let Go" and "Talk to Me."

Karen could see a new excitement in me during this period. Frankie and I were even playing handball at the Chicago Health Club together. We could sense that this was going to be the big one—the one that had the potential to give us a platinum record without the aid of the *Rocky* franchise. Perhaps we'd never again have to hear, "'Eye of the Tiger,' didn't Frank Stallone sing that one?" Whenever I'd talk to John Baruck, I'd glow over the new songs and Jimi's vocal strength. My catchphrase that I'd add at the end of every conversation was, "Order the Porsche, John!"

What I didn't see at the time was a growing jealousy in Frankie's eyes as I became closer to Jimi. I was blind to this as Karen and I showed Jimi a good time in Chicago one day at a five-star restaurant or took him sightseeing. I truly thought it was one for all, all for one, but it was really the beginning of a problem that would get worse and worse—this rivalry between Frankie and Jimi would grow more intense as each month passed.

For now though, we were a band happy to be going to Los Angeles to record our fifth album at the Record Plant on 3rd Street with the producer of our dreams.

Tracking went smoothly; we were cutting one or two tracks a day. I thought it was curious that Frankie didn't play guitar on the basic track of "The Search Is Over," preferring to overdub his part. But you didn't question Frankie. That was an unwritten law known to all.

We would sometimes eat together at the fine French restaurant, L'Orangerie, next to The Plant at the day's end. Frankie had purchased some major camera equipment and set it up in the studio the first day. I think his enchantment with photography disappeared as fast as it came. It would be fascinating to one day see these photos.

For some reason around this time I decided to take one of the band member's offer to try cocaine. There was a curiosity in me, I guess, and I wondered if it might even help my creativity. In the next few weeks of preparing for *Vital Signs* it seemed that I was asking for more and more "bumps" until finally I did what I never thought I'd do—I purchased a gram.

It was the dead of Chicago winter and there had been a snowstorm that I was carefully attempting to navigate through on my way back from rehearsal. I had a bronchial condition at the time so I was chugging a synthetic codeine cough syrup called Tussionex. I had also had a couple of tokes at the carpet warehouse. As I approached the exit curve onto Mannheim Road off of the Eisenhower Expressway I failed to slow down enough and went careening into the guardrail, smashing my bumper and wheel well, ruining a rim. I got my bearings and limped home thanking God that I hadn't hurt someone or myself.

When I got home Karen was sleeping soundly in the bedroom adjoining the master bath. I poured myself a whisky on the rocks in a large crystal tumbler to try and calm my nerves and come down from the trifecta of cocaine, codeine, and cannabis.

As I stood at the toilet and urinated, I multitasked and nursed the drink. Suddenly the tumbler slipped from my hand and fell with a deafening crash onto the toilet, shattering not only the glass but the porcelain toilet as well.

Karen was up in a flash to witness the carnage. "What the hell is going on here, Jim?" she shouted. I sheepishly told her the whole story. I had been keeping my brief dalliance with recreational drugs from her, so she was not only mourning the loss of the toilet but absorbing the shock of my secret. We had always shared everything—both good and bad.

I tearfully fell on my sword, promising I would never do that seductive powder again. "Swear it, Jim," she said sternly. "I swear, Karen." To this day I have been true to my word.

Finally we were done tracking, or so we thought. Near the end of one day I was in the piano booth finishing an overdub when I heard Frankie playing a magical, arpeggiated guitar part in the main recording room. He played it over and over as it gradually took shape. I started playing some majestic chords over the progression: B–A over B–E over B–A over B…and a song emerged. I caught the action on my cassette recorder and asked Frankie to join me in the isolation booth. Over the next three hours, we hammered it out as Ron deliberately stayed out of the way until he felt it was time to step in.

I had transferred the title, "I Can't Hold Back" from notebook to notebook for at least two years—the phrase had existed as merely ink stains on a page waiting for the right moment. This was it. Of all the songwriting sessions I have had in my life, this one stands out as the high point. It was unplanned, unforced, and totally egoless. Frankie contributed what he does best, his editing skills and his amazing guitar parts. I brought what I do best, melodies and lyrics. Ron contributed his gifts as an arranger. Listen to his production of "Isn't It Time" by The Babys to hear the way he could make a simple rock song into a magnum opus.

Frankie had now switched from electric to acoustic guitar. A week earlier I had scouted out a pristine, vintage 1961 Gibson J-185 for him at Norman's Rare Guitars in Reseda—natural blond finish, no less. This is the crystalline guitar you hear Frankie playing on the opening riff of the final mix of "I Can't Hold Back."

With this magical sound in my ear I began singing, "There's a story in my eyes."

Immediately Frankie unreeled, "Turn the pages of desire."

Oh shit—that was brilliant!

I rejoined with "Now it's time to trade those dreams for the rush of passion's fire."

Then I began to play what we will call the pre-chorus, but it's really more like a secondary chorus because it's easily as memorable as the chorus itself.

"I can feel you tremble as we touch, and I feel the hand of fate, reaching out to both of us."

This is one of those sections that came to me FedEx from heaven. Pure romance.

Finally, when we had most of the music and about half of the lyric done, Ron Nevison walked into the crowded iso room. His eyes danced as he fired off suggestions. "Try this, instead of going from the bridge to the chorus, try going to the pre-chorus and then to the chorus."

Each time I'd say, "That won't work."

"Try it," Ron would bark.

Guess what? It worked. Ron threw every section into a musical Cuisinart and spun out an arrangement so unusual that songwriters and bands to this day marvel at it. I believe it is one of the reasons "I Can't Hold Back" has enjoyed such longevity: it keeps you guessing where it will go next.

It was mutually decided that we would stay one extra day to cut this song. As I jogged along the beach the next morning, the missing words started to emerge as I sang them into the cassette machine. "I see a shooting star go by—and in the night the silence speaks to you and I…" Hmm—nice! I also settled on the exact melody of the "I can't hold back" hook as I dodged skaters along the shore.

We all arrived at Record Plant Studio with a certain glow in our eyes. We knew we had one chance, one session to get it right. This time everyone in the group was unanimous that this was a very special song. I was very hard to please that day as far as settling on a final take. I knew this album depended on a great AOR (album oriented rock) track to give us credibility on the album rock stations. Yet it would need to have enough pop appeal to get us on top 40 radio as well. I was sure this was the one.

We did take after take with Jimi singing live with the track from an iso room in the attic. I was in the piano booth; Marc occupied the main room that Ron had mic'd up extensively to capture all sound fields. Frankie was in iso room number 2.

Finally, after about ten takes Ron said, "That's the one. Come in."

I didn't feel it was "The One," but I filed with everyone into the control room and heard the playback. I wasn't sure. Then Ron played it back one more time at ear-splitting level trying to convince me. I still wasn't sure, but everyone else felt it was the magic take. It turns out that it was the magic take, but I think my expectations were so high that nothing could have pleased me that day. It wasn't until overdubs in Sausalito a few weeks later that I really was able to enjoy the track's divinity.

While in Sausalito I decided I needed to shed about thirty pounds, so I went on a doctor-supervised diet along with Kevin Sullivan (Frankie's road crew bro) and our guitar tech Joe Campagna. We went to this quack in Mill Valley and he shot us up with some potent shit each morning before we went to the studio. He said it was B complex, but he wasn't playing with a full deck. There had to be some kind of speed in it. We would be flying down the highway back to the Record Plant Sausalito, buzzed out of our brains with our plastic packets of rabbit food for the day (500 calories total).

One day upon getting to the studio, Ron informed me that the nine-foot Steinway grand piano was tuned and ready for me to do the final overdubbed take on "The Search Is Over." Sheeeitt! I thought the track I had done in L.A. would have sufficed, but Ron felt I could do better.

With shaky hands and speedy head I tried to ignore my recently shot-up condition. The track still sounded naked without Frankie's guitar parts, so every chord I played was exposed for all it was… and wasn't. As I played, the room started to undulate. After the third take, finally Ron's voice said gently over the talk back, "Okay, Jim, we got it." I made the sign of the cross and lay down on the floor next to the Steinway.

I ended up losing the unwanted thirty pounds and looked trim for the upcoming videos for "I Can't Hold Back" and "The Search Is Over." Every time I hear "The Search" I think of that magic cocktail I had before that take. I must say the piano part still sounds great!

We took a couple of weeks off and repaired back to Chicago. Karen could see a renewed enthusiasm about the band and the project at hand similar to the spark she recognized in me when Survivor was just coming together in '78.

The second day I was home Karen came to me very cautiously and seriously and informed me that she was quitting her interior design job. I was very surprised to hear that she was leaving this very rewarding job—the job that made me feel secure that she was busy and fulfilled while I was out on the road or in the studio.

She tearfully admitted that things with her co-worker were getting out of hand and the long hours they spent together were beginning to threaten our marriage. She said that they didn't "do anything" but it was clear to me that their relationship had gone beyond professional.

I was shocked, lost for words. I was in total denial of this possibility for years. My surprise was beyond the fact that I trusted her completely, but also because I thought her co-worker was gay!

"You're my best friend, Jim. I had to tell you." Karen told me that she had ended this relationship and decided to leave the job for many reasons. She found it more and more tedious to work with the limited resources at the design firm, trying to create magic in peoples' homes with the old pieces of junk that were lying around the outdated showroom.

When things settled down I held her in my arms. I told her, "Ya know, I'm kinda glad this happened. Now I can put any guilt away that I had been carrying for that one thing I did back in '74."

I was referring to a girl I met in Dallas, named Sheila, who had been watching the Jim Peterik Band one night at the club where I was playing. I was all of twenty-three and feeling my oats after a dynamite show. Karen and I had been virgins on our wedding night. I had fought off temptation for years leading up to our wedding day and now since I had miraculously achieved that goal I wanted to reward myself by feeling what it was like to be with another woman.

Sheila was groupie-cute, long honey-blonde hair, dressed in an ultra-short miniskirt, high-heeled sandals, bangles, and beads. This looked like Jimbo's big chance. She set her sights on me and followed me back to the hotel. About fifteen minutes later, the deed was done and she left without ceremony. During our little sprint everything on her anatomy seemed to be in the wrong place. Very awkward. She felt wrong. She even smelled wrong. Not bad, just unfamiliar and foreign to me. I learned a huge lesson that night that some of my fantasies were best kept as fantasies and that flesh without feeling was empty indeed. If nothing else this experience helped me to define who I wasn't—and by contrast, who I am.

For the next few weeks on the road, I was wracked with guilt. When you are that young you have no idea how you will react to different circumstances. Committing this act brought out all of my Catholic upbringing, the sanctity of marriage, the sins of the flesh, the ravages of hell.

I got through the rest of the tour somehow but it was a blur. I guess my "night of passion" got around—groupies aren't necessarily the pillar of trust—and, suddenly, Jan, one of my background singers, was hitting on me relentlessly. Hey, if I did it once…but I was less than interested. All I could think of was the way my mother would always throw my dad's affair in his face when she needed a weapon.

"It's been ten [then fifteen, then twenty] years now, but I still remember the day I found out, like it was yesterday," she would say through bitter tears.

Now I had just repeated the sins of my father.

I did the predictable thing. I sent Karen flowers the next day for no apparent reason. Then I went to the Dallas hospital and got a shot for the flu I had at the time. I thought it might do double duty to prevent any disease I may have picked up.

When I got home I went straight to my parents' house. I told them what had happened. My dad took me aside and said, "Whatever you do, don't tell Karen!" My dad was surely remembering his own admittance of his affair and the sickle of guilt that my mother constantly wielded above his head. Somehow I knew I was going to be unable to follow my father's advice.

In the confines of our tiny apartment, I acted perfectly normal. Traditionally, Karen and I would make love soon after I got back and this day was no exception. This would be my test to see if I could put my guilt aside and move on.

Lovemaking went smoothly—business as usual, until I withdrew from Karen sooner than usual after climax. It was nothing I noticed, but women have that sixth sense.

"What's the matter, Jim? That's not like you."

Shit. I'm busted!

At that point I went against my father's advice and told her what had just happened. I was sobbing. She was crying.

When the crying stopped, Karen asked tentatively, "Do you love her?"

I said, "Love her? ... I didn't even know her!" To this day it was the only time I strayed from my faithfulness to Karen.

That was all Karen seemed to need and she forgave me—just like that. It wouldn't be until Karen admitted her near-miss with her partner at the design firm that I could finally forgive myself.

On the Road Again

MY FIRST INKLING that Survivor's *Vital Signs*
album was going to be huge was in San Diego. I was there with Karen
for the very first Music and Tennis Festival, organized by former
world-ranked tennis pro Dave Austin.

I was a hack tennis player, as were most of the other rockers in
attendance at this three-day fest, but our embarrassing serves and
volleys did nothing to inhibit us from wearing the latest state-of-the-
art tennis wear by Nike and others.

There I was with Rick Nielsen and Robin Zander of Cheap Trick,
Fergie Frederiksen, fresh from his induction into Toto, Phil Ehart of
Kansas, Mike Reno of Loverboy, David Pack of Ambrosia, Dave Jen-
kins of Pablo Cruise, Stephen Bishop, Garry Tallent and Max Wein-
berg of Springsteen's E Street Band, Alan Parsons, and many others,

all playing doubles on state-of-the-art clay courts with a certified tennis pro.

Each night there would be a rehearsal for the big charity concert on the last day. The tennis pros, including celebrity players such as John McEnroe and other luminaries, would try to outdo one another each night for the most over-the-top rock outfit as they posed and preened for all they were worth. It was good fun indeed, as we taught the tennis pros the "Rock 'n' Roll for Dummies" versions of "Eye of the Tiger," "Eye in the Sky," and the perennial favorite, "Under the Boardwalk."

As I was standing just outside of the hotel waiting for my car, a massive Harley rumbled by. It was driven by what looked like a lawyer in Hells Angels gear, with the proverbial hot leather chick draped around his neck in the back.

Blasting from their stereo in all its distorted, low-fi glory I heard, "I can't hold back, I'm on the edge…" Whoa—our song was on the air. Jimi's pure tenor cut through the noonday atmosphere and sounded sooo sweet to these ears.

Over the next few days, I found that my image had changed. Suddenly I wasn't just the "Eye of the Tiger" guy. I was assailed with compliments from musicians and athletes who were digging the new one.

As the single raced up the charts, management landed us a U.S. tour, again with REO Speedwagon. That tour was followed almost immediately by a tour with Bryan Adams. Bryan sat next to me on one flight and said, "That song, 'Search Is Over,' that's really a good one. How did you guys do that?"

Jimi became the front man I knew he would be. But Frankie's jealousy of this new kid on the block began to show. He was careful never to be upstaged by Jimi and seemed to discourage our new vocalist from freely moving around the stage, at all, and, all the while, he kept pushing me further into the background.

I no longer had even one guitar song to play. Frankie would shoot me daggers across the stage if I spoke to the audience. During our *Live in Japan* video you can see me pathetically playing my towel, stretched out as if it was a guitar, on the encore.

Our "I Can't Hold Back" video became a staple on MTV. The video concept, which, again, Frankie tried (unsuccessfully) to modify two days before shooting began, showed Jimi in a Tom Cruise take from the film *Risky Business*. We rode an actual Chicago elevated train dressed as all manner of characters: Frankie was the tough greaser, Stephan was the nun, Marc was the bum, I was the straight-laced business man in a three-piece suit and slicked-back hair, and Jimi was just Jimi, playing a hot make out scene with Leeann, the video's heroine.

During its taping, I ran into Frankie sitting in the balcony of the Park West, weeping openly, as he watched Jimi filming his live sequence for the video. I'll never really know for sure why he was crying.

The second single, "High on You," pushed *Vital Signs* into platinum territory and when the third single, "The Search Is Over," went number one, Epic Records joined us on the road for a platinum party.

Just then we played the biggest show we had ever done in our career: playing to 60,000 rabid fans at the enormous Hiram Bithorn Stadium ballpark in Puerto Rico. I remember a rickety school bus driving Survivor, Night Ranger, and Men At Work to the venue. The night air was electric as we started the opening strains of "Eye of the Tiger" and thousands rushed the stage. It was pure triumph. When I explored San Juan after the show the strains of the number-one song in that country filled the streets: "The Search Is Over." Despite my growing dissatisfaction, the thrill of success could not be denied.

Next, we conquered Japan, recording and filming a live concert at Budokan arena, which had been made world famous by the immortal 1978 chart-topper *Cheap Trick at Budokan*. The concert video was complete with behind-the-scenes high jinks, exploding cigarettes, and adoring and adorable Japanese fans. The cries of "Frankie, Frankie, Jimi, Jimi" filled the night air at every show.

Karen came with me on this trip. Being tall and blonde and gorgeous, she became a celebrity in her own right with the Japanese fans, receiving a constant stream of handmade scarves, mats, and ornate fans.

Me, Jimi, and Stephan on a train in Japan.

Karen and I loved every aspect of Japanese culture (though we discovered, to our dismay, that those tempting "chocolate truffles" were, in reality, salty, fishy, bean jam buns!) and elected to stay an extra week in the ancient capital of old Japan, Kyoto.

Our stay in a traditional Japanese inn, called a *ryokan*, meant sleeping on *tatami* mats and having authentic dishes such as *sukiyaki* and *shabu shabu* prepared right in our room.

We learned that we were supposed to leave the water in those deep bath tubs (their tradition is to shower first, scrub, and then get in the tub leaving the water clean). Instead we "took a bath" American style and let all the precious water out afterwards. The hotel management was very upset.

Visiting the ornate, stone temples of Kyoto was enjoyable, and so was rocking with the '50s-influenced teens in the streets of Roppongi. From there, Karen and I flew to Hong Kong to continue our vacation.

Our week of contemplation and serenity would soon come to an end. When we got back to the States, there was an unwelcome envelope waiting for me. Frankie and I were being sued for copyright infringement on our song "High on You."

It took six months and $50,000 to put this frivolous suit to rest. I have to say Frankie was a true friend through all of this, even when I made some bonehead statements in deposition. Later, when I accepted an unsolicited cassette from an opening act, he wisely jumped all over me. "This is how we got sued in the first place!" I learned the meaning of the phrase, "Where there's a hit, there's a writ."

Now we hit the road again with REO. These were exciting times. It seemed every hit was followed by another and we were developing that momentum only seen in the top bands in the pantheon. After a call from Sylvester Stallone, Frankie and I received a script for *Rocky IV*. I sat at the pool in Alabama reading the saga of the Russian threat to our hero, Rocky Balboa. I started sketching phrases in my trusty notebook.

> *"Two worlds collide, rival nations*
> *It's a primitive clash*
> *Venting years of frustrations*
> *Bravely we hope against all hope*
> *There is so much at stake*
> *Seems our freedom's up against the ropes."*
>
> Copyright 1984 Easy Action/EMI Music ASCAP/Rude Music BMI/Sony/ATV Melody BMI/
>   Three Wise Boys Music LLC BMI

Frankie and I had the road crew deliver a Wurlitzer electric piano to my room, and we worked like mad putting together the chord changes that became "Burning Heart," the main title track for the *Rocky* franchise's next smash.

Musically the song was finished but it was tough finding the right title—and a hook that pleased Stallone. Originally we called the song "The Unmistakable Fire." The chorus started "In the human heart— just about to burst." Sly wasn't happy. As we sat in music supervisor

Robin Garb's office Frankie said, "We're gonna call it 'Burning Heart.'" I'm still unclear whether that was Robin's or Frankie's idea but I thought it was a brilliant solution.

A few weeks later found us in Sly's office on the movie set playing him the mix of "Burning Heart." "I like it," Sly said. "But it still needs something—another hook." Thinking on my feet, I suggested, "How 'bout after Jimi sings 'In the burning heart,' you hear an explosive *whack!* to set off the title." "Yeah, that's it," he intoned. The next day we were back at Rumbo with my Ides keyboard player Dave Arellano, who created the now-familiar sonic boom on his ARP synthesizer.

The song came out simultaneously with the movie and again jumped to number one, totally torpedoing our fourth release from *Vital Signs*, "First Night." But those were good problems to have.

On the surface, things looked good, but there was a growing drug problem among band members that made every band meeting a nightmare. We would arrive at a decision one night only to see everything change the next day. Survivor was now a totally dysfunctional family fraught with ego and jealousy. Sound checks were a thing of the past. We'd show up onstage like strangers and try to project a chemistry that wasn't there. It was in this chilly and airless climate that we once again, robotically, entered the recording studio to record our sixth album, *When Seconds Count*.

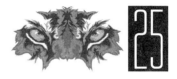

Venting Years of Frustrations

I REPAIRED TO THE SAFE harbor of home trying my best to make the transition from road dog to good husband, but returning home also meant dealing with my mother's declining health. My mother was suffering from Parkinson's disease and my sister Alice Anne and I had to find her a home caregiver. A parade of different Polish immigrants, all named Helen (!), marched through my mother's house every week.

Mother was starting to have visions, perhaps the early stages of dementia, but fortunately she was still very much aware of my burgeoning success. To lift her spirits, I'd play her new songs in our Formica-and-vinyl-clad dinette.

Karen and I were pulling closer together now that she was working from home with her own interior design company—one that

I christened "Interior Motives." Cards were made up and Karen seemed at her most fulfilled.

We talked about starting a family. Karen was now thirty-four and her biological clock was ticking. Up to this point, every time we'd see a family with a young child screaming in apparent anguish or crying for attention, we'd say in unison, "Oh those poor people!" We seemed to be united in our view, for many years, that children were not necessarily on our horizon.

But now I felt the tug of wanting to bring a new being into the world who reflected our love and, hopefully, the best attributes of us both. I felt that creating a new life was something we were put here on earth to do. I wanted to continue that musical gene pool that started with my grandfather's concertina and continued with my dad's saxophone. I took this mission seriously.

We agreed tentatively to start trying to conceive in earnest, charting Karen's most fertile periods, relaxing, and willing it to happen. It was tough work, but someone had to do it—and it brought us closer in our quest to create an original life.

Speaking of conception, around that same time Frankie and I started writing for the album that became *When Seconds Count*. The process began very creatively with Frank coming down to Tanglewood Studios to work on songs. Tanglewood was a studio co-owned by my Ides of March cohort Larry Millas.

It was located in Brookfield, Illinois, across from a stone quarry and a half block away from roaring freight trains. We would have to suspend recording every half hour or so to allow the dynamite blasts from the quarry to cease, then stop again to allow the train to rumble through.

But it was all good fun. The writing period was always my favorite and Frankie always brought his A game. It was at Tanglewood where "Is This Love" took shape with studio second engineer Frank Pappalardo programming the Linn drum machine. Later, Marc Droubay would play the part verbatim on acoustic drums, only now adding his unmistakable swing.

After completing that song we wrote the title track, "When Seconds Count." I had created two totally different verses and Frankie helped me decide which to go with. I think we made the right choice.

Soon Jimi Jamison joined us and together we wrote "Rebel Son" (my personal favorite from this album) and perhaps our most quintessential power ballad, "In Good Faith." This was the first time that Frankie and I brought anyone else into the writer's circle. I personally felt that Jimi, being such a great singer, would have something to offer as far as melodic ideas. Also, I felt politically it would be a good move to involve him in the income at the publishing end. We were also impressed by some of the rough cassettes Jimi sent us with raw ideas.

But who would produce this next effort? The choice was again clear. With *Vital Signs* selling double platinum, we went with Ron Nevison. This time though, Frankie wanted to co-produce. Apparently he felt his production input on *Vital Signs* had been unheralded. I had major problems with this notion, feeling that this should have been seen as part of Frankie's overall contribution to the band's success.

I felt that my input, especially during preproduction, was easily as valuable as his. Plus, I felt, though I dared not express it at the time, that I was being overly generous with writer's splits with Frankie, generally splitting songs fifty-fifty, which rarely reflected our individual input. In my opinion, except in some circumstances ("Caught in the Game" and "Take You on a Saturday" come immediately to mind), his writer's share was not commensurate with his contribution.

But Frank certainly did not weigh my generosity of spirit into the equation when he lobbied for, and got, co-production credit with Ron on this new album.

It was in this frame of mind that Karen and I decided to take a long overdue vacation on Paradise Island in the Bahamas before I left to record in L.A. But our time away was anything but Paradise. The weight of the years with Survivor was taking its toll on me. You can only swallow so much before you choke. And, boy, did I choke.

I decided not to take my trusty acoustic guitar on this trip so that I could totally detach from my professional life. Bad idea. I felt like a man without a mission, like I was short one arm, like life had no meaning.

Karen watched me spiral down on this trip 'til I was a weeping mess as I tried to sun myself by the pool. In our quest to get pregnant, sex became rote and decidedly unsexy. And all of this at $500 a night! I had night sweats and crying jags as Karen watched helplessly.

This was a man who had let his life get totally out of his control. The team of handlers—managers, road manager, booking agents, financial advisors, and suck-up sycophants—put me totally out of touch with who I once was. And I bonked.

In the '50s, the professionals may have called it a nervous breakdown. All I knew is that I was miserable beyond anything I'd ever known and did not at the time know why.

When I landed, I immediately sought the help of a friend and counselor, Dr. Domeena Renshaw. Domeena, one of the world's most eminent experts on the human condition and sexual function, had helped us previously in our marriage when Karen and I were looking to recapture the magic of our courtship and early marriage. At that time, we did a monthlong program that basically rewired our sexual chemistry. It worked so well that Domeena became the only person I wanted to advise me as to why my mental state had gone up in flames.

For the next few months, I saw the doctor regularly as we skinned back the onion revealing layer upon layer of disappointment and frustration. As Domeena drew out more and more from my subconscious I realized just how badly I was letting myself down by not living authentically. I was a tiger without the stripes...and I had no one to blame but myself. Frankie and I were two alpha males, but I had totally subjugated my personality for the survival of the band. My dysfunction showed in the way I handled both my band and my marriage. I was a man in free fall caused by an almost total eclipse of my natural abilities in leadership. I learned at this point to take more control, more responsibility for my actions, and to live in much less fear. I wasn't there yet but I started coming back to life. By the time I headed to Los Angeles to begin cutting the new album at the new hot studio, One on One, I felt like a wounded warrior, still in recovery, but definitely on the mend.

I was able to compartmentalize my frustration of being left out of the production circle and guitar duties and concentrate on what

I did best—keeping a steady hand on the arrangements that would bring out the heart and soul of my beloved songs. Karen, now her own boss, came out to visit me more regularly as we continued our child quest.

When the album wrapped and I was back home preparing for our first real headline tour, it soon became apparent that no degree of sexual timing or creative positions were causing the desired effect of pregnancy. Karen went for an exam, first, to see if her infertility was a medical condition.

We went to a noted fertility clinic and after trying the most obvious techniques of timed intercourse and testing the number of little swimmers in my semen (plenty), they had me go into a room with a *Penthouse* magazine and produce a sperm sample. This was then injected into Karen. Pretty romantic stuff! Nothing happened.

It turned out she had a quite advanced case of endometriosis—a malady where the lining of a woman's uterus goes outside the uterus, causing infertility.

She entered La Grange Memorial Hospital and after having a procedure, we were again open for business and eager to resume our activities.

The Survivor tour was our first as headliner playing small to midsize theaters all over the country. Some were beautiful in-the-round venues (such as New York's Westbury Music Fair), and some were rundown theaters that had seen their better days during the vaudeville era. I was positioned behind a fake, white grand piano that cleverly housed my electric keyboard.

These should have been great times, but not for me. After the show, I'd look forward to wandering through the cool parts of whatever city we were in, dining alone at some warehouse-turned-restaurant, observing life as it whirred by.

I felt nothing in common with any of my bandmates and, indeed, they really wanted nothing to do with me. I mostly hung out with Joe Campagna, our guitar technician. One memorable night we had an amazing Italian dinner in Greenwich Village, New York, where I picked up the tab. He still brings this night up when I bring over a guitar that needs adjusting.

Songwriting was how I kept my sanity on the long road trips with Survivor in the '80s. My perch on the tour bus was the shotgun seat next to our trusty driver, an ex-gospel singer who went by the handle Bass Man. As we crisscrossed the country I would document all I saw and felt as America whizzed by, making entries into my trusty spiral notebook and singing into my Sony handheld recorder the pieces of future songs.

Jealousies would rise up constantly, especially when management set up a radio promotion with Jimi and me. We had an amazing on-air chemistry that must have made Frankie crazy. At one station, Jimi told the disc jockey how much he was influenced by the Stones. I retorted, "Yeah, Fred and Barney." Ironically, it was Frankie who took himself out of the running by refusing to do radio promotion on the road.

Jimi Jamison and I had a comfortable chemistry that Frankie and I never shared. Frankie would get in a rage when he felt I was giving Jimi special treatment. One afternoon Jimi didn't show up for a sound check for a Bryan Adams show. I told Frank that I let him slide because he only got a couple of hours of sleep due to the tour schedule. (Frankie felt the sleep deprivation had more to do with late night partying.) No matter what the reason, to me the singer of a band is sacred. Without his strong voice at the helm we could not function. He was the mouthpiece of the songs—the voice of the band. It was after this incident that Frankie stopped coming to sound checks—if there were any at all.

One memory haunts me to this day and speaks to the discrepancy I had with Frankie as to a rock 'n' roll band's responsibility to its audience. We had recently got some great news from our manager, John Baruck, that Survivor was scheduled to do a headline tour of the many Six Flags amusement parks throughout America. These were shows for the whole family; the parents would bring the kids, ride the rides, eat the cotton candy, and then go to a rock show. Six Flags was booking some of the best rock bands in our strata so we were chuffed. The first show in St. Louis went well. But when we hit the stage in Atlanta, after about the second number Frankie cried, out of nowhere, "Fuck! Fuck! I'm feeling good! Are you all feeling

Me with Jimi Jamison.

good?" I saw mothers and fathers covering their children's ears as Frankie's F-bombs flew through the skies.

The very next day Six Flags canceled the rest of our tour. We lost approximately $100,000 in income. And now other promoters became wary of hiring us for other family-friendly events.

After the tour, I felt exhausted, and yet elated that it was over. Karen and I set our sights on our family mission, but still with no tangible results. I had my sperm count checked. It was normal. It was just not our time yet. God must have felt the timing wasn't quite right. As usual God keeps his own schedule. I love the line I use in "Beautiful Mess" from *Lisa McClowry Sings Acoustic Alchemy*: "to make God laugh tell him your plans!" The universe seemed to sense that I had a little more learning to do before I could take on the role of father. God may have also sensed that Karen would need some extra shoring up when that time came—so I'd have to be strong for two. We consoled ourselves by saying that if bringing a little miracle into the world was not in His game plan, then we could accept that. After all, finding each other back in '68 was miracle enough for both of us.

Sun Sinkin' but the Fire's Still Burning

THE CHRONOLOGY OF MY LIFE has always been marked by album releases. It is the benchmark around which everything else revolves. When asked how I remember so much detail and so many dates from my past, I reply that I just think of the record I was working on, find the release date, and work backward.

For Survivor, in 1987, it was a time of reassessment. Our second tour of Japan went well enough, though Jimi landed there with extreme laryngitis and barely croaked out the first show. As a result, every vocal had to be re-dubbed for the live video.

Playing dates back in the States, Marc Droubay's attitude had deteriorated. Perhaps this was due to alcohol consumption or unhappiness with the musical direction Survivor had taken since Jimi's arrival. Marc was a disciple of the kind of hard rock played by Led Zeppelin with his hero, John Bonham, pounding the skins.

In his bunk on the bus, you could hear Marc playing rare bootleg cassettes of Zep in their prime. "Kid, listen to this—it sounds like a train wreck!" he would say to Frankie, his eyes wide. Clearly he was unhappy with the pop songs that had become our hits: "High on You," "Is This Love," and especially "The Search Is Over."

At one outdoor show in Philly, Marc had ingested a good portion of the Glenlivet whiskey required in our show rider before going onstage, and he continued swigging between songs throughout the set. When it came time in the set for "The Search Is Over," he caught the eye of his pal Dave, the drum tech, and proceeded to play the song with a lounge-y cha-cha beat. The daggers I shot him failed to penetrate as the song samba-ed on. Of course, the sold-out house didn't notice a thing, too wrapped up in the lyric and Jimi's crooning, but it was the last straw for me. I couldn't see going back in the studio with a drummer who had no respect for the songs I was writing. After the tour, Frankie and I discussed our next move. We decided that if Marc was that unhappy with the group's musical direction then perhaps he should move on.

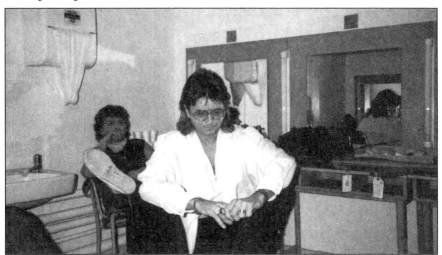

Marc and me in the dressing room.

Stephan had recently suffered a major medical setback on the road when he started bleeding internally and had to be replaced for a few shows by the head of our road crew, the storied Rocko Reedy, the guy who gave Survivor its first gig. What was first thought to be a ruptured pancreas turned out to be a bleeding ulcer. He needed some major time off to heal. I remember visiting Stephan in the hospital, bringing him a Sony Walkman and phones. Stephan was the classic victim of the rock 'n' roll lifestyle. He chugged his Carlo Rossi morning to night and chewed Excedrin by the handful for a chronic toothache. He would become drunk and unruly on international flights, one time en route to Germany goose-stepping down the aisle shouting "Sieg Heil, you Nazi bastards!" almost getting us banned for life from Lufthansa. Having said this, Stephan had a heart of pure rock 'n' roll gold. But for his own health and the health of the band we had to let him go.

After informing our rhythm section of our decision, Frankie, Jimi, and I set off to find the right producer and a new rhythm section (Sound familiar?) to play in the studio for our next, and what would turn out to be final, album for that era.

The bass slot was filled by an old friend of Frankie's and mine, Bill Syniar, formerly with the Chicago band Tantrum. Bill was always solid and right in the pocket and he was also a hell of a great guy.

We also brought in Kyle Woodring, a fantastic young drummer that we discovered at Royal Recorders, located in the old Playboy resort in Lake Geneva, Wisconsin, when he was recording with a band called Jewel Fetish.

Frankie, Bill, Kyle, Jimi, and I laid down the demos for the new album at Royal. The songs were really flowing: "She's a Star" (a rocker Frankie brought to me for completion), "Desperate Dreams" (which I wrote aboard a 737 from Philly), "Hello to You," "Didn't Know It Was Love," "Rhythm of the City," "Here Comes Desire," "Girl's Grown Up," and a tune that grew from a song seed that Jimi brought in—"Too Hot to Sleep," which became the album's title track.

This was the material we played for a producer Frankie and I both admired for his recent work on Foreigner's *Agent Provocateur* album: Frank Filipetti. We felt from a sonic standpoint he could not be touched, plus his arrangement skills were very evident on my favorite track, the lush, keyboard laden "That Was Yesterday."

I also was blown away by Filipetti's work on James Taylor's masterful *That's Why I'm Here*, which was the album I played for guests at my house when I wanted to show off my state-of-the-art stereo system.

Frank Filipetti was equally impressed with our new batch of songs and a deal was struck. He recommended a drummer he had worked with who had played on some of the biggest songs in the Hall & Oates catalogue: Mickey Curry. Filipetti didn't have to say it twice because Sullivan and I were presold on Mickey's powerful, rock solid drumming on some of the biggest hits by Canadian sensation and touring buddy, Bryan Adams. Filipetti felt that Kyle Woodring was not quite ready to do a full, state-of-the-art rock album. Besides, he was more comfortable with someone he had already worked with such as Mickey Curry. Kyle was crushed but took it like the pro that he was. Kyle, who would eventually join Survivor a few years later, tragically and inexplicably committed suicide in 2009. His shining spirit and talent will always be remembered.

Mickey had just the rhythmic pocket we needed to bring everything up a notch. Marc Droubay had the John Bonham swing and bluster, but Mickey brought the fire that Marc was starting to lose under the weight of frustration, nonstop touring, and, some would say, increased alcohol consumption.

The decision of where to record was settled quickly. Filipetti knew Right Track Studios in Manhattan like the back of his hand. He should have—he helped design it! The giant automated Solid State Logic console stretched on for what looked like miles in the Studio A control room. The crude plywood floors gave the drums and guitars a rough immediacy like we had never known before—even punchier than the Nevison days at the Record Plant.

The band took up residency at a posh Manhattan hotel paid for by the Scotti brothers (but to be eventually deducted from our record royalties). I would have preferred to stay at a less grandiose hotel, but Frankie's taste ran to the lush life of a rock star.

Recording ran smoothly, at least until it was time for Jimi to do vocals. By this time we were back in Lake Geneva at Royal Recorders. It was much cheaper to stay at the former Playboy resort, and Royal's hourly rate was a fraction of Right Track's.

Jimi became convinced that Frankie was bugging his room, listening in to his conversations, and stealing clothes from his closet. He felt that Frankie was trying to push him over the edge and make him believe he was going crazy.

Jimi was crippled by paranoia and actually believed that Frankie had set up a sting whereby Frankie's guitar tech offered to sell him cocaine, hoping he would reveal himself by purchasing the drug. To this day, I don't know if any of this had any foundation in truth, but it made for an almost impossible atmosphere in the studio.

As a songwriter, I am especially proud of my lyrics and was totally thrown for a loop when Frank Filipetti came to me one night and strongly suggested lyrical and title changes in the songs we had just recorded. I had never been challenged like this, on any of the albums I had written for, with any band I was ever in.

Filipetti unceremoniously handed me a few sheets of paper with his suggestions. "Girl's Grown Up" (a clever lyric about a solid woman behind a crazy rocker) became the uninspired "Can't Give It Up." The pop gem "Hello to You" became the generic "Tell Me I'm the One." "Here Comes Desire" stayed the same in title only and was restructured to fit the facelessness of most of the rewrites. Some great lines in "She's a Star" were lost for all time. ("In a Porsche, looking pretty" comes to mind.)

I took comfort in that the lyrics that were left unmolested truly reflected my sensibilities: "Desperate Dreams" ("one girl lost in a reverie, lost love found in a memory"), "Too Hot to Sleep" ("I wanna know that I can count on you to pour a little gasoline on the fire," "a cold Corona and a twist of lime"), and a song that originated from a celestial jam back in Chicago, just before we flew to New York.

Frankie started playing a neat, muted guitar figure. I began playing some support chords on the keyboard, using what I call "Ice Cream Changes"—the structure reminiscent of many songs in the innocent ice cream parlors of the '50s: A major to F# minor to D major to

E major then back to A major. There's just something about that simple run of chords that brings back the ghosts of so many great songs. It was magic as the melody developed in the room with Jimi eventually singing the opening words I created on the spot: "When I'm all alone, on a distant path, and my ticket home has been torn in half—oh, I can hear your voice—girl, I can feel your touch—across the miles tonight." Goose-bump city.

We knew then and there we were experiencing the creation of a classic. I had jotted down the title a few weeks earlier, browsing through the greeting card section of Marshall Fields department store in downtown Chicago (now sadly bought out and renamed Macy's) when I saw the plastic marker card that read "Across the Miles," referring to cards to loved ones far away. (This song was beautifully covered by Uriah Heep in 1998 with lead singer Bernie Shaw reportedly breaking down as he sang this ode to the heartbreak of separation.)

The issue of Jimi's involvement in the writing of this song was perhaps the main reason for his exit from the band a few months later, claiming he was part of the song's creation at that Chicago warehouse.

In addition to criticism of my lyrics from Filipetti (to this day I believe Frankie Sullivan had a lot to do with swaying Frank into demanding lyric changes), our pal from Styx, Tommy Shaw, added his own special brand of negativity, saying that some of my lyrics were "not rock 'n' roll," when he came up to Lake Geneva to do background vocals.

I had known Tommy since the days he played with MS Funk. Now though, Tommy and Frankie were as thick as thieves, hanging out together and going out at night. Tommy may have been another factor in the lyric changes. He called the lyric to "Hello to You" "wimpy."

I was bucking a lot of negativity coming my way. Jimi was claiming writing credit on songs that Frankie and I had no recollection of his being involved with. He made it clear at the time that if he didn't receive the credits he claimed, his days would be numbered with the band. He often brought up his ambition of recording a solo album. I was caught between a rock and a hard place: If I caved in to Jimi's demands I would alienate Frankie; if I didn't we might lose our singer. Frankie and I discussed it and decided to chance it and not cater to Jimi's demands—to just let the chips fall where they may. This is probably the single worst decision I ever made in my professional life.

When I listen now to "Burning Bridges," one of my favorite tracks on *Too Hot to Sleep*, it's no wonder that the lyrics of the song we wrote were delivered with an urgency I've never heard before or since from Jimi. He was literally singing his story:

> *"You can call out my name but I won't return*
> *I'm a fugitive of love and this heart's been burned*
> *Whoa-oh, Burning Bridges behind me*
> *You can follow me down but it's plain to see*
> *I'm a victim of the burn and it's third degree*
> *Whoa-oh, setting bridges on fire."*

Copyright 1988 Easy Action/EMI Music ASCAP /Rude Music BMI/Three Wise Boys Music LLC BMI

The *Too Hot to Sleep* album came out to little fanfare, except in Europe and Japan where it was heralded as a masterpiece and Survivor's best to date. The first single "Didn't Know It Was Love" landed with a thud in spite of a very cool video filmed at an outdoor amphitheater. The second release, "Across the Miles," was also supported by an expensive video. One scene made Frankie, Jimi, and me look like we were spinning shakily on a hot dog rotisserie.

What now? Where do we go from here? Was this the end of a long tradition? We circled the wagons. Frankie and I were crushed by the apathy surrounding *Too Hot to Sleep*. Even with my lyrical disappointments, I felt it was a great album. Why couldn't we get the record company to get behind it? Was the musical tide turning? Was melodic rock becoming passé? Were the anguished, atonal sounds of alternative rock taking over? History would soon supply the answer.

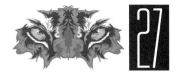

Another Part of the Plan

1988 WAS A YEAR of miracles for Karen and me. It will go down in my private history as perhaps the richest time of my life—the year most fraught with victory and tragedy, wins and losses. Survivor was tottering on its last legs, devastated by a distinct apathy from the press and public regarding our latest disc, *Too Hot to Sleep*, which we felt featured some of our best work.

Unfortunately, timing is everything and this was the period that the rock music world started to change. Mullets gave way to long, straight, greasy-looking hair. Gold lamé, eyeliner, and spandex were out; flannel and droop-assed jeans were in. Sunburst Les Paul guitars were put in storage in favor of grungy, purposely out-of-tune sounding, cheapy Fenders like the Duo Sonic model and the Jaguar. The wide-legged rock stance changed to the one leg in front of the other pose—kind of like surfing without the board.

The music was all about angst now. Love songs were pretty much out the window and power ballads were suddenly a thing of the past. Melodies were frowned upon and heroin was taking over in some circles as the hip drug of choice. Northwest bands such as Nirvana, Pearl Jam, Soundgarden (the best of the breed in my opinion), and others were setting the tone: The record labels were eager to see what rough beast was slouching toward Seattle to be born.

I wanted no part of this scene, plus I had no credibility to even try to compete. I was overall a happy, satisfied, and content guy with a loving family and a wonderful wife. What did I know or care about teen angst? Plus my heroes, songsmiths such as Carole King and Gerry Goffin, Leiber and Stoller, Bacharach and David, and Lennon and McCartney, wrote music and lyrics light-years away from the three-chord grunge that was starting to sludge up the airwaves and bullet up the charts.

In a way, 1988 was the perfect time for me to reboot my life and hit "undo." I'd had it with the band politics of Survivor. I was sick of not having my opinions valued. When *Too Hot to Sleep* failed to burn up the charts, a part of me was relieved.

One sunny afternoon on my thirty-seventh birthday, November 11, 1988, Karen decided to seduce me. Maybe it was her idea of a birthday gift. It certainly became the gift that keeps giving! We had a really bright bedroom with windows on two sides of the lofted ceiling room. We slept in a distressed bamboo canopy bed (which now resides in our Saugatuck second home along with our brass wedding bed), and it was a really romantic setting. Afternoon delights seemed to be our style throughout our marriage.

Karen and I had about a year ago given up on our "child quest" ambitions. We were really tired of the mechanics of trying to get pregnant and failing. We decided we'd rather be successful at making love than failures at procreating. The miracle, as we repeated like a mantra, was finding each other in the first place.

It was in that mindset that we had a wonderful lovemaking session on that day. Just after we had finished the act, Karen did something I had never seen her do before (or since)—she turned over on her stomach and put her hand between her legs. I asked her what she was doing. She gently said that she heard somewhere that if you turn over right after sex that the sperm could more effectively travel to the uterus (and she had recently been diagnosed with a tilted uterus) and that this would increase our chances at pregnancy.

I was amused and confused. "Karen, I thought we gave up on that a year ago!"

She said that she just had a feeling she should flip over. Okay, fine.

I felt a new freedom that year with the hiatus of Survivor. A disgruntled Jimi Jamison was off doing a solo album for the Scotti brothers much to our dismay at the time. Frankie was doing all he could to keep control of me, attempting to unite us through chaos and shared enemies such as our then-manager John Baruck. But I'd have none of it. I was so done with the Sturm und Drang of rock 'n' roll.

One afternoon in late November, Karen and I decided to take advantage of perhaps the last mild day of the year by taking a bike ride at the Arie Crown woods in Hodgkins, Illinois. It was mid-afternoon by the time we got there to ride the park's winding, pea gravel trails. In our helmets and padded-ass shorts, we made quite a pair. As the skies grew darker and the wind whipped up menacingly, we decided we'd better make haste back to our car before the sunset. We started really pedaling hard.

Suddenly we found ourselves speeding down a fairly steep decline in the grade of the road—*Wheee!* I was in the lead when suddenly out of nowhere there appeared a chain across the exit/entrance to the park. I saw it too late and careened into it. I flew about twenty feet over the chain and landed on my head. Luckily, Karen was far enough behind me to avoid the same fate.

She came over to me, as I lay there unconscious. Next thing I knew I was in the back of an ambulance roaring down Mannheim Road to La Grange Memorial Hospital. I could feel warm blood running down my face as I started to come into semiconsciousness.

Next thing I remember was the vague image of the kindly face of Dr. Janda. He was stitching up my face as if he was mending a ripped shirt. I felt nothing. The world was a blur. In the accident I cracked my skull open, ripped up my face, and broke my left wrist and a few ribs. The doctor said if I had not been wearing my helmet, I'd be dead or paralyzed. Karen's fast action just after my fall was a godsend. She is grace under pressure personified and I'll always love her for that day.

I recuperated for one full week at the hospital, shot-up with the best drugs science could design. I actually wrote some great songs under the influence of the opiates I was receiving. When I got home, I was still really out of it. The concussion had totally messed with my memory. Suddenly, as Karen and I were visiting our next-door neighbors I started sobbing uncontrollably. I couldn't stop. I was wailing! I went back to the hospital for an extra week—I had been released too soon and my electrolytes were way out of whack.

Things were still kind of blurry when I got back home, but I was a happy and thankful guy. I could have been dead or incapacitated for life. Though I was still a little dizzy, my perspective on life was razor sharp. When Frankie would call and try to inflame me with the latest "disaster," I would say, "Well, that's really no big deal. It will all work out." Once you've dodged the bullet, things don't seem nearly as catastrophic as they once did. Frankie had his mojo working—but it just wouldn't work on me from then on.

Karen and I went about our lives together, drawing even closer because of the shared events of the last month. Soon after I returned home we visited my mother a few times. She was still living at home, attended to by the parade of Helens. Mother was suffering from dementia, a product of her mid-stage Parkinson's disease, so it was not a huge surprise that, while we were chatting in her dinette, she said, "Who's that little blond boy in the corner? Right over there. Don't you see him?"

Karen and I gave each other that bemused look that said we both knew Mom was hallucinating, but she just kept insisting that there was a very cute blond boy sitting right in the corner of the kitchen.

About a week later we again visited Mother Peterik. As we sat down she said, "There he is again, the little blond boy. Seems whenever you come over to visit, there he is." *Crazy lady*, we thought.

But in late December, Karen realized her period was quite late in arriving. She said nothing at first—she had been late before. Then, on New Year's Eve at our friends Rich and Peggy Brom's house, we were eating pizza when suddenly she began to feel nauseous.

She went to the doctor the following week for a pregnancy test. I sat on pins and needles hoping with every fiber of my being that we had conceived. I distinctly recall sitting in the living room of our La Grange home when the phone rang. Karen answered it in the kitchen.

All I heard was the following one-sided conversation: "Hello doctor! [Pause] So you're sure? Are you sure you're sure? Really? Well what do we do now?"

I was up in a flash hugging her. I couldn't believe my ears. What the doctors had called a near impossibility had happened. Against all odds we had connected in the most sacred and intimate of all human experiences. This was the blessing I had been praying for. Karen had been more ambivalent about it so I must have been praying for two.

It turns out that my mother had seen our future son, playing calmly in the corner of my boyhood dinette, when she was caught in some kind of cosmic time warp between the here and hereafter. This was long before we even realized we had conceived. I will never again assume to know the existence of the unknowable again.

The next months flew quickly. Without the constant demands and crises of Survivor we even found time to vacation on the Florida Keys when Karen was about four months along. For some reason our sex life went into high gear. Perhaps it was a combination of her raging female hormones and my belief that a girl is at her most womanly when she is pregnant.

One day my buddy Jeff Carlisi called me up and asked me if I'd like to join him at a rock benefit event in Indianapolis based around racing school. He raved about the last one he'd attended with the likes of Bon Jovi where you'd get lessons, then get to race cars around the track at breakneck speeds—all for charity. It sounded good to me, reminding me of the drag races I got to tag along to with Alice Anne and her various boyfriends.

When the day arrived, before heading to the airport, I first visited my mother, who by that time was at an assisted living facility in La

Grange called Colonial Manor. In the weeks prior to this my mother had been in and out of coherency, battling her dementia.

She was stationed on the sunny porch on the south side of the home. When she saw me she lit up. "Jimmie! It's so good to see you!" I could barely believe the transformation. She was alive, attentive, and sparking with renewed interest in the world around her. I told her that I was on my way to racing school in Indianapolis. I thought I sensed a disapproving look on her face but she said nothing. She knew what a spacey driver I was, often distracted by musical ideas at lightning speeds. We talked on about the family and anything else that crossed our minds. It was the best talk I had had with her in years. I left the Manor buoyed up by her renewed life.

Carlisi greeted me at the airport and we went to a reception where I met the other rockers such as Don Dokken, of Dokken, who was raving about his new seven-string guitar. After my second glass of champagne I received an emergency phone call. Somehow my nephew's wife, Kathy McCabe, tracked me down. My mother had passed away. Stunned, I made plans to return early the next morning. My mother had known her days were numbered. I believe to this day that she chose this particular day to die, to keep me out of that damn racing car and prevent my certain demise. She used similar, though not as dramatic ploys to prevent me and Karen from getting motorcycles—such as making sure the West Coast shipping strike would cause us to cancel our order for twin Vespas. Thank you, Mother— I'm still here and I've never raced since.

Karen and I wanted a fresh start for our new family. We spent idyllic days cruising the western Illinois suburbs on our Yamaha Chappy minibikes (Mother somehow approved those little Shrine Circus bikes) for property to build our new home. We came across an area in Burr Ridge that really spoke to us. It was upscale but not fancy, gated, or ostentatious. The homes were nice but not grotesque in their pretension. The residents were mainly hard-working professionals and a few high-end sports figures. We purchased the perfect half-acre lot and began finding the right architect to build what I called our future "launching pad."

A pregnant Karen looks out the window during the building
of our "launching pad."

So as Karen was growing a baby, we were also creating a house. After three completely different house plans with two different architects, we found the perfect combination of design elements. On the cover of *Builder Magazine*, an amazing great room was pictured. I said, "Let's base the whole house around this room." It was a huge room with twenty-foot ceilings and square windows along the top. This is when the house plan really took shape. There was also going to be a workout studio above the four-car garage.

Ultimately, the planned sweat shop turned into a recording studio just weeks before the house's completion when Larry Millas, my friend and musical partner, said, "You know, Jim, you're leasing all that cool recording equipment to River North Studios downtown. The lease is up. Why don't you bring it all home?"

That made a ton of sense and I immediately called our architect, Stan Glodek, and caught him just in time to create a separate entrance to the studio. That studio has barely gone one day in twenty-three years without a session rocking just yards from our bedroom door.

Fortunately a Lifetime Fitness club sprung up just two blocks away to take care of our workout and yoga needs!

I can look back and smile now at the little dramas along the way to the birth of our child, such as the seemingly endless thirty-minute wait in the lobby as Karen went through amniocentesis to test for the presence of birth defects in the fetus. One of the happiest moments of my life was when the doctor brought me into that tiny room where Karen was being scanned with a device that showed the new being inside, heart beating for all it was worth. Karen wore a beaming smile on her face. There it was—new life—a life that our love created! We could not yet tell the sex of the child (no "outdoor plumbing" was yet in evidence) but we walked on air out to the car when the procedure was over and had a great dinner.

I was on the road when Karen's dad, Rudy, accompanied her to the test that screened for any further abnormalities and in which the gender of the child could finally be determined. As soon as I landed at O'Hare, I called Karen. She reported that all was A-OK with our baby boy. What? Come again? Did you say *boy*? I was overcome with joy and doubt at the same time.

I immediately went to the airport bar and ordered a cold gin martini while I wrapped my head around the news. I had kind of thought it was going to be a girl, who would be raised more or less by her mother and tutored in the feminine things of life. Now I find out it's a boy and all at once I wondered if a nontraditional rock-and-role model could really raise a lad properly.

I couldn't fix a sink or build a tree house. I wasn't the throw-and-tackle kind of guy, but my overriding emotion was pure joy. I knew I was up to the challenge of showing my son, by example, what I thought it meant to be a good person, and I convinced myself this would be enough.

One evening, as we waited and waited for Karen to go into labor, we rented the remake of 1950s horror classic *The Blob*. This is perhaps the grossest movie visually of all time with undulating gobs of goo sliming its way into unsuspecting folks' bedrooms. This is all it took to send Karen into labor. (Hint to all: To induce labor, rent *The Blob*.)

Karen and I had idealistically, though as it turned out, misguid-edly, decided to try a home birth. But after sixty hours of labor at our home in La Grange, Karen could take no more. Our baby's life was in danger and so was his mom's. The home doctor said it was time to drive down to his home base of operation—Weiss Hospital on Lake Shore Drive in Near North Chicago—to birth the baby.

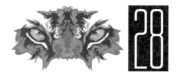

The Path from Dark to Light

I WAS IN THE DRIVER'S SEAT, Karen in shotgun, and Esther and Rudy (Karen's dear parents) in the backseat. I remember going ninety-five mph down I-55 in a blind dash to save two lives. I had never been more focused and determined.

In the hospital room our doctor tried every method known to man except for the Jaws of Life to extricate our future son. But our baby had his own ideas—still does. He presented himself in "brow position" and was just too bulky to come out. Karen was swooning in pain, having been denied pain meds or spinal blockage to ease her intense labor pains. (Our doctor/quack did not believe in such crutches.) But our doctor was getting panicky. You could see it in his eyes and the sweat that soaked his shirt.

Finally, he turned to me and cried, "He won't budge! What do we do now?"

I looked at him with a stunned stare of disbelief and said, "You're gonna find a doctor in this hospital that knows what the fuck he's doing."

Soon a wonderful female doctor, who appeared like an angel, took one look at the situation and said, "Let's get this baby born."

Amen to that. She gave Karen a much-needed spinal injection and her pain-tortured face turned soft and kind again. Colin James Peterik came kicking and screaming into the world by cesarean section at about 11:30 a.m., approximately sixty-six hours since KP and I watched *The Blob* together back home.

Our son, born on October 31, 1989, was christened as such for my love of that name when Colin Blunstone burst onto the scene as the dapper lead singer of The Zombies.

I did not really care to see what was going on behind the curtain, but as soon as the baby was extracted I got to cut the umbilical cord. It was a tougher membrane than I expected, but I got the job done. By this time "Dr. Homebirth" had scurried away never to be seen or heard from again.

As Karen held Colin in her arms there was a deep look of satisfaction in her eyes. The baby had a certain Peterik familiarity about him that everyone picked up on, but there was a beauty in his eyes that was all Karen.

The second day as she lay recuperating, Karen started to feel intense pain and cramping in her calves. The doctor said it was most likely muscle strain from all the pushing to get the baby out.

She had to stay in the hospital for an extra week for recuperation and observation while I took Colin home to La Grange to start our life together. For some reason, though I should probably have been terrified, I felt totally in control—just me and this lump of baby protoplasm. Since he was flesh of my flesh, flesh of Karen's flesh, all things seemed possible.

Holding Colin in my arms was unlike anything I had ever experienced—way better than holding the Grammy statuette, or getting that second encore before Led Zeppelin took the stage. Now I was fulfilled. My dear mother's hallucinatory vision was now flesh and blood. Now Karen and I could truly start our

Karen, me, and baby Colin.

second act—not just as friends and lovers, but as parents. We didn't realize it, but through our love and years together we had been rehearsing for this moment ever since The Turtles concert in 1968.

The traumatic events of giving birth to Colin would soon have far-reaching effects on Karen's life and mine. Still, the miracle of life was set in motion and I had an undying faith that the rest would take care of itself.

Colin cried practically nonstop. It turned out he was colicky, which is a digestive disorder in infants. The only thing that would make him stop wailing was to hold him over my shoulder and apply what I called "Rhythm Therapy," where I gently pounded his back and sang calypso songs. ("The Banana Boat Song" comes to mind— "Day-o!") It usually worked.

On our first night alone together Colin was still screaming. I lay on my back in bed and held him on my chest. My beating heart must have calmed him down because he slept soundly until he woke me up for a 2 a.m. feeding. I had prepared Prosobee formula in advance, so I would feed him in the kitchen as I worked on lyrics to new songs, such as the one I was writing in his honor, "Child of a New World." This routine continued for weeks on end. I also learned to change his diaper in forty-five seconds flat. My dear friend Tim Dam said it looked like I was casually trussing a turkey.

Every day, while Karen's wonderful parents took over the watch, I visited KP at the downtown hospital. She was in bad shape physically and mentally. I brought her flowers one morning and a homemade card with one of my drawings that showed us picnicking in a carefree way with a bottle of wine. I was noted in my family for saving money on Hallmark cards by doodling my own through the years. Without knowing it, I made drawings that looked rather like John Lennon's doodles. Karen glanced at my card often, many times through tears, in the weeks to come. It reminded her that there was life waiting for her after all this was behind her.

I didn't realize it then but Karen was starting to show the classic symptoms of post-partum depression. When the doctors felt she could finally come home she spent hours weeping and saying things so uncharacteristic of her like, "My life is over. Things will never be the same." She was, of course, referring to the changes that were to take place by bringing this new person into the world.

I really couldn't quite understand it. All I saw was hope and light. This was the child I had prayed for. This was the one to reflect all that we were. All Karen saw was the end of life as she knew it. All the while her leg pain kept getting worse and worse.

While I was taking a walk one day with Colin in my front carrier I saw a young doctor who lived down the street, Dr. Jack Payne. I described Karen's leg cramps. Without blinking he said I should get her to the local hospital immediately where he would check her out.

I brought Karen there post-haste and not a moment too soon. She was diagnosed with life-threatening blood clots caused by the pregnancy and difficult delivery and received emergency injections of the blood thinner heparin, that just may have saved her life. If a clot had made its way to her heart she would have been a goner. And it had been on its way. Jack Payne was another in a long line of angels looking over our family.

Karen started feeling better, with less and less leg pain, but emotionally she was still on tenterhooks. Colin's constant crying drove her up the wall. To this day when she hears the demanding wail of a baby, she goes into that very dark place for just an instant. I suggested she see Dr. Domeena Renshaw, the therapist who put our sex life back on track nearly two decades earlier and more recently helped me come back after my Bahamas breakdown.

Dr. Renshaw talked Karen through the many emotions she was feeling and prescribed her a mild antidepressant. Karen may have taken it for only a few weeks, but just talking to this empathetic professional did wonders for her. Gradually, smile-by-smile, she started acting more and more like her old self, though it took roughly a year and a half 'til she was finally out of the woods and walking in the sunlight again.

We would look forward to our trips to the construction site of our new house. I brought a guitar to check out the acoustics as Karen took careful measurements for carpet and drapery. We went to various stores to pick out appliances and furniture.

About that time, Karen noticed a peculiar, smooth, hairless spot on the back of her head about the size of a quarter. Then the spot grew larger. Soon she was learning ways of swooping her hair around to hide her growing baldness.

As the hair loss worsened she was diagnosed with a condition called alopecia. The doctor said there was no way of knowing if all her hair would fall out or just part of it. It turned out that in the course of the next five months Karen would lose every hair on her head and body in this most extreme example of alopecia universalis.

There is no known cause or cure for alopecia, as we learned, but in some cases there is a trigger. Sometimes a catastrophic event starts a chain reaction that makes your immune system think your hair is a foreign object and thus rejects it. It could be divorce, the death of a loved one, an accident, sickness, or, as in Karen's case, a life-threatening labor and delivery.

Just before she lost her last tuft of hair she went shopping for wigs without a clue of where to find a really quality product. Her first wig looked like a dead animal had somehow perched on her head. She came home with it on and burst into tears.

Karen went to Dr. Fiedler, the hair-loss guru in Chicago, who has sold the dream of hair regrowth to many men and women, usually with little success. After thousands of dollars of pills, salves, and ointments not a wisp of hair reappeared.

I thought she looked amazing even without hair, so I think that fact helped her with her self-esteem. Gradually she started leaving the house and got back into the mainstream of life—even with that fright wig on her head. Karen knew that she had to find a product that reflected the real her. She began a quest to find the ultimate hairpiece, which led her to the National Alopecia Convention in California. It was there that she noticed a woman with the most gorgeous hair she'd ever seen—lustrous, long, and natural. If only she could find a wig that looked like that woman's God-given hair, Karen mused. At that point the woman said hello to Karen and proceeded to whip her hair right off her head! The brand of hair prosthesis this woman wore would change Karen's life.

By the year 2011, with her company, New Life Hair, Karen had become one of the leading dealers of the Freedom Hair of New Zealand vacuum hairpiece for long-term hair loss, generally due to alopecia. Karen was one of the first in the country to purchase and use a laser scanner, which replaced the messy old plaster wrap for molding her clients' heads to create the natural, unprocessed human hair wig she sells. She has become a role model for hundreds of women (and an inspiration to many hairless men as well) who have lost a lot of self-esteem in the process of losing their hair.

In 2006, after four days of hiking the rugged Milford Track in New Zealand, Karen and I visited the headquarters (no pun intended) of Freedom Wigs in Dunedin on the South Island. We toured the factory where trained professionals sorted, braided, and tied the thousand strands of unprocessed human hair and crafted a latex-based cap to hold the wig like a vacuum to the scalp. Just like Karen, people can go about their normal day's activity, the wig becoming just an extension of themselves. Sports, swimming, sex—all back on the menu. It gave Karen her life back and now she is giving lives back to so many. Karen truly took adversity in her life and found a life-changing silver lining. It's the proverbial lemons to lemonade. I could not be more proud of her and her shining spirit.

Motherhood was starting to suit Karen better. The fact that I loved the process of changing and feeding Colin made it possible for her to enjoy his smiles and growing awareness of the world around him.

He was very obviously musical. So many of the early photos and video footage of Colin finds him perched in front of his Casio synthesizer or on my lap selecting keys on our grand piano. He would sing along to the hits on the radio in perfect pitch. Frankie Sullivan witnessed CJ singing along with the radio one day and remarked that he had the musical gene. On our thirty-minute trip to and from Montessori preschool each day, we would listen not only to the current rock radio station, but also to classic rock and oldies. The songs he writes these days strongly reflect the rich stew of influences he heard emerging from that dashboard radio. It became commonplace for Colin to hear his father take a call from a local radio station and be put on the air as we drove to school. (When Colin first played me back his first solo CD released in 2011 called *Detroit Club* I was not prepared for the emotions waiting inside me. As I've often said, the strongest emotions sneak up on you and take you by surprise. As "Your Name Song" and then "Idaho" played I was suddenly overwhelmed and started sobbing and wailing uncontrollably right there in the front seat of the car as we listened in the driveway. I thought of all those rides in the car together going to school, the road behind him and the endless road that stretched ahead of him. Suddenly I felt his goodness and the divinity of God's creation and saw the miracle of how Karen and I had transformed our love into the flesh and blood of this amazing boy. Colin looked at me with an edge of panic in his voice, "You okay, Dad?" "Yeah, son," I croaked through my tears, "Real okay.")

We were now dug in at our Launching Pad. I called it that because I felt our family could do absolutely everything from that one location. Just like Larry had suggested, the enormous Neve model 8068 recording console was installed in the space above the garage. A special platform lift had to be created to transport the two-ton behemoth over the railings on the upper level of the house. Same with the refrigerator-sized Studer A800 multitrack tape transport.

Remember, this was before the digital age took over and miniaturized the mechanics of recording. The warm analogue sound we heard that first day of recording was more than enough reward for the very difficult delivery—pun intended.

When Colin was able to walk he came with me into the studio and began to chase a balloon. I told him to please stop. He continued. Suddenly he fell into a bank of vintage guitars I had on stands in the studio and about ten of them went over like dominoes. The headstock of one of the Fenders chopped into the side of my priceless 1942 prewar Martin D-18 acoustic guitar.

This was the first and last time I totally lost my temper and yelled at Colin for being so careless. He went screaming out of the room and down the stairs where I found him shivering and shaking on the sofa, apparently traumatized. I swept him in my arms and told him how sorry I was for losing it so completely. This incident taught me a lesson about self-control and the damage a parent can do to a child's self-esteem. It never happened again.

Having adjusted to my new normal, and with Survivor no longer occupying my time, I thought about what I wanted next from my career and began to reconnect with what I most enjoyed about being a songwriter. Independence brought back all the youthful enthusiasm that had been ground down by the endless battles with Frankie. I was also still driven to write hit records and have my songs heard. Perhaps my biggest regret of the Survivor years was that I had let Frankie guilt me out of co-writing with other artists. At the start of the '80s, before I allowed Frankie to condition me, I was writing great songs with people like Sammy Hagar, Henry Paul, and 38 Special and having hits—and having a great time, too. I'm a people person and a natural collaborator who loves the stimuli of meeting and working with new people, pooling our stories and experiences and coming up with something fresh. I couldn't wait to get back in the game.

As fate would have it, 38 Special was going through its own internal issues at the start of the '90s. My good songwriting buddy Don Barnes had left the band (temporarily as it would turn out) to try his hand at a solo career. But Donnie Van Zant, Jeff Carlisi, and the gang were ready to move forward, joined by veteran talents Danny Chauncey and ex-Jack Mack and the Heart Attack lead singer Max Carl. With Jeff, Danny, and Max, I co-wrote the upbeat rocker "The Sound of Your Voice," which turned into a major AOR radio hit for 38 Special and gave them their last crack at the Top 40. We also crafted a great vehicle for Donnie in "Rebel to Rebel," a tribute to his fallen brother, Lynyrd Skynyrd's Ronnie Van Zant (soon, I would be co-writng with the third Van Zant brother, Johnny, for several albums by the reborn Lynyrd Skynyrd). This latest success with 38 Special reaffirmed my long-held belief that we should have never stopped writing together in the first place. It was great to renew this connection of music and friendship, which continues into the present day.

Another connection was reignited in late 1991 when I ran into my friend and champion John Kalodner at a Cheap Trick album release party at the Hard Rock Café in Chicago. Their next album, *Woke Up with a Monster*, would contain two songs that I wrote with Rick Nielsen, "You're All I Wanna Do" and "Never Run Out of Love."

After catching up a bit I mentioned to Kalodner that it was my dream to write with Steven Tyler of Aerosmith, who were about to go into the studio to cut their follow-up to their mega platinum *Pump* album.

John, who had signed the band, called Steven the next day and a week later I was in Boston being picked up at the airport by Aerosmith's limo. I put my suitcase and guitar in the trunk and sat down in the backseat next to the biggest pair of lips on the planet. It was a surreal moment, where because of his iconic status and media concentration, Steven appeared to me as a life-sized cartoon.

Gradually the awkwardness melted as we talked rock 'n' roll. He mentioned that he was originally a drummer and used to play along with my Ides of March hit, "Vehicle."

When we got to his farm/studio we got right to work on a song seed I brought with me from Chicago called "Brass Balls." He loved the idea and we chased it all afternoon. I have never been pushed so hard to write a great lyric before. It was eye-opening as the song kept getting better and better—cleverer—more descriptive as the hours flew by. I learned a lot that day from my caricature teacher. The song never made it to their next record, but I have a great demo of it, featuring Steven singing and banging the drums with me on guitar. I wouldn't trade the experience for anything. These are the kind of experiences I never could have had if I were still locked in with Survivor.

Timing is everything, though, and the truth is that the hits weren't coming as easily as I'd hoped. There was a time in the early '90s when I thought the gravy train had stopped for good. Grunge had taken over the airwaves and melodic hits like my "Hold on Loosely" and even "Eye of the Tiger" were considered "so yesterday." The only places where my musical values of a great melody, inspiring or meaningful lyric, and soaring vocal were being heard in heavy rotation during this period were in the adult contemporary hits of artists like Celine Dion. And for whatever reason, I wasn't getting the same opportunities as writers like Desmond Child or Diane Warren, who very successfully transitioned from the '80s to the '90s, to pitch big ballads to the pop divas. My quarterly earnings from publishing dipped to a fraction of what they had been in the '80s.

I panicked and began to sell off some of my precious guitars. The most significant sale was my prized 1958 Gibson Les Paul Sunburst electric. I had purchased this guitar for $6,000 back in 1980, and I became well known in collector's circles for owning a mint-condition example of this sought-after guitar. I decided to sell it for the money I could make on it, and also in part because this guitar brought with it a tragic legacy. A few years after I had purchased it, the former owner (owner of the tiny Bobill Music in Waukegan, Illinois) killed his wife, his two-year-old child, and then turned the gun on himself. I couldn't play this guitar without thinking of this horrific legacy. I ultimately sold it to Norm's Rare Guitars in Reseda, near Los Angeles, for $22,000. Today that guitar is worth in the neighborhood of $250,000.

Concurrently, The Ides of March got an offer from our hometown of Berwyn to reunite for one giant show to be held in July of 1990.

Every Ide to the man said the same thing, "I'll do it as long as all the original members do it—it's got to be 100 percent." It was.

I was in a position finally to be my own man, unencumbered by the need to get Frankie's blessing before I made a move. In the recent past, if I did something outside the band like producing a song demo for my publisher, Frankie would dog me on the phone, asking me what I was doing, tying me up as long as he could. It had to be all about him. His possessiveness of my talent was obvious and he would often call me three or four times a day with nothing to say. He seemed determined to keep his hooks in me even though we were not actively playing during this period. Once my son was born, Frankie became a footnote and no longer wielded any power over me. Now I had proven myself as a man and would continue to prove what I could do in a Frankie-less arena.

The Ides agreed to do the show and headline at Berwyn's big event, Summerfaire. We started the laborious and often hilarious process of "restoring the vehicle" as it were. I love to watch the footage of that first rehearsal with us all hovering around an ancient turntable re-learning our repertoire as if we were our own cover band. Neil Young wasn't kidding when he said, "rust never sleeps."

After three months of rehearsal, The Ides were ready to take the stage. We were greeted by a crowd of 20,000, which filled the Cermak Plaza parking lot and beyond, as far as the eye could see into our old hood next to Morton West. We didn't know it then but we were facing a street that would be rechristened "Ides of March Way" in 2010. The magic of old was still there: Larry glancing in my direction as always, Bob bounding around the stage, Mike slamming the skins as only he can, and new member and former "big Ides fan," Scott May, lording over his powerful B3 organ. We closed the show with our 1970 hit "Vehicle" after which the crowd demanded more. After the triumphant third encore we ran out of songs. We loaded up our cars and headed to our old haunt, Salerno's Pizza, for a real, authentic Berwyn celebration. It felt like old times and I felt like the Jim Peterik of days of yore: confident, well-respected by my band members, and admired by the audience as the front man. Jimbo was back.

That supposed "one off" gig has now stretched to twenty-two years of constant touring by The Ides. After all that rehearsal, we couldn't play just one show, plus we're still having way too much fun. We recently released *Still 19*, our first album of totally new originals since our last album the first time around in 1973, *Midnight Oil*. I will be an Ide 'til the day that I die. As long as I can draw a breath, I will be singing, "Great God in Heaven, you know I looooove you."

Caught in the Game, Again

IT'S KINDA FUNNY. When people started prodding me to write my memoirs back in 2010, I usually told them, "Naw, nobody wants to read a book about a happy guy with a great wife and very few problems, conflicts, and crises." But in the process of writing this book I came to realize more and more, that my life was full of all that; it's just that I never focused on the negative parts. I always sort of hid in a cocoon of creativity. Songwriting was my drug of choice and it was more effective than anything you could score on the street.

But never did I need more escape fuel than I did in the next period of my life—the dark ages, 1993 to 1996. Frankie had finally found a way to suck me back into his world. I really had thought I had left the Survivor years far behind. I was happily playing and recording with my old homeboys, The Ides of March.

I was changing diapers, driving Colin to preschool with a rock 'n' roll soundtrack blasting, taking home videos, recording in my own studio, and watching Karen break out of her doldrums into an even better version of herself. Life was good.

Then I got the call. "You're not gonna believe it. Fuckin' Jamison just stole the name Survivor and is playing shows using our fucking name!" Really?

Even in my state of bliss I did not like the sound of this. Perhaps this time Frankie really did find his crisis point—the one that would reunite us against a common foe.

I had tried unsuccessfully to trademark the name Survivor back in 1978 when I started the band (I was blocked by a Chicago jazz band called The Survivors), and now Jimi was taking advantage of that weakness, claiming he had as much right to use the name as did Frankie and me. I was sickened as I heard and saw footage of Jimi with his band of Memphis cronies playing huge festivals in the summer of '92, performing all the Survivor hits, even the ones he did not originally sing, and inserting covers of hits by The Doors. Yeah—the frickin' Doors. I was livid.

There's nothing that makes you realize the value of something more than when it's taken from you. Suddenly the name Survivor represented the blood, sweat, and platinum of the many years it took to achieve success. All at once I realized that the band I had started, the name I had created, the songs I had written, the fans and friends we had made, were being defrauded by a wannabe version of Survivor. Not that Jimi wasn't a big part of that success. I truly believe that if he had asked us to re-form at that time, I, for one, would have seriously considered it.

So Frankie and I contacted a Wisconsin law firm to address the blatant infringement that had just taken place in America's dairy land and they instituted a cease and desist order on the bogus Survivor.

There were subpoenas, countersuits, court appearances, depositions, and orders to quash. I learned more about law than I ever wanted to know. I'd sift through piles of old playbills, royalty statements, and show reviews for backup evidence that the name Survivor was already a known entity long before Mr. Jamison joined the band.

Promotional photo of the '90s Survivor trio.

While this was going on Frankie and I decided to form our own "official" version of Survivor. Before our original lead singer Dave Bickler agreed to return to the band, we went through a who's who of potential lead singers.

Mark Free (now Marcie Free, in one of the most famous of all gender reassignments in rock 'n' roll) was in serious contention, as was Mitch Malloy. We auditioned countless drummers and bass players including Kyle Woodring from the *Too Hot to Sleep* demo days (he got the gig) and future Styx drummer, Todd Sucherman. I'm really not sure why we did not consider Marc and Steph at the time unless it was a matter of geography or unavailability. Or just too much blood on the tracks.

With our new lineup—Jim Peterik, Frankie Sullivan, Kyle Woodring, Bill Syniar (our *Too Hot to Sleep* bass man and long-term buddy), and the venerable Dave Bickler—we played one warm-up gig at a packed-to-the-gills Synergy club in West Chicago and then packed off to Germany for a much-demanded tour.

The clubs in Munich and Berlin—in fact, in every town we played—were filled to overflow with rabid Survivor-philes eager for a slice of the pie they had been denied for so many years. (Here's a classic JP/Sullivan verbal exchange from a few years previous. Me: "Frankie, Tony Scotti wants us to fly to Germany over Christmas to do some shows. Let's do it!" Frankie: "If you can give me the right reason for why we should do it—I'll go." Me: "Because we don't have anything better to do." Frankie: "Wrong answer—no dice." If I had really been thoughtful about it I would have given him the "correct answer" I'm sure he was looking for—"So we can build the Survivor name overseas and create a strong market for our group worldwide." But I didn't have the wherewithal.) The crowd in Munich sang along with every line. The male-dominated audience pumped their clenched fists above their heads as if they were at a freedom demonstration. Survivor was a kind of call to arms for them. To be honest, I never knew just how big we had become in Europe until that tour. Certainly, our nonexistent royalties never reflected that. The Scotti brothers seemed to have a way of charging everything back to our debt, especially the hard to trace European royalties.

Back in the States, our lawyers were getting rich on our game of "Name That Survivor." Frankie, Dave, and I went into the studio (my "Launching Pad" studio, by the way) to record two new tracks for a repackaged greatest hits album. In one song I resurrected an old title from the *Premonition* days, "Hungry Years," and breathed new life into it propelled by a freight train drum track by Kyle. In the second song, "You Know Who You Are," we used our three-part harmony blend to its fullest. This track is perhaps the greatest example of the synergy of our voices since the opening phrases of "Heart's a Lonely Hunter" from *Premonition*.

The album's liner notes were exclusively quotes from an interview with yours truly. This was a typical pattern: I would be willing and available for interviews; Frankie would be obstinate and hard to reach. Then when the piece would come out and it would lean on my quotes, Frankie would go bat-shit. Hey man, had you been available...!

Meanwhile, back in court, the verdict came down. Frankie and I basically lost our bid to stop Jamison from using the name. Our attorneys sucked. The judge in the case was quoted as saying how much she enjoyed the videos of Jimi onstage that she watched during the case. "I've had worse afternoons than this!" she chirped. The fucking judge was seduced by Jimi's onstage charisma! Blind justice indeed.

The two-headed beast called Survivor crisscrossed the country, sometimes narrowly missing each other in neighboring towns. My Survivor was getting sloppier by the show. Frankie was blowing leads and playing out of tune. Dave's vocal maladies of old were coming back to haunt him. I was going through the motions, like a wooden Indian, standing behind my keyboards, which were relegated to the back of the stage, often with no lights.

We called it the No Boundaries tour. We had T-shirts printed up but the design featured different color letters for the title. Some letters showed up more than others and for all the world it looked like the "No Undies" tour. Hilarious and sad.

Concurrently, we were recording demos at my place. Songwriting was still an area I thoroughly enjoyed. I encouraged Frankie to come over to write because this was one of the few times we really could bond. It was our refuge. He always brought his best attitude with him to these sessions and for those sacred hours it was like old times.

We created and recorded a cadre of unreleased gems: "Velocitized" (actually sung by Jamison in a brief period of temporary reconciliation), "Someone Else's Sleepless Night," "Fire Makes Steel" (one of Frankie's best titles and riffs), "One Step Ahead of the Flames" (a song I was inspired to write as I watched Lieutenant Dan running desperately from the flames in the Oscar-winning film *Forrest Gump*), "No Boundaries," "Credits Roll," Dave's powerful "Angeline," Frankie's "Anymore," "Rocket Science," "Innocence of Love," and many more. There is a good album's worth of material sitting somewhere unreleased from this era.

But the shows were a nightmare, marred by poor set-up, shoestring production budgets, and spotty performances. I was on my last legs as we headed into 1996. It's almost as if Frankie designed the touring to be as miserable as possible to flush me out, like one of those stress tests at the doctor's office where they put you on an exercise bike just to see if your heart will pop. We had no record deal and zero interest from the record industry. I felt like a canceled check (or was it Czech?).

Karen and I were quarreling nonstop over the way she felt Frankie was again controlling me. In fact, she was losing respect for me. In a marriage, respect is everything. It was even affecting our love life. Being Frankie's whipping boy isn't exactly sexy. Things were coming to a head. The juggernaut of life was careening out of control to Independence Day. It turns out that day, which was just around the corner, would give rise to a game-changing standoff.

Turning My Back on the Thunder

BEING ON THE ROAD with Survivor "Mark Two" was a struggle for me, to say the least. Decisions were basically made for me by Frankie and his newly appointed yes-man, Pat Quinn.

Quinn was a veteran of road managing other bands and he was a real pro. Unfortunately he was Frankie's pro. It seemed like every move they made was designed to flush me out of the band. Once a world-class act—veterans of Oscar nights, Grammy awards, and platinum sales—our dignity fell to a new low.

Frankie, prone to be a man of extremes, went from demanding limos and first-class airfare to renting U-Haul vans on their last leg. Pat booked us at "no-tell motels" that you could rent by the hour, to change clothes in or grab a catnap, just to save a few bucks. One room in particular in Canada was co-leased by a cadre of exotic insects arranged on the wall like abstract art. After shows I would commiserate with our drummer, Kyle, and oft-times Dave Bickler. Pat Quinn would insist to anyone who would listen that "Frankie *is* the band."

Basically I went back on the road not because I wanted to, but because I felt I had to in order to legitimately prove our claim to the name against the Memphis version of Survivor.

Still, tensions were mounting. After a show in Germany, the promoter complained in loud and broken English that our set was short. Frankie then loudly berated me in front of the band for having "the nerve" to suggest that if he refused to add any songs maybe we could add a big drum solo to add time to our set.

After he humiliated me in front of all the guys, I felt self-conscious and was sure the band thought I was a real jerk for suggesting this option. But, actually, it was quite the opposite.

"Can't believe he ripped you like that—what a jerk" was the consensus. Frankie just made himself look bad. Over and over again.

To pad the set Frankie took to playing an endless blues solo in the middle of a dog of a song I helped him write called "Anymore." For me just standing there vamping endlessly on three chords was soul-crushing. If Frankie could have just relied on his natural abilities, good looks, and stage presence (like when I saw him with Mariah all those years ago), I could have easily continued to share the stage with him. And would it have killed him to even once make eye contact with me during a show?

In early 1996 we met with Joe Thomas, a Chicago producer who was interested in financing a new Survivor album. Joe was fresh off album success with Peter Cetera and a Beach Boys tribute album called *Stars and Stripes* featuring a who's who of country music stars including Willie Nelson. We played Joe some of our latest demos, which sounded nothing like the songs of our halcyon *Vital Signs* days: "No Boundaries," the bluesy "Anymore," "Round and Round," and "Give It Up." As Joe's eyes glazed over I asked the tape operator to play a song that recaptured the essence of vintage Survivor. The song was "The Love We Never Made," which I had recently written with British singer and Bad Company interim front man Brian Howe. On the opening strains Joe's eyes lit up. "This is what I'm looking for from Survivor!" he practically shouted. "Why did you play this last?" I did not want to tell him that Frankie didn't even want me to bring that song because not only did he not write it, but it didn't reflect the bluesy direction he wanted to go.

At that moment Joe Thomas saw the writing on the wall and took a pass on the band.

We continued playing really atrocious venues around the U.S. until we got a great offer to open for Fleetwood Mac at a festival near Toronto.

We had just played a small fair in Indiana. Frankie was in charge and decided we'd leave for Canada at 10 a.m. the next morning. My cries of "Isn't that a little late with customs and all?" went unheeded.

Then on the way we got lost. When we finally got on the right road we realized that our destination was in another time zone so we lost a valuable hour. Then we were detained at customs for improper paperwork and questionable van contents. Everything had to be taken out and searched.

We limped into the fest site two hours late for our actual show time. The promoter in desperation had put Fleetwood Mac onstage. I listened to "Rhiannon" as I sat miserably on the mud floor of our changing tent, dejectedly sucking on a bottle of beer.

Once Fleetwood Mac finished and after the equipment change we had exactly fifteen minutes to play before curfew would force them to shut the event down.

We squeaked out "High on You" and part of "Eye of the Tiger" before the power was shut off and the disappointed crowd filed out.

When Frankie and I boldly went to the production tent to demand payment, the promoter, looking menacing, even in his wheelchair, said, "I've got good news and bad news for you. Bad news is I'm not paying you a penny for that piece of shit show. The good news is that if you're lucky I won't sue your asses for breach of contract!" I tried to protest but Frankie just said, "Let's go."

At another memorable fest in early '96, we did our afternoon sound check and went back to our hotel to shower and change. The skies became threatening and rain was imminent.

At the hotel the promoter kept calling over and over. Frankie refused to answer the phone, knowing it was the promoter desperately looking for an early start to beat the rain.

As we pulled up at our contracted time the opening act was just coming off stage. Then the sky opened. The bottom line is we could have played that show if Frankie hadn't been intent on missing it.

At one Chicago area fest he got in fisticuffs with a promoter who took loud exception with the short set we had just played. The last time I saw Frankie that night he and his hapless brother Kevin were being questioned in a paddy wagon.

Around about June 1996 things really started to become intolerable for me. At one show, at Indiana's Club Dimensions we had to get local rocker Dave Carl to sit in for Frankie, who had reportedly fallen through the roof of his garage while doing a repair. His bruises were horrendous and some wondered if he had actually been beaten up.

Finally, there was a gig on July 3 at a roof garden in Iowa. The show was what I had become accustomed to: a short set of songs with that now fifteen-minute solo on "Anymore" and an encore of Robert Johnson's blues shuffle "Sweet Home Chicago" (!). (We could have easily encored with one of the many great songs from our own catalogue that our fans came to hear.)

It was during Frankie's solo that I decided, then and there, that instead of standing on the side of the stage dutifully playing three chords behind Franklin Park's answer to Eric Clapton, I would venture over to Frankie's side and try to engage him in a little jam. You know: eye contact, musical interaction, perhaps even some excitement.

Frankie shot me repeated angry and withering glances and then attempted to physically push me back to my side of the stage. The crowd observed this interaction with mild amusement. Some probably thought it was part of the show; others saw it as the stand-off it really was.

I was livid. I performed the rest of the set like the pro I am even when Frankie came to my side of the stage and skillfully turned my volume down on my guitar! (He had to be the loudest onstage.) The audience by now knew that something wasn't right with this once regal band. By the end of the set there was about half a house left to watch the encore—the endless "Sweet Home Chicago" blues jam.

After the show, with the whole band back on the tour bus, Frankie stormed in. He threw an Ides album at me to sign for a fan. I remember shaking so badly I could barely hold the pen steady. Then he looked me coldly straight in the eye and menacingly drawled, "I'm gonna draw a line down the middle of the stage. Never cross that fucking line again!"

Those were among the last words I ever let him say to me. I sat in that bus still shaking, quaking with anger. I decided then and there that the line I drew between us would be far longer and deeper than any line Frankie had ever imagined.

Unless, of course, this was Frankie's plan all along—to make playing with this band so completely intolerable that I would have to exit for my own sanity.

And if that was his plan—mission accomplished. On the 4th of July we had a show booked down South with 38 Special. I had told Karen about the imaginary line and summed up my frustrations, which were leading me to a breaking point.

My bags were packed in preparation for Karen to drive me to meet the band at O'Hare. Then I told Karen, "I'm not getting on that plane. Not today or any other day. It's over. I'm done. I can't take one more day of Frankie's Napoleonic bullshit. My self-worth is in the Dumpster. I've lost all respect for myself and what I've let happen to me."

Karen tried to settle me down and started loading bags into the car. She had heard similar words from me before.

I said, "No, you don't get it. I am not getting on that plane! It's over!"

Finally, I got a panicked call from Frankie at the terminal. It must have finally dawned on him that I wasn't showing up. Suddenly his voice was gentle and pleading. He said, "Come on, man, you gotta do it. Things will be different."

I said, "You mean like the way things would be different when you convinced me that you had turned over a new leaf back in 1993? Well, nothing changed and nothing will."

I hung up the phone with a bang. Karen came over and hugged me like she would never let go.

"You're really not going? You mean I'm getting my Jim back again? I've never been prouder of you in my whole life," she said, beaming.

"Karen, look at the calendar. What day is it?" I asked.

"July 4th," she replied.

I said, "Not only that, my love, it's Independence Day."

A Man and His Will to Survive

THERE I WAS. Alone with my sudden decision. Actually it wasn't as sudden as it seemed. It was eighteen years of frustration in the making. For years the end seemed to justify the means. Not anymore.

I went through the day in a fog. I felt badly about leaving Dave and Kyle in the lurch. Would they be able to do the show? Would I or they get sued for breach of contract? I found out much later from Don Barnes of 38 Special (Survivor opened for them that day) that they did indeed play the show and it was a total disaster. Did I feel badly for Frankie? If I did, my feelings of extreme anger and righteous indignation made up for any guilt or sentimentality. In his every action and general behavior he had been challenging me to quit for some time. At a one-on-one meeting a few weeks prior he angrily suggested, "If you don't like it, why don't you just quit?" I had finally called his bluff.

That night, Karen and I walked over to the park in Burr Ridge for the fireworks. As the colorful sparks flew and the sonic booms filled the night, I felt as if I was in a daze. On one hand I felt giddy with newfound independence. On the other hand I was scared as hell. What would the consequences be of my sudden and unannounced departure? All I knew was I had reached my breaking point and it was the only decision I could possibly make.

The next day, Karen suggested we repair to our second home in Saugatuck, Michigan. This house is our refuge even in peacetime so now it was like a sacred asylum. I felt I could dodge the inevitable calls there from band members, managers, business managers, and attorneys.

Walking down the brick streets of Holland, Michigan, I caught a glimpse of myself in a store window with Karen and a five-year-old Colin. What I saw bowled me over. It's not like I looked any different but somehow I saw myself differently. I was proud of what I saw. I saw a little swagger in my walk that I hadn't seen in years. I was proud of myself for having the balls to say enough is enough. "Don't worry, Sullivan; I won't cross your line again!"

The image of that reflection stayed with me through the next year of lawsuits, countersuits, threats from business managers and attorneys, and mistruths from Sullivan on his Website. He claimed on the Internet that I had "emotional problems" and also said I had retired from the music business!

This reflection gave me the strength to realize that no matter what the consequences, I had made the right move. I was liberated from human bondage. As dramatic as that sounds it is absolutely what I felt. The angry faxes would now stop; the constant calls as to my whereabouts, the glares, and the interminable Cosa Nostra–style band meetings where Frankie would hold court like a Mafia don. Plus all the wasted hours waiting around at rehearsals 'til he felt like starting.

One day Frankie's brother Kevin (a really good guy, by the way, and a longtime member of the Survivor road crew) sheepishly appeared at my door in a half-hearted attempt to collect the master tapes of the demos we had done (for free at my studio), which were still in my possession. He also demanded the Roland Space Echo unit that Frankie claimed was his. Well, I gave him the damn Space Echo, but Kevin left without the tapes.

Life went on that year at the Peterik household as I adjusted to a Survivor-less existence. I was experiencing shortness of breath, which my doctor said might have been posttraumatic stress. (I had thought it may have been emphysema from all that secondhand smoke I had inhaled through the years on tour buses and in clubs.) Karen kept me grounded, assuring me that my breath would return and I had done the right thing by leaving the band. She was the very rock I needed.

One awkward moment happened when Jeff Carlisi and Don Barnes of 38 Special asked me to come to Lake Geneva, Wisconsin, to write on the road with them and play a few songs with them at their show. The writing went great. We holed up in a hilariously Wisconsin-chic motel suite complete with moose horns on the wall and all manner of '50s kitsch, including tiny colored lights everywhere and a bear rug. We were in stitches the whole time as we wrote what would become songs for their 1997 release *Resolution*. This is where "Fade to Blue" and one very special song were completed.

Karen and I were asked to "tell our story" to a Catholic youth ministry conference. It was a very off-the-cuff presentation. I told the tale of how we met and how she inspired many songs including "Vehicle" and "The Search Is Over." As we showed photos of our lives together on an overhead projector Karen noticed the prism of light that illuminated the screen. She got that faraway look in her eyes and as I sat in amazement she started to speak. "You know, in a way Jim has always been a totally focused single beam of musical light. Through our days together I have been his prism breaking that beam into a thousand different colors, diffusing it into other interests besides music: art, sports, fitness, backgammon, and, I guess you might say, the art of life." The audience and I sat stunned then broke into applause. Here is the song that that spontaneous moment brought forth, co-written with 38 Special and released in 1997 as a part of their *Resolution* album:

"Without direction I walked the night
I was alone—a single beam of light
One glance and you changed my blues
To a prism of light—a thousand hues
Now I will climb to the rainbow's arc
Who knows I might find a halo for your heart
Whenever I'm lost for words
And my whole world is falling apart
You are my saving grace
You are the light of a love everlasting
I've found a hiding place
In your arms
My one and only saving grace"

Written by Jim Peterik, Don Barnes, Danny Chauncey, Jeff Carlisi

Copyright 1997 Jim Peterik Music/Bicycle Music ASCAP, Don Barnes Music ASCAP, Timbre Rich Music BMI, Turbo Tunes ASCAP

At show time I made a startling discovery. The promoter who had put on the July 4th Survivor show (my infamous no-show) was the very one staging this Wisconsin fest—a definite "Oh shit!" moment. I did everything I could to avoid him. I half thought he'd hand me a writ then and there or have the sheriff collect me and take me to the station.

But none of that happened. He came over, shook my hand, and welcomed me to the show. Not one word about my nonappearance. With that I took the stage confidently with 38, armed with my new aqua-blue American Showster Chevy tail-fin guitar. I called this my "Screw-You" guitar 'cause I knew that Frankie would have hated this blatantly showy piece of gear, especially if it was hanging around *my* neck.

Soon after that I began my pilgrimages to Nashville to write with some of Music City's finest songsmiths. Over the course of 1996, thanks to the efforts of a song plugger and publisher named Karen O'Connor, I wrote with the best of the best: Henry Paul (then of Blackhawk), Skip Ewing ("If a Man Could Live on Love Alone"), Bob DiPiero ("American Made"), Craig Wiseman ("Live Like You Were

Dying"), Gary Burr ("Love's Been a Little Bit Hard on Me"), John Greenebaum ("Third Rock from the Sun"), and so many more. Interestingly, the song "Eye of the Tiger" did little to get my foot in the door in the tight clique of Nashville songwriters and artists. It was my creds with 38 Special that really did the trick. I couldn't believe what an impact "Hold on Loosely" had down there. And "Rockin' into the Night."

I even started my yearly appearances at the Nashville Songwriters Association International (NSAI) Tin Pan South weeklong convention. Practically every club in town is filled with what we call "writers rounds" where three or four songwriters of note (!) tell stories behind their biggest hits and play them in an unvarnished, unplugged fashion as the guitar is passed around the circle. It's a great time and highly recommended to everyone.

Through the next years up to the present I played at the Bluebird Cafe, The Rutledge, the Listening Room, 12th and Porter, and the Factory with a who's who of singers and songwriters: Bonnie Bramlett, Brett James, Keith Burns, Gunnar Nelson, Roger Cook ("Long Cool Woman in a Black Dress," "You've Got Your Troubles," accompanying himself on a humble baritone ukulele—and always bringing down the house), Bob Welch, Joie Scott, Michael Peterson, Kelly Keagy (Night Ranger), Dennis Morgan, and so many more. I fall in love with Nashville more with every passing year. I am currently producing seventeen-year-old country star in the making, Hunter Cook, and co-producing with Frank Pappalardo an amazing "new country" singer/songwriter, Andrew Salgado.

One of the highlights of my career as a songwriter came in July 2006 when Bart Herbison, the head of NSAI, invited me to be a part of a songwriters' junket to Washington, D.C. to play in person for the members of the Senate (Jim Bunning, Mark Pryor) and House of Representatives (Lloyd Doggett, Howard Coble, Jim Cooper). Bart wisely figured that if some of the nation's best songwriters came in person like wandering minstrels right into the offices of the lawmakers of America, that they would feel our passion and personal commitment and help us with some of the goals.

Together with hit writers Monty Powell, Danny Wells, Lee Thomas Miller, Brad Parker, Steve Bogard, Lynn Chater, and Suzanna Spring we marched into numerous offices where appointments had been set up, and we proceeded to change some hearts and minds. The capper was always "Eye of the Tiger." No amount of arm-twisting could have had the impact we had simply armed with a couple of acoustic guitars, our voices, and belief in the various causes we were stumping for regarding songwriters' rights. One of the biggest victories that our trip brought about was the changing of some very exorbitant and archaic taxing laws for songwriters selling their publishing catalogues. I got to take advantage of our musical lobby only a few years later when I sold a portion of my publishing.

Just as I was starting to enjoy my newfound independence and getting ready for Christmas day with my family, I got a loud knock on my door from a particularly seedy-looking man with an envelope in his hand. I opened the door as he shoved the envelope in my hand and said, "You've been served." It turned out to be a lawsuit from Frankie suing me for $7,000,000! Merry Christmas!

I pored through the pages of lies and impossible demands and felt sick to my stomach—the very band I named and assembled was now suing me for all I had and much, much more.

I called my attorney to make some sense of it. In the course of the next few months it was nothing but replies, counter-replies, depositions, motions to quash—the usual menu of dishes that make no one but the lawyers rich.

At the end of the day I had to severely limit my use of the name Survivor and turn over the master tapes of the demos. I would have done this without the drama and wasted dollars of a lawsuit if we had been able to meet peacefully. In exchange for waiving a fee the band still owed me, I received the right for my record royalties to be paid directly to me. This was big. I figured if all my monies had to be siphoned through Survivor, getting paid would have been an endless fight. Frankie ended up with the master tapes that my money paid for. (Some things never change. I was never paid back for all those original demos we made to land our record deal. And I never saw a nickel for co-producing the *Eye of the Tiger* record.)

When the lawsuit was finally settled (it never got to court), I was all the more determined to prove what I could do on my own. I started to dream up a super show made up of many of the musician friends I had made in the last thirty years; those I had toured with, written songs with, hung out with and enjoyed good times and bad in this crazy music business.

I started making a short list, which became longer and longer as I thought of all the great people I knew. One prerequisite for inclusion on this list was that they were positive, well-meaning people, respected and valued by me, who played music for the love of it, without the egos that often go along with stardom. I decided to call it Jim Peterik and World Stage and immediately filed for a trademark. (Time does teach us something if we care to listen.)

The first official Jim Peterik and World Stage concert was held on January 21, 2000, at the Norris Cultural Art Center in St. Charles, Illinois. I was ready for this. My band was made up of the best of the best in Chicago: Ed Breckenfeld on drums (remember his great band The Insiders?), Klem Hayes on bass, Christian Cullen on keyboards, Joel Hoekstra (now with Night Ranger and the Trans-Siberian Orchestra) and Mike Aquino on guitars, and The Ides of March brass (John Larson, trumpet; Chuck Soumar, trumpet; Dave Stahlberg, trombone; Bob Bergland, sax; and Chuck "Tito" Soumar doubling on percussion). The backup singers were headed up by Thom Griffin of Trillion fame.

The guest artists on that first show were Kevin Cronin of REO Speedwagon, Henry Paul of Blackhawk and The Outlaws, The Ides of March, Kevin Chalfant of The Storm, Joe Thomas (Beach Boys), Kelly Keagy of Night Ranger, and Don Barnes of 38 Special. Opening up for World Stage was an artist I was mentoring, the amazing Leslie Hunt, then just seventeen. Amazing singer-songwriter Jeff Boyle was there for the very first show and many more after. My dear friend, R&B singer Marzette Griffith, who I had been producing since he was the main singer in the Epic Records group Essence, became a regular fixture. Mindy Abair, recently of Aerosmith touring fame, became one of my latest and most visible converts. The mighty Jack Blades brings not only Night Ranger songs to the stage but the gems of his other band Damn Yankees. Talk about a twofer!

Part of my concept for World Stage was not only sharing memories of past glories but also allowing even the heritage artists to play
both their smashes of the past and their latest output as well—hits
of the future as it were. In addition, I wanted to spotlight new artists, giving them a stage to present their unique talents. Through the
years I introduced the world to Cathy Richardson, Joe Vana, Toby
Hitchcock (of Pride of Lions—more on that later), and a girl who is
just now finding her way to major success, Lisa McClowry.

Since introducing herself to me at a *Songwriting for Dummies*
book-signing in Oakbrook, Illinois, Lisa has become a major player
in my life story, her voice and spirit inspiring countless songs much
in the way Jimi Jamison brought out the best in my writing. The
word "muse" is too often bandied about carelessly, but the term certainly applies to Lisa and her divine energy and five-octave vocal
range. If I was Burt Bacharach she would be my Dionne Warwick.
Through her unique interpretations of the songs I write or we co-
write she has become the voice of my voice.

The *Jim Peterik and World Stage* CD was finished and ready for sale
just days before the first show. It contained collaborations with the
above artists in addition to duets with Dennis DeYoung, Buddy Guy,
Rick Nielsen, and Tom Keifer.

Just as I was about to take the stage I received a message from
Frankie Sullivan, which was delivered to me through a mutual friend.
Two words: "Entertain Me!" I recognized these words immediately
as the rallying cry Frankie and I always got from our manager Frank
Rand before we took the stage with our respective bands many years
ago. Though well-meaning, Frankie's message threatened to throw
me off my game that night. It was as if he was still with me as I was
trying to exert my independence. I had to put it out of my mind as I
took the stage.

The show was groundbreaking. The house was sold out with
people swarming the lobby in search of last-minute tickets. Lasting nearly four hours (with a short intermission), it was a night of
"hard acts to follow." Highlights for me were Kevin Cronin's "Roll
with the Changes," Kelly Keagy's "Don't Tell Me You Love Me," my
own "We Wish" (which I prefaced by reciting the chilling antiwar

The first World Stage cast—Kevin Cronin, me, Henry Paul, David Carl, Cathy
Richardson, Jeff Boyle.

poem, written in 1969, by Kendrew Lascelles called "The Box"), my
duet with Cathy Richardson on the song from the *World Stage* CD,
"Diamonds for Stones," and "Vehicle" with a hilarious impromptu
dialogue between me and Marzette before the last verse. The encore
with all performers onstage was "Eye of the Tiger."

The four hours went by in a flash. It was a rock 'n' roll love fest.
This show set the high-bar standard against which all other World
Stage shows would be measured.

I guess I wasn't the only one touched by that evening's experience.
As I signed at the merchandise table after the show, my stage manager Toby Bermann's mother Terry came up to me in tears. She had
just gone through life-threatening surgery and almost died on the
table. She said, "I'm glad I stayed alive if only for this night." Such
was the impact on the many who witnessed this gathering of angels
called World Stage.

The Fire Within Still Burns

SURVIVING THE APOCALYPSE. A bit dramatic I'll admit, but that's the way it felt coming into the new millennium. The world was supposed to end on that New Year's Eve in the year 2000.

Karen, Colin, and I and our dear friends Joe and Julie Cielinski and family were huddled in front of the TV as Dick Clark counted the seconds down 'til the ball dropped in Times Square. I was hoping with all my might that my newfound happiness would not be cut short due to the annihilation of the species.

Colin, at age ten, was right in front of the set wearing his pointy celebration hat and half-heartedly blowing on a noisemaker. On his lap was piled every possession that meant anything to him: his beloved Pokémon cards, assorted rare Beanie Babies, some Power Rangers nostalgia, and a few Crazy Bones. If he was going, they were going with him. He was ready!

Needless to say, we are still here so I guess Armageddon had been postponed and it was back to business as usual. After the triumph of World Stage and the brisk sales of the *World Stage* CD, I looked for other mountains to climb.

The Ides were sailing on, getting better and better shows as our reputation grew. We played Vegas with The Turtles, Peter Noone, Chubby Checker, and The Grass Roots. I told Mark Volman of The Turtles that I had met my future wife at their Chicago concert in 1968. He said he was so sorry for causing that.

Around that time I was approached by my friend Dave Austin. He was the ex-tennis pro who organized the music/tennis festivals in which I had participated. He was approached by his agent at Wiley, the company that publishes the popular, yellow-and-black branded *Dummies* book series, to put together the right team to write *Songwriting for Dummies*. I was flattered when he told me I was first on his list.

At first I was eager, but in a few days I started to wonder if my craft would suffer because of the analysis that would occur in the process of writing this "how to" manual. I like to think of songwriting as divine magic. By deconstructing it I was afraid that unknown quantity would be analyzed right out of existence.

On the other hand, what a great opportunity this would be to share the knowledge I had gained through years and years of non-stop songwriting; a chance to tell the stories behind the hits. I had the potential of tapping into a wellspring of hidden creativity in us all and re-inspiring the more established writer. I said yes.

With the help of Dave Austin, who supplied coaching tips, and various editors, I embarked on the seemingly impossible task of teaching someone how to write a song. Along with that goal I set forth to also share what I knew about the business of songwriting: how a song makes money, how to set up your own publishing company, the purpose of organizations such as ASCAP, BMI, and SESAC, and how to go about finding homes for your beloved songs by finding artists to record them. I wanted to explain the art of collaboration, the daily cataloguing of ideas, how to conquer writer's block, and how to wear your musical influences invisibly by creating your own style. I wanted to tell stories that orchestrated my dreams like the fateful call from Stallone or the compliment from my songwriting hero, Burt Bacharach, after he heard me perform "The Search Is Over" with full orchestra at a songwriters convention that honored Burt and his brilliant lyricist, the late Hal David. He came over to me after the set and said to me, "'The Search Is Over'—what a song." I said, "Burt, I can die now!"

I started the book in the most romantic of settings. In 2002 Karen and I and a few friends embarked on a bicycle journey for REI Adventures that went from Vienna to Prague. Each day we rode about thirty-five miles through the rolling hills of Central Europe, stopping at designated inns for home-cooked dinners of goulash, pork, sauerkraut, and dumplings and a well-deserved rest in a nice cozy bed. I noticed in the towns we stopped in that the young Czech men were all sporting blond-streaked hair like mine at the time and wearing the same wild clothes that I favored. I realized that I was not as unique as I thought—rather a chip off my Czech heritage. We all had the same "wild and carazzy" fashion sense!

In one tiny town I found a bakery with the name of the owner in big red letters outside: Peterik. I was literally miles from where my grandfather was born.

The day before we reached Prague we were staying in a village whose big claim to fame was an ancient castle called Český Krumlov. While the others toured the town I stationed myself in the town square sipping cappuccinos and starting to analyze this alchemy called songwriting so I could teach it to others. At the end of the day I had scribbled about 100 pages.

Songwriting for Dummies is now in its fourth printing. We recently published an updated version that gives the song examples a facelift with more current examples and up-to-the-minute facts on changes in technology, online resources, and music law. Because of this book's success I am now considered a best-selling author.

In early 2001, I was contacted by the Frontiers record company in Italy, which is headed by a savvy music fanatic named Serafino Perugino. He suggested that I record an album by putting together a supergroup with the shards of some now splintered bands, with me writing and playing keyboards and guitar. He said it could be like the Survivor I had once envisioned, with me sharing lead vocals with another higher-voiced singer. I replied that I already had a super-group with World Stage and would rather do a group made up of heretofore unknown artists. He liked that idea.

Traditionally the hardest band member to find is a great vocal-ist. I had no idea where to start looking. There were plenty of great vocalists I could have considered—Kevin Chalfant, Mitch Malloy, Derek St. Holmes, and Mark (now Marcie) Free, to name a few—but I was looking for someone I could surprise the world with, much like when Dave Bickler was suddenly thrust upon the rock scene back in 1980.

One day my very talented niece (actually Karen's niece), Kelly Moulik, came to visit from her home in Kenosha, Wisconsin. Out of the blue, she said, "Uncle Jimmie, I just did an audition for a new Dick Clark pilot TV show that would feature unknown singers doing sound-alike versions of the current stars. There is one singer that you've just got to hear. His name is Toby Hitchcock."

Now when Kelly tells me something like this, I listen—hard. This gal knows her stuff and is a tremendous singer in her own right. Kelly is Karen's late brother Andy's daughter, one of a set of twins. Christi is her sister. Kelly is now well on her way to becoming a star.

When I got serious about finding a singer for my new project I thought of Kelly's recommendation. But by this time she had lost Toby's contact info. I started looking again for a guy that could han-dle the demanding melodies that I write.

In the summer of '03 The Ides played the popular Popcorn Fest in Valparaiso, Indiana. It was an afternoon show so we saw the audi-ence clearly. I noticed a guy in the front row who was particularly attentive. After the show he came up and introduced himself as Toby Hitchcock! It turns out that Valparaiso was his hometown. Talk about destiny.

He gave me all his contact info and I called him the next day to sing a duet with Kelly on a song I had just written called "No Long Goodbyes." I wanted to see what this kid (and he was a kid, twenty three years old at the time) had to offer.

On Monday he came by my studio with Kelly. When I saw him I thought, *Wow, we've got to get his teeth fixed before any photos are taken.* Suddenly he and Kelly burst out laughing as he took out the plastic set of fake chompers he had inserted into his mouth as a gag. That was Toby all the way.

When he first opened his mouth and sang on mic, a chill rushed through me. I heard echoes of all the great vocalists I had worked with through the years—Dave Bickler, Jimi Jamison, Don Barnes, Dennis DeYoung, Tommy Shaw, Sammy Hagar—they were all represented in one voice. But beyond that, there was a new sound all his own that the world had yet to hear. He nailed the vocal in two takes. It was a thrill for me to know that this was his first time singing in a real studio, on a professional microphone.

Now Serafino wanted to hear this kid I was so excited about. Instead of sending him the duet I had just done I wanted to represent him on the kind of material I envisioned for this debut CD. Back in 1984, while working on *Vital Signs*, I started a song that I couldn't quite finish: "Love Is on the Rocks." With the passage of time I found the perspective and inspiration I needed to complete this song.

Toby sang it flawlessly, with passion and perfect pitch. Not only that, we found our voices blended like one. Serafino flipped. "Maestro! Kissing your hand, my hero, you have found your singer!" he gushed in an e-mail. Serafino's letters are like no other's; in his wonderful broken English, he says things like, "This song is a piece of art, my hero!" I love this guy.

Serafino and his henchman Mario even came over from Italy to meet with us personally. We met them in Nashville at a fantastic state-of-the-art studio called The Sound Kitchen in the Nashville suburb of Franklin, then owned by Dino and John Elefante (former lead singer of Kansas). It was here that I'd cut a CD for Mecca, a band I produced, that featured the vocal talents of Fergie Frederiksen, of Toto fame, and Joe Vana, as well as many other tracks through the years.

The dog and pony show had been all set up by the time the Frontiers honchos entered the control room. Larry Millas was manning the playbacks. The studio had provided us with muffins, coffee, and juice. Toby and I had even rehearsed a never-recorded song from the early Survivor days called "Rock 'n' Roll Boom Town," which we were ready to give them a taste of unplugged in the control room. (That song has yet to be recorded.)

As soon as Serafino saw Toby he exclaimed, "You're just a baby!" He could not believe how young Toby was. He was used to us grizzled classic rockers who were the stock-in-trade of his roster.

We treated them to playbacks of some of the songs we had just recorded. Besides "Love Is on the Rocks," they heard, for the first time, "It's Criminal" (Mario exclaimed, "It *is* criminal!") and "Interrupted Melody." This clinched the deal. After every playback Serafino shouted at Toby in mock anger, "You're fired!" That's how much he loved him.

This first Pride of Lions album was pivotal for me. All the Survivor fans of the world would be looking at this one to see how Jim Peterik could do without Frankie and Jimi. So much was on the line. This was my chance to show what part of Survivor I really was. Besides rescuing some older songs from oblivion ("It's Criminal," "Interrupted Melody," "Love Is on the Rocks"), I started writing brandnew songs in the style on which I made my reputation—using big guitars, even bigger keyboards, soaring melodies, and lyrics bearing an overall positive message.

With my longtime musical partner, Larry Millas, I wrote perhaps my favorite song on the CD, and a fan pick, "Gone." This song is a great example of the duet aspect of Pride of Lions. It combines my dark baritone voice with Toby's fluid tenor. One of my favorite moments is when Toby sings the bridge, "Is she wearing that sundress that goes with her eyes?" I get goose bumps every time. With my lyrically gifted buddy Steve Salzman, I wrote the blistering "Unbreakable." It was my ode to the resilience of the human spirit. ("Grip the knife in your teeth as you climb the mast, take your life by the reins and hold on!")

The self-titled debut of Pride of Lions went over like gangbusters in Europe and Japan, topping critics' polls in many countries. Germany, Italy, Spain, France, Belgium, and Tokyo were evidently ready for this new spin on melodic rock. The thing about Europe and Japan is that once you have been a star there, you are a star for life. The fans remember and reward you by supporting your latest effort. I had built up a very large fan base as a member of Survivor.

Serafino had made it very clear to me what he did and did not want as a part of the sound of POL: "No blues, no slide guitars, no harmonicas, no female singers, no wah-wah pedals, no horns, and no jamming." He wanted hooky songs with soaring, melodic choruses. I heard the words "Too bluesy!!" many times as he responded to my new output of songs.

He was right on with his recipe for the very market he was shooting for with Pride of Lions: mainly males between the ages of thirty and fifty-five who never got enough of the '80s sound. We delivered that—in spades.

The week the CD was released in Europe, Toby and I were on a flight to Italy armed with backing tracks from the album, to which we would sing live vocals at promotional appearances. I would also play live keyboard parts. Of course, I'd always rather play with an entire band but because of economics this was the best arrangement.

It was mostly about the interviews anyway. Toby and I did a huge record store in Milan where we were happy to see our new product displayed prominently with giant posters with our images. Toby had never experienced anything like this so it was double fun for me to watch the events through his wide eyes.

From Italy we went to France and experienced the same type of enthusiasm from the retail stores and fans alike. We played one very large record store in Paris where the fans swarmed to see us and get a signed CD after the set.

That afternoon Toby and I found ourselves stationed in the dank basement of the club in Paris we were about to play that night. A steady parade of rock journalists came by to ask us questions about the new CD, the genesis of the project, and future large-scale touring. Again, Toby was unaccustomed to the interview process where you have to make every interviewer feel like you are answering a question for the very first time. This is an acquired art and not for everyone. Toby learned the game relatively quickly.

From there we went to Germany where we did a big rock TV show. We would hear strains of "It's Criminal" and "Gone" through the

Toby Hitchcock in Germany, during the Pride of Lions tour.

streets, blaring from loudspeakers in front of record shops and from car radios. For me, it felt like a sweet victory. I'd created another group, logo, and identity that had the earmarks of success and longevity.

After the release of the first CD, Pride of Lions issued a single that was inspired by the terrorist bombing of an elevated train in Spain that killed hundreds of innocent victims commuting to their place of work. As I watched images of the tragedy I was moved by the black ribbons that practically every house in Spain displayed in their shared mourning. I had gotten to know the people of Spain on our first trip there and especially enjoyed their style of humility and tranquility.

The song I composed was "Black Ribbons," which was released as a single all over Europe and Japan. All proceeds went to a fund that aided the families of the deceased. We even traveled to Spain to perform.

I brought Karen, Colin, and his buddy Jake Cielinski (Jake was there in front of the TV at the Y2K party) to Barcelona. Colin experienced firsthand why they call Barcelona the skateboard capital of the world. He and Jake skated on practically every concrete structure the city had to offer.

Through the back alley streets of the city, people pointed at me and Toby and exclaimed, "Pride of Lions!" not "Survivor." That's how popular we are there. At the concert, the packed house gave us a five-minute ovation after we performed "Black Ribbons."

Our second album, *The Destiny Stone*, was equally successful. It featured a slightly more theatrical style, not unlike some earlier Styx with shades of Genesis, particularly on songs such as the stately and romantic "Back to Camelot" and "The Destiny Stone," named after an actual stone located in Scotland, which for centuries kings and commoners alike would mount in order to contemplate their problems, while often divining answers to their questions and learning their destiny.

In 2004, on the heels of this release, Pride of Lions traveled to Belgium to take part in the weeklong music festival The Lokerse Feesten held each year near Brussels. We were pie-eyed as we wandered the grounds the day before our performance and watched a wide variety of acts take the giant, extravagantly lit stage. I had seen a lot of high-tech stages in the '80s when Survivor toured with REO Speedwagon and Bryan Adams, but this was something else again. The stage towered over the massive crowd of 20,000 as we watched Suzanne Vega sing one of my favorite songs, "Luka," to the masses.

Pride of Lions, which besides Toby and me consisted of Ed Breckenfeld on drums, Klem Hayes on bass, Mike Aquino on guitar, and

Christian Cullen on keyboards, took the stage at 7 p.m. Since this show was to be recorded for a live DVD, I brought Larry Millas along for front-of-house sound and to assure that everything would be just right.

The show was practically flawless, featuring the most popular songs from the first two Pride of Lions albums: our opener, "It's Criminal," our first single and video (featuring my future artist, Lisa McClowry, as Toby's love interest in the video) "Sound of Home," and "Man Behind the Mask." Our set also included the towering ballad, "The Gift of Song," a tune I had sent to Michael Jackson's engineer, Bruce Swedien, years earlier in a slightly different form. When Michael heard the song, he said, "Bruce, he is singing about my life." Michael especially related to the line, "But on that midnight rise to fortune, I was blinded by the footlights of the stage. Now face to face with my reflection, at last the child has come of age."

We, of course, performed a few from my back catalogue, most notably "Vehicle" and "Eye of the Tiger." For a new band to convince an audience of 20,000 to stand up and cheer after most of the songs is a daunting task—but we did it. Toby's showmanship and charisma were powerful. Going out into the crowd during "The Gift of Song," he personally touched everyone with the sound of his voice.

The DVD came out to great reviews and sales. We were one step closer to being an act to be reckoned with in Europe. It captured the magic of that night for the world to see. We caught lightning in a bottle.

Our third studio album, *The Roaring of Dreams,* came out in 2007. While writing material for the CD, my personal life was colored by the deteriorating health of Karen's brother, Andy, who had been diagnosed with inoperable liver cancer and cirrhosis.

I had known Andy since I first met Karen back in '68. He was a sweet, good-looking kid, but always in some kind of trouble usually connected with drug use. Soon after I met Karen I ran into Andy and a friend of his at Cermak Plaza panhandling for drug money. He was ten years old. He was a natural musician and could have really gone somewhere if his mind wasn't focused on his next cop. By age eleven, he was snorting angel dust, a powerful sedative also known as elephant tranquilizer, and dabbling in heroin.

"You should try angel dust, Jimmie, it's really a great high," he would tell me, with glassy eyes. I would always try to help him, buying him his first professional bass guitar—a shiny, brand-new Fender Precision bass. Within a week, it was gone; the money he received from its sale went up his arm.

Giving him another chance in the mid-'70s when he swore he had cleaned up, I had hired him as a roadie for Jim Peterik and the Chi-Town Hustlers. Then, about a month into the tour, I found a complete "kit" in the back of my Fender Dual Showman amp head: needle, spoon, heroin, matches, the works. This was all I needed to get arrested and ruin my reputation forever. I reluctantly had to send him back to Chicago.

By 2007, Andy was finally clean, relatively sober, and living on welfare in Milwaukee, Wisconsin. But the damage to his liver had been done. In 2000 he was diagnosed with hepatitis C but did not tell anyone. That disease turned into severe cirrhosis and, finally, cancer. By the time the doctors found the tumor it had spread to other organs. A transplant was not an option.

The whole family—his mom, Esther; his dad, Rudy; Karen; Andy and Karen's other brother, Phil; both of Andy's twin daughters, Christi and Kelly; and I—were gathered around Andy at the hospice. As the priest came in to give last rites, we held hands and sang a teary "Amazing Grace" and prayed as Andy drew his last breath.

The day after he passed, Andy came to me in a dream and said how beautiful everything was in Heaven and then said, "You know, Jimmie, you can have heaven on earth!" With that, he sang me a melodic hook that included the words, "Heaven on Earth."

I shook myself out of slumber, grabbed a guitar, and wrote the song, then and there, in the middle of the night. "Heaven on Earth" became the opening song on Pride of Lions' *Roaring of Dreams* album. I think of dear Andy every time I hear or play the song. It totally rocks.

I took a few years off from Pride of Lions while I was producing and writing for Jimi Jamison's solo album *Crossroads Moment* and while co-producing and co-writing for the second Kelly Keagy (of Night Ranger) album.

Writing for and producing Jimi Jamison was literally a dream made real. My biggest regret was not being able to work with his incredible voice when I severed ties with Survivor. I always told myself if I ever was offered the chance I'd drop everything to work with Jimi again.

The dreamed request came from Serafino in 2009. I could barely believe my good fortune. As a songwriter I had done some of my best work writing for Jimi. Now I had a second chance.

I dropped everything.

I hit the keyboard immediately with the ring of his tenor strong in my imagination. With every line of lyric and melody I would fantasize how it would sound with Jimi singing it. And those ideas and songs flowed thick and fast from my outpost cottage in Saugatuck with my Yamaha keyboard overlooking the lush willow trees just outside my window. "Crossroads Moment" was the first. Then song after song appeared seemingly out of nowhere.

At the beginning of 2012, my juices were again flowing in the direction of writing and producing the strongest Pride of Lions record yet. Toby had just released his solo album, *Mercury's Down*, produced and written by Swedish musician Erik Martensson. It was a good album, much harder and heavier than my style, so there was no conflict there with the sound of POL. Toby turned in his usual great vocals.

My competitive side kicked in, however, and the motive of topping that solo album was a good one for bringing out the best in me as a songwriter and producer. Pride of Lions remained basically the same for our next album—Ed, Klem, and Mike—but this time around I did most of the guitar and keyboard work myself. I also asked Kelly Keagy, the powerhouse drummer with Night Ranger, to play on about half the tracks for an even harder edge.

Toby came to Chicago in April and did all of the eleven vocals in four days! I worked a bit differently this time. In the past, Toby had come in and learned songs on the spot. This time, he had been living for weeks with the demos I made.

Previously I rarely did demos for Pride of Lions. I would write the songs, and then record them with the whole band. I would be crushed if Serafino rejected a tune, not only because I believed in the song, but also because I had just spent a lot of money cutting the track.

This time, after I wrote a song, and felt it was a good fit for the project, I would go into my studio where Larry would program a drum pattern in the style and meter of the song. Then I would flesh it out, playing the keyboards first, then bass, then guitars, and then add extra guitar leads and hand percussion.

At the end of the session, I had a real decent-sounding example of the song. At that point, I'd sing a falsetto vocal. Toby has such a broad range I could never hit all of the melodies I write for him in full voice. Then, I would send it to a great singer in town, Marc Scherer,[5] who would learn it and sing over the track. Finally, I'd send it to Frontiers for approval.

This time around Serafino passed on only two songs. Much of the work I did on guitar, bass, and keyboards on the demos ended up on the final versions of the tracks for our fourth album, *Immortal*. I had not played so much on an album since the Ides of March days and I had a blast!

The songs all have something to say. I've found that in the past, my most enduring songs had some sort of message people could relate to in their own lives. This, I believe, is the element that gives a song wings. Sure, it has to have a good hook, melody, and beat, but what keeps people coming back for more is the message.

The leadoff cut "Immortal" contains the key line, "For the thousand times we fail, it's the one thing we did right, that leaves a mark forever on this world, and makes us Immortal." I've been wanting to say this all my life: There is no positive action that doesn't cause a positive reaction. Sometimes it is the smallest kindness that makes the biggest difference.

---

[5] This year I finish production on Marc Scherer's first solo album for the Frontiers company. Inspired by his spine-tingling four-octave tenor I feel I'm writing some of the best lyrics and melodies since those first songs I wrote for Jimi Jamison.

"Delusional," the first single off the album, is about letting a young person follow their dream by giving them the encouragement they need to succeed. The subtext is about the tendency of modern society to sometimes carelessly medicate those who do not quite fit into the mold of the well-behaved and focused person. There are certainly cases where medications such as Ritalin and Adderall are a godsend to those with severe attention deficits. But in many cases kids should be allowed to be themselves—eccentricities included. As a child when I would get wound up and hyperactive or drowning in worry, my dad would tell me to "go climb a tree." Much of my obsession with music may have been "smoothed away" by medications. My chronic problem with worry and anxiety might have been alleviated but at what price to my creative side? (I recently recut "Delusional" in "new country" style with Hunter Cook. It works really well in this genre—I've heard it said that country music today is basically '80s rock with fiddles and mandolins. I know one thing for sure: It's one of the few genres where a great song still carries the day.)

This song has received a lot of attention because it addresses such a widespread concern. The video directed by Greg Bizzaro outlines the life of a skinny kid who dreams of being a football star only to be discouraged by his macho coach and team members. They shake their heads and throw him a T-shirt emblazoned with the word DELUSIONAL.

The video also shows a young girl who dreams of being a pop singer, "She sings into her hairbrush in front of the mirror," only to be put off by her all too realistic mother who throws her the DELUSIONAL shirt to wear. In the video for the song, our young heroes are played by Peter Claussen and Maggie Perez, both of whom did a marvelous job depicting the frustration that comes with following your dream when others refuse to believe.

The video closes with an emotional crescendo as Maggie joins the band and shares the mic with Toby. When Pride of Lions perform their live concerts, Maggie often walks on stage right at the end of "Delusional" and reprises her video role. She sings the last word of the song, "Delusional!" and brings down the house every time.

The great and widespread response we've received to *Immortal*, "Delusional," and the video has proven once again what I've always believed: Good music and strong, positive messages are timeless. A great song, even a single, honest and heartfelt verse or line, can reach across time and touch or inspire listeners of any generation.

The Search Has Come Full Circle

GROWING UP AS A TEEN it came down to the three Bs—the Beatles, Burt Bacharach, and The Beach Boys. In '65 The Ides made a pilgrimage to the Arie Crown Theater in downtown Chicago to watch our heroes The Beach Boys perform. In their matching striped shirts and white jeans they were the "Un-Rolling Stones" and we loved them all the more.

An unexpected phone call came one day in the mid-1990s from Frank Pappalardo. Frank was another good friend and terrific engineer who had worked frequently with Larry Millas. He said, excitedly, one day: "Jim, you're never going to believe who is taking a nap on the studio floor!"

Of course, I agreed that the studio floor was an odd place for anyone to take a nap, but Frank assured me that "Brian Wilson is like that."

"Frank, back up," I said. "You mean to tell me that you are recording Brian Wilson?"

Frank explained that his boss, Joe Thomas, had gotten to know Brian Wilson and had convinced him to move to St. Charles, Illinois, buy the house next door, install a studio in the basement, and make a long-awaited comeback album. Joe had been partners with my musical partner Larry Millas back in the mid-'80s in River North Recorders on Fairbanks in Chicago. (In the '40s the basement of the building was the iconic Chez Paree nightclub, ground zero to performers such as Tony Bennett and Frank Sinatra.) I leased my Neve 8068 console and Studer A800 twenty-four-track recorder to the studio for years before installing it in my own studio in '88.

Joe had also launched Platinum Entertainment, a big Gospel label, and a subsidiary of Polygram. Joe made a lot of contacts, and most recently made his mark as producer of Soundstage, the very popular PBS rock concert series taped at the WTTW studios in Chicago.

At that time, he had made friends with Brian Wilson, through his channels, and ultimately became musical director and promoter of Brian's first world tour. Brian, who was impressed with Joe's credentials, agreed to make a record.

Frank became the main engineer and urged me to call Joe. He felt that I should be involved with the project. I felt nervous, though. I explained that I could never sit in a room with Brian Wilson. I told Frank, "He's my hero and he's the ultimate songwriter. What would I be doing?"

Frank emphasized that Brian really needed a co-writer. After the phone call, it became clear that Joe was definitely enthusiastic about the idea of a collaboration—just as Frank had predicted. I showed up at the studio and Brian, Joe, and I wrote two songs for the 1999 album, *Imagination*.

The first song was "Your Imagination." Steve Dahl, a disc jockey, was also a contributor to our first collaboration. He came up with some of the lyrics, so it was a four-way undertaking; the second original we created was a "three-way."

It was about Brian's little girl, who was about one year old at that time. Brian and his wife, Melinda, had this very sweet baby, Daria

Rose. She kept crawling around and landing on Brian's lap. I told Brian that his daughter "looked like an angel." I even wrote down the phrase "Dream Angel" because I thought those words sounded so nice together.

I asked Brian what he thought and he said that theme sounded like a great idea. Then we sat down at the piano. Joe did a great job of bringing the elements of Brian Wilson and Jim Peterik together and adding his own magic.

Brian Wilson is a self-taught genius, though he has had his share of tragedy. He is deaf in one ear. He has survived the deaths of his younger brothers, Dennis, who drowned in '83, and Carl, who died of lung cancer in '98.

Brian has battled the ebb and flow of mental illness and is the father of seven children. His first marriage to Marilyn Rovell produced Carnie and Wendy Wilson. In the early '90s, these two singing daughters became two-thirds of the trio Wilson Phillips. It has been said that his second wife, Melinda, a former car salesperson and model, shifted Brian's life in a more sane and creative direction, after years of isolation and self-doubt.

Many people wonder what Brian Wilson is really like. In my opinion, he is very sweet and very kind. He doesn't say a whole lot, but when he says something, you listen.

He would sit down at the piano and play some of his most famous chord progressions, from "God Only Knows" or "Don't Worry Baby."

I was sitting there in the presence of greatness, pinching myself. I grew up listening to Brian. When I was eleven, I pressed my transistor radio to my ear to listen to him; and, now here I was, composing with the architect of The Beach Boys. This was pretty surreal stuff. It was the thrill of my life.

Then, Joe Thomas calls me up and asks if I want to appear on *The Late Show with David Letterman*. Are you kidding me? That was one of my dreams, because Karen and I watched this popular talk show host nightly. I took off to New York City dressed up in my red silk shirt and jeans. I grabbed my 1956 Telecaster.

We were sitting in the green room and Brian asked me if I was nervous.

Me and the master, Brian Wilson, with his main henchman, Jeffrey Foskett.

"Not really, Brian. Are you?"

He said, "Yep."

As legend has it, the studio in the Letterman suite is freezing. We did a run-through with Paul Shaffer and the band. The guitarist Sid McGinnis was fascinated with my Telecaster; it was the guitar that he had always wanted. After we did the run-through, Letterman came by to shake everybody's hands. He was not unfriendly, but certainly not warm—just nice and civil.

Paul suggested that we play "Vehicle" before the next commercial. Paul knew me and my music. I had performed at a Farm Aid show about a year earlier, so he knew me from that event, too. David, however, said, "No. We have to go out with a Brian Wilson song."

I could understand the logic, but I admit I was disappointed at the time. This was my chance to sing "Vehicle" on the David Letterman show. But I now think that the band made the right choice by playing a classic Brian Wilson number.

Flash forward a little more than a decade and I found myself writing songs for The Beach Boys. Joe called me again, prefacing the conversation with, "You'll never guess what I'm doing…" He was producing what is perhaps the final album of the original Beach Boys.

Of course, there were challenges with this project. First of all, The Beach Boys don't get along. They have legal battles regarding what they can call themselves. But Joe, who is a great mediator, got everyone together in one room. He reminded everyone involved that each musician had a lot to gain by cutting one more Beach Boys album with all of the original, living members.

The group included Brian Wilson, Al Jardine, Bruce Johnston, Mike Love, and even David Marks. David was only about thirteen when he joined the group, to replace Al Jardine, who left to attend dental school. David had stayed to record four albums, then returned in 1997 for another couple of years, but also went on to form The Marksmen.

Anyone who ever called himself a "Beach Boy" was essentially on this project. Joe also said, "Do you remember the song, 'That's Why God Made the Radio'?"

That was one that Brian, Joe, Larry, and I had written about ten years before.

At the time, I was sitting at the downtown Chicago Italian ristorante called Bice with Brian and Joe Thomas. I was expounding on how good a hit record used to sound coming through the oval speaker on my 1964 Plymouth Valiant on the limited bandwidth AM radio. Brian agreed, then added, "Guess that's why God *made* the radio." I jotted those words down immediately and sang a primitive melody into my hand recorder. The title immediately suggested a melody. Larry's verse template set the whole song into motion. We developed the song over the next few months.

Joe explained that that song would be the title cut of the new Beach Boys album. It would be their first release and the name of their new tour. Joe called me several weeks later and said that they were still looking for some new songs.

Larry Millas, invigorated by the acceptance of "That's Why God Made the Radio," came to the studio one day bursting with a new melody and words.

"I got a new one we should write for The Beach Boys." A cappella he sang, "Isn't it time to catch another wave..."

I loved it immediately and in the dressing room at an Ides gig in North Dakota I developed enough of the song to be able to present it to Joe and Brian. The song became "Isn't It Time" at Brian's request—he and Mike Love didn't dig the "wave" reference. The hook became "isn't it time to dance the night away" and it became The Beach Boys' second single from the album.

Now every time I see Brian and the boys singing our song onstage or on cable, I pinch myself. Is this really young Jimmie Peterik, 2647 Oak Park Avenue, Berwyn, Illinois; the boy who only dreamed this would happen?

The dream continues as I write these memoirs with Brian, Larry, and I again writing songs for Brian's new solo album for Capitol. Life just keeps getting better.

My whole family was on the VIP list when The Beach Boys performed at the famous Chicago Theatre in May 2012. We got to hang out with the guys backstage. Brian remembered my name! Al Jardine was such a gentleman as was Bruce Johnston and musical conductor Jeff Foskett, who brought me side stage to talk to Brian as he did his preshow chill. I got to ask David Marks about his Lake Placid Blue Fender Jaguar. He confirmed it was the same one he used on "Fun, Fun, Fun."

We sat in row three waiting in high anticipation for my big moment. The hits went by in a beautiful blur: "Help Me, Rhonda," "Fun, Fun, Fun," "Little Deuce Coupe," "God Only Knows," and "Good Vibrations"—basically the soundtrack of my life—when finally Mike Love introduced the new single. "Here's our latest, 'That's Why God Made the Radio.'" I squeezed Karen's hand to the point of her wincing in pain; when our song hit the swoon-worthy chorus she casually draped her leg over mine in a reprise of her cheeky move at the Turtles concert back in 1968.

My son Colin whispered to me, "This has got to be a pretty cool moment for you, huh, Dad?"

I could tell he was living it, too, perhaps imagining a moment like this someday for him in the not-too-distant future. "It doesn't get much better," I replied. But what I was feeling was way beyond words.

Suddenly my life came into sharp focus. All I had been through seemed just then to be part of some master plan. I truly had been waiting for this moment, to quote my song, "ever since the world began." I saw the panorama of my existence in crystal vision—through the eye of the tiger.

■ ■ ■

I ALWAYS HAVE SAID, "I'll sleep when I die." I feel I am right now at the most exciting time of my life. Sure, I like to look back and reminisce but it's even more fun moving forward and creating new memories. "Youth is wasted on the young" it is often said, and in a way I agree. We didn't know at the time just how precious those early days were. I now have the life experience and perspective to enjoy fully the people around me and treasure every day as the gift it is. I try to avoid the pitfalls of the past but knowing full well that perfection is nobody's friend—you will always fall short.

The Ides are living the dream celebrating our fiftieth anniversary this year, playing up to fifty shows a year: festivals, fairs, casinos, corporate events, and benefits. The family has recently added the renowned trumpet player Tim Bales and Grammy-nominated reed man Steve Eisen.

A typical ninety-minute Ides set is a high-energy affair featuring not only Ides of March classics such as "L.A. Goodbye," "You Wouldn't Listen" (our first Top 10 from 1966), "Flipside," featuring the lead vocal of Larry Millas, and of course our big claim to fame, "Vehicle," but also includes Ides reimaginings of songs I have written for and with others. We love doing a medley of 38 Special hits including "Caught Up in You," "Hold on Loosely," and "Rockin' into the Night." We also put the Ides' spin on "Burning Heart," "Heavy Metal," "The Search Is Over," "Is This Love," and of course our brass-charged version of "Eye of the Tiger," which never fails to bring down the house.

I was on the road recently with my smooth jazz ensemble, Jim Peterik's Lifeforce. This expression of my softer side has just released its second CD, a double disc featuring the who's who of the smooth jazz world. It's made up of Eddie Breckenfeld on drums, Klem Hayes on bass, Jeff Lantz on keyboards, Mike Aquino on guitar, Steve Eisen on sax, and either Lisa McClowry or Leslie Hunt on vocals along with yours truly. We often feature guest performers such as Mindi Abair, Steve Oliver, Casey Abrams, and many more.

When I first met Mindi Abair on a smooth jazz cruise I was mesmerized—blonde hair, great gams, tight jeans, and electric charisma as she stalked the stage with her alto sax. I was hooked. We got along like old pals and I started making pilgrimages to her bungalow in Hollywood to jam, write songs, and try to get into trouble at her favorite haunt, the iconic Hollywood mecca, Lucy's.

One of the first songs we wrote, "'Sall Good" appeared on my second Lifeforce CD, *Forces at Play*. Now in 2014 two of our newest collaborations feature on her latest release on Concord, *Wild Heart*: "Amazing Game," featuring Trombone Shorty, and "Train" on which she shows the world she is a double threat with her urgent lead vocal.

She is a musical force to be reckoned with.

After a particularly strong show out of town I wandered alone as I often do to reflect on the night and find something decent to eat. I was drawn to one of those campy theme restaurants that tries to recapture the spirit of the innocent '50s, complete with soda fountain, neon Coke signs, a juke box, and young gals on roller skates in shorty poodle skirts taking your order. One cute lass skidded up to the luncheonette counter where I was sitting. We chatted as I ordered practically the whole menu: a cheeseburger with everything, fries, onion rings, and a chocolate milkshake. (I usually feel that I can get away with eating almost anything after one of my aerobic shows.)

I thought the innocent flirtation was going really well. Then she said, "Are you from around here? I'd really like to set you up—with my grandmother." Oww—did I say Oww? Not even her mother, mind you! I laughed 'til I cried all the way to the hotel. There are some moments in life that truly tell you just where you stand in this world. Life has a way of keeping you humble.

One of my greatest joys is joining forces with my heroes. After a Lisa McClowry show in Milwaukee where she opened for one of Karen's and my favorite "chill-out" groups, England's Acoustic Alchemy, I told them that I always dreamed of adding lyrics to their evocative moodscapes and melodies. Miles Gilderdale, one half of the duo (along with founder Greg Carmichael), replied in his Dudley Moore lilt, "Well then, why not have a go at it, mate!"

This was the start of a year of giving voice to the music of Acoustic Alchemy, culminating in the 2012 release, *Lisa McClowry Sings Acoustic Alchemy*. Lisa sings it like she lived every phrase. The single release, "Brand New Hallelujah," based on Alchemy's "Passionelle," is perhaps the CD's pinnacle with its telegraphic guitar work and Lisa's near-operatic bell-ringing chorus. I see this work as having wings.

Among the acts I am producing is an immensely talented group of siblings, Ariel, Zoey, and Eli. Besides having their own syndicated show we are now in development of *Steal the Show*—featuring Ariel, Zoey, and Eli—with Jim Peterik. Each episode combines elements of reality show and music video along with celebrity interviews as the camera follows the always compelling action of a recording session at my own World Stage Studios. In the process the audience gets to learn a lot about the process, fun, high jinks, and challenges of recording hits.

I'm also passionately involved in a relatively new nonprofit organization called Special Talents America, headed by Greg Bizzaro, with the help of many talented and devoted people. At their third annual talent show I was one of the judges watching some of the most talented young people I have ever seen. It was hard at first to believe that every one of them had special-needs disabilities. There were singers, dancers, harpists, banjo players, and more showing the world what it means to overcome a handicap. All of us judges picked out a sixteen-year-old girl with high-functioning autism named Breanna Bogucki as our *numero uno* singing the anti-bullying anthem made famous by Taylor Swift, "Mean."

First prize was the opportunity to have yours truly and singer/ songwriter/painter and STA member Lisa McClowry write and produce a custom song for her. The result is the moving ode to acceptance in high school society, "I Was Born Yesterday," which has become a hit on iTunes and a rallying point for special-needs individuals worldwide. A major music video produced by the award-winning Jaffe Films has just hit all media outlets. The world loves Breanna Alyssa, as she is now known (her first and middle name). I intend to be involved in this organization for many years to come.

"Eye of the Tiger" has been the gift that keeps giving. It is the feature song in the new *Rocky: The Musical* that has taken the theater community by storm. The song and Survivor have recently been given a special award by Sony/Legacy Recordings for upwards of 2.5 million downloads as it cozies up on the charts with the likes of the new breed—artists that were not even born when the song came out: Taylor Swift, Katy Perry, Mumford and Sons, and Imagine Dragons.

Finally, 2012 brought about a reality that would have seemed the stuff of dreams when The Ides and I were trudging down the halls of Morton West High. The very street, Home Avenue, that runs in front of our alma mater is now officially for time and tide renamed "Ides of March Way." Presented to us by the mayor of Berwyn and attended by 500 in the very auditorium where we did school assemblies back in the day, it was one of the most rewarding days I can remember. All the Ides gave their thanks and related touching anecdotes, including our late trumpet player, John Larson, making what turned out to be his last public appearance, and ex-member and trumpet player Chuck Soumar. Spearheaded by our schoolmate Rich Brom (who recently helped us create The Ides of March Scholarship Program for the Arts at Morton West) and promoted by Chuck Soumar, it was a moment that will live with me forever—especially whenever I walk past that proud school full of memories.

As I crisscross the world doing shows (I recently did a concert in China for an audience of more than 80,000—the crowd seemed to know every word of my songs, phonetically at least), there is one philosophy that drives me and keeps me on track. I guess you'd call it my life's mission statement. It's pretty simple:

1. Identify your gift.
2. Develop that gift with all your passion and might.
3. Share that gift with the world and make the world better.

I have been beyond fortunate to have Top 10 songs in four decades and two centuries. I have more than 1,000 published songs. I can only take partial credit. It often feels like I am simply taking dictation from some higher power and tapping into the blood, sweat, and genius of my ancestors. I believe we all have a special gift bestowed upon us by our maker and by every leaf and branch on our family tree. If you follow your heart you can't help but make this world a better place. And isn't that the sweetest gift we can give?

Acknowledgments

Jim Peterik

THE LIST OF PEOPLE in my life who have helped and inspired me would fill the pages of a separate book. I will attempt that list on my website.

For this book I will limit my thanks to those involved in its physical creation. My heartfelt thanks go out to:

Lisa Torem, my collaborator and advisor.
Glenn Yeffeth and his incredible team at BenBella Books.
Bill Gladstone, my literary agent.
Marc Hauser, cover photo.
Baker & Taylor: George Coe, Steve Harkins, and entire staff.
Chris May, personal assistant.
The author would also like to thank Paul Braun, Jeremy Holiday, Henry Perez, David Chackler, Bob Bergland, Larry Millas, Scott May,

Mike Borch, Kevin King-Templeton, Harvey McCarter, Mark Levinson, Roy Ferrer, Gene Steinman, Kristie Schram, Clark Besch, Steve Salzman, Mark Alano, Dave Austin, Bob Bittinger, and Terry Becker.

Also to Frankie Sullivan. Despite or because of our differences we helped each other create music that will live beyond us.

A very special thanks to the Man, Sylvester ("Call me Sly") Stallone for giving a relatively unknown band and writing team a chance at the title—and for giving me the phone call that inspires my life and the lives of millions of others. A Rocky story in and of itself.

Sincere thanks to all those who weighed in with reviews, personal stories, photos, and endorsements.

These extensive "Other Voices" reflections and the discography will appear on this book's website and www.jimpeterik.com.

Also check out Facebook.com/officialjimpeterik and twitter.com/jimpeterik.

Lisa Torem

FIRST OF ALL, I would like to express special thanks to BenBella staff: Sarah Dombrowsky, Alicia Kania, Katie Kennedy, Adrienne Lang, Monica Lowry, Lindsay Marshall, Jenna Sampson, and Glenn Yeffeth for clarifying the compelling copy and making sure that the visuals supported and moved the story along in the best possible way. Your expertise, creativity, and patience are so appreciated.

To Viv and Phil: I'm grateful to have been born into a family where the love of language was highly valued. Mom, your diagramless puzzles and triple-word Scrabble scores still impress. Dad, I miss your ostinatos on "Besame Mucho" and all of those other Latin/swing classics. My precious memories of your heartfelt writing and lovable piano playing only get stronger. Your kindness for all, love of education, and compassion for the underdog has always inspired me.

My girls: Emily, thank you for pointing me in my true direction. Your prizefighter spirit and gentle nature for all living things make me proud. Allie, you're the bravest lady I know. Your multitalented soulfulness is contagious. Madeline, we don't always rock out to the same tracks, but you've taught me how to stretch and appreciate the beauty outside the lines. Susha, thank you for your honesty and curiosity. Everything moves forward with your blessings.

Thanks to Jeremy Holiday, Henry Perez, and David S. Chackler for constant encouragement and utmost attention to detail. Thank you, Jim and Karen Peterik, for living an honest, creative life and allowing us to laugh and cry along with you. Many readers will see themselves in your stories and grow as a result of your lasting partnership. Thank you for putting your faith in me.

Chris Torem, thank you for the thousands of details you tend to so I can be who I am. Thank you for finding my glasses, my keys, and never questioning my desire to bond with Galápagos sea lions or sea birds in Antarctica.

To John Clarkson, Pennyblackmusic: You're the best friend a writer could have. Thank you for laboring over my drafts even when shattered, and pushing me beyond my limits. To Webmaster Richard Banks and the writers: You're a community of angels.

Finally, thank you to the Beatles, Eric Burdon, The Chordettes, Donovan, Herman's Hermits, The Ides of March, Jethro Tull, The Kinks, Jim Peterik, The Survivors, The Ventures, Question Mark and The Mysterians, The Zombies, and all those other fantastic groups and artists whose work has created such rock-solid happiness.

Chiseled in Stone
Postscript by Jim Peterik

THE QUESTION I'M ASKED MOST, just after "What comes first for you, the lyrics or the music?" and "How did that *Rocky* thing come about?" is "Are you ever going to get back with Survivor?" Well the "When hell freezes over" line has already been used so I say, "No, I like my life too much right now to change a thing." And that's the truth. I'm living my dream and consider myself a very lucky s.o.b.

My reasons for not needing to be a member of my most successful band are many. First off, I have the greatest band of brothers in the world already, The Ides of March. I also have a nod to my melodic rock heritage with the powerful Pride of Lions. But more than anything, as a lifelong songsmith, many of my children (my songs) have found success in the world on their own. I think more people know the song "Eye of the Tiger" than they do the band that recorded it. Same thing with "Vehicle." That's the power of a great song.

On any given week you can hear one of my songs at sporting events, played by marching bands, in commercials, in supermarkets, on the Internet (that amazing eighth-grade class singing "Eye of the Tiger"), in video games such as *Rock Band* and *Guitar Hero*, on TV in shows such as *American Idol*, *Glee*, *The X Factor*, *America's Got Talent*, *The Voice*, *Dancing with the Stars*, and others. You can hear my songs in countless movies and television series such as *Family Guy*, *The Simpsons*, and so many more. 38 Special is still together and doing 200 shows a year featuring the songs I co-wrote with them. Sammy Hagar is still encoring most nights with "Heavy Metal." And The Beach Boys have been playing "That's Why God Made the Radio" and "Isn't It Time" every night on their worldwide tour.

This is how my songs stay alive. This is how I stay alive. I'd rather keep creating new songs and producing new artists who share my vision, than go around the country doing the same ten songs night after night. I turned down a stint with The Beach Boys for the same reason—only with that I wouldn't even be playing my own songs.

I live to see my songs find homes all across the world in every imaginable form. That is truly my biggest reward. This is success to me.

KEEP ROCKING!

—*JIMBO*

Celebrate 50 years of The Ides Of March, the legendary Chicago band with all four original founding members, including Jim Peterik, together since 1964, with this deluxe three-disk box set.

st Band Standing: 50th Anniversary Collection features two CDs representing best of the band's recorded output (all original masters) from their 1966 "You Wouldn't Listen" to their number one 1970 smash "Vehicle" all the y to the premiere of five brand new brass heavy tracks, including the first ase from this set, "Last Band Standing".

e third disk is a DVD featuring the Ides live in concert at Chicago's House lues. Included on this disk will be rare footage, interviews with the band a music video of "Vehicle" and "Last Band Standing."

st BAND STANDING: 50TH ANNIVERSARY COLLECTION ILL BE AVAILABLE IN STORES AND ONLINE IN 2015.